T0358523

ROUTLEDGE LIBRARY EDITIONS:
ECONOMETRICS

Volume 17

AN ECONOMETRIC MODEL OF THE U.S. COPPER AND ALUMINUM INDUSTRIES

AN ECONOMETRIC MODEL OF THE U.S. COPPER AND ALUMINUM INDUSTRIES

How Cost Changes Affect Substitution and Recycling

MARGARET E. SLADE

Routledge
Taylor & Francis Group

LONDON AND NEW YORK

First published in 1984 by Garland

This edition first published in 2018
by Routledge
2 Park Square, Milton Park, Abingdon, Oxon OX14 4RN

and by Routledge
711 Third Avenue, New York, NY 10017

Routledge is an imprint of the Taylor & Francis Group, an informa business

British Library Cataloguing in Publication Data
A catalogue record for this book is available from the British Library

ISBN: 978-0-8153-9640-6 (Set)
ISBN: 978-1-351-14012-6 (Set) (ebk)
ISBN: 978-0-8153-5009-5 (Volume 17) (hbk)
ISBN: 978-1-351-14036-2 (Volume 17) (ebk)

Publisher's Note
The publisher has gone to great lengths to ensure the quality of this reprint but points out that some imperfections in the original copies may be apparent.

Disclaimer
The publisher has made every effort to trace copyright holders and would welcome correspondence from those they have been unable to trace.

An Econometric Model of the U.S. Copper and Aluminum Industries
How Cost Changes Affect Substitution and Recycling

Margaret E. Slade

Garland Publishing, Inc.
New York & London, 1984

Library of Congress Cataloging in Publication Data

Slade, Margaret E., 1940–
    An econometric model of the U.S. copper and aluminum
industries.

    (Outstanding dissertations in economics)
    Thesis (Ph.D.)—George Washington University, 1979.
    Bibliography: p.
    1. Copper industry and trade—United States—
Mathematical models.   2. Copper—United States—
Recycling—Mathematical models.   3. Aluminum industry
and trade—United States—Mathematical models.
4. Aluminum—United States—Recycling—Mathematical
models.   5. Substitution (Economics)—Mathematical
models.   I. Title.   II. Series.
HD9539.C7U5695   1984   338.2'743'0724   80-8628
ISBN 0-8240-4185-2

All volumes in this series are printed on acid-free,
250-year-life paper.

Printed in the United States of America

AN ECONOMETRIC MODEL OF THE DOMESTIC
COPPER AND ALUMINUM INDUSTRIES:
HOW COST CHANGES AFFECT SUBSTITUTION AND RECYCLING

by

Margaret Emily Slade

B.A., Vassar College
M.A., University of California, Berkeley

A Dissertation submitted to

The Faculty of
The Graduate School of Arts and Sciences
of The George Washington University in partial satisfaction
of the requirements for the degree of Doctor of Philosophy

May 6, 1979

Dissertation directed by

Anthony Marvin Yezer
Associate Professor of Economics

TABLE OF CONTENTS

LIST OF FIGURES

LIST OF FIGURES (Cont.)

LIST OF TABLES

ACKNOWLEDGEMENTS

I take great pleasure in thanking a number of individuals who have assisted me, in one way or another, with this research project. I therefore greatfully acknowledge:

Professor Anthony Yezer, who directed this dissertation, for his helpful and timely comments and encouragement throughout the duration of the project;

Professors Salih Neftci and Allyn Strickland, members of my committee, for their useful suggestions for improving the research;

Dr. John Schanz, from Resources for the Future, for helpful discussions on the conception and scope of the project;

Dr. Dennis Cox, copper commodity geologist with the U.S. Geological Survey, for his knowledgable reviews of the sections on technology and supply;

Drs. Allen Clark and Richard Meyer of the U.S. Geological Survey for encouraging this research;

And my daughter, Emily, for putting up with late meals and a tired mother during my entire graduate student experience.

In addition, many other professors, colleagues, friends, and members of my family have given their time and encouragement; without them this dissertation would not have been possible.

CHAPTER I: BACKGROUND AND INTRODUCTION

I:1 Changing Mineral Industry Costs

Much attention has been focused on changing energy economics
in the last decade. The Arab oil embargo and Organization of
Petroleum Exporting Countries (OPEC) price increases of 1973-74
forced the realization that we cannot count on secure supplies and
cheap prices of petroleum in the future. Subsequent price increases
for all energy sources have caused inflationary pressures worldwide
and have directed attention to the long-term nature of the problem.
The need to assess the short-, mid-, and long-range consequences
of rising energy prices is obvious. Because energy is an essential
input to virtually all industrial production, almost all industries
have experienced higher energy-related costs. Particularly hard
hit have been the mineral industries. These industries are highly
energy intensive and process intensive. The energy intensiveness
of mining, refining, and smelting means that mineral-industry
energy-related costs have been rising faster than costs in other
sectors. The use of energy in these industries primarily for basic
physical processes means that energy savings are difficult to achieve.[1]
The burden of higher energy prices is not borne equally by all of
the mineral industries. For example, primary-aluminum production

---

[1]   In the short run, most energy savings come from changed han-
    dling, transportation, heating and lighting, not from changed
    basic physical processes, but basic processes account for 85%
    of energy use in metal production. (See Fusfeld, 1976).

is several times more energy intensive than is primary-copper production, and secondary production of these metals (production from scrap or
recycling) requires one tenth to one twenty fifth of the energy needed
to process the equivalent metal from ores. The unequal effects that
increased energy prices have on mineral-industry costs will therefore
cause changes in their competitive positions and substitutions in
the use of their products.

Higher energy prices are possible because total resources of
fossil fuels are finite and unequally distributed geographically and
because many low-cost sources have already been exploited. Resources
of non-fuel minerals are finite, unequally distributed, and of differing quality as well. In fact, whereas there are energy sources such
as solar power that are virtually unlimited, all mineral resources
are limited and nonrenewable. [2] As high-quality mineral deposits are
depleted, higher costs are incurred by those industries that must
process lower quality ores. Not all metals are equally abundant. For
example, aluminum constitutes 8% of the earth's crust whereas copper
accounts for only .006%. Mineral industries involved in the production
of scarce metals might therefore experience rising costs,[3] while
those that process abundant metals are temporarily unaffected by the
depletion of low-cost deposits. Therefore, changing ore quality will

---

[2]   The stocks of copper and aluminum are not lost when used,
      but their concentration in high-grade mineral deposits is
      dissipated.

[3]   Following Skinner (1976), we define a metal to be geochem-
      ically scarce if it constitutes less than .1% of the earth's
      crust.

also cause changes in metal-use patterns.

This study is an attempt to estimate, in quantitative terms, the short- to mid-term consequences of rising energy prices and falling ore quality for two domestic mineral industries -- copper and aluminum. The effects of changing cost factors on substitution between metals will be assessed, the potential for increased recycling (because of higher energy and other natural-resource costs) will be examined, and the reserve positions of the two metals will be studied to see whether lower grade ores will have to be mined (requiring more energy-intensive techniques and thus higher costs).

II:2 Estimating the Effects of Cost Changes

Changes in energy economics affect the mineral industries in
three important ways. First, increased energy prices cause increased
mineral-processing costs, directly (through the purchase of fuels)
and indirectly (through the purchase of factors that require fuels in
their production). Metal prices must rise, but, because the energy-
intensiveness of metal production varies, they rise by unequal amounts.
Second, because the processing of ores is more energy-intensive than is
the processing of scrap, higher energy prices may increase the potential for recycling. But, as a higher proportion of available scrap
is recovered, the energy-intensiveness of secondary production
increases, dampening the original incentive to recycle. And third,
increased production of a scarce metal means that ores of lower
quality, which require more energy inputs per ton of refined metal,
must be processed. Therefore, for scarce metals, higher production
means higher energy costs.

The three effects just described can be expected to change
relative metal prices. Changed relative prices cause purchasers to
substitute one metal for another and to substitute nonmetalic
materials for metals. This process is dynamic, because time is required
for the effects of changed costs to filter down to the ultimate consumer. Therefore, the mid- and long-term consequences of higher
costs can be expected to be considerably greater than those experienced at first, and cost changes that occur today will affect metal-
use patterns for years to come.

4

We can expect changes in the competitive positions of all the mineral industries as cost factors vary. However, this study concentrates on two domestic mineral industries -- copper and aluminum. These two metals are substitutes in many end uses. They also differ in the energy-intensiveness of production and in their domestic and world reserves. Copper- and aluminum-industry problems should be representative of those faced by the mineral processing sector as a whole, and, because the two industries are unequally affected by higher energy prices and falling ore quality, they should exhibit diverse responses to the changed situation.

To make quantitative estimates of metal usage, substitution, and market shares as cost factors vary, two econometric models were constructed and estimated, one of the domestic copper industry and one of the domestic aluminum industry. The models are linked by copper and aluminum prices, derived demand from the copper- and aluminum-using sectors of the economy, and the copper-aluminum elasticities of substitution in each sector. To forecast the short- to mid-term (ten year) consequences of higher energy prices and falling ore quality for copper and aluminum prices, market shares, and the fraction of consumption of each that is supplied by recycled metal, model simulations are performed. The copper- and aluminum- industry forecasts resulting from these simulations depend on the exogenous-variable forecasts used. Alternative assumptions about future energy prices are made, and the sensitivity of future metal price, consumption, production, and substitution to the choice of energy-price forecast is analysed. The consequences of alternative assumptions about the quality of ore deposits to be mined in the future are also examined.

I:3 Model Overview and Study Outline

Two econometric models have been constructed and estimated,
one for each industry -- copper and aluminum. Figure I:3:1 illustrates the inter-metal market relationships that link the industry
models through the demanding sectors. Because most metal is used
as an input to industrial production, the demand for it is derived;
that is, metal demand is prompted by the demand for metal products.
In the copper-aluminum substitution (CAS) model, there are five copper-
aluminum-using sectors as well as two sectors that use only aluminum.
In each sector, the demand for the metals combined is derived from
the sector's production function. The demand equations are neoclassical marginal productivity equations, and sector demand depends on
copper and aluminum prices, aggregate economic activity, and the
price of the sector's output. The way in which the sector demand for
copper and aluminum combined is divided between the two metals depends
on the estimated long-run elasticity of substitution in that sector.
Just as price is an output from the industry models, consumption (as
determined by the derived demand and elasticity of substitution equations) is an input to the models. However, the process of price and
consumption determination is not sequential; it is simultaneous, and
the variables -- price and consumption -- are jointly determined.

7

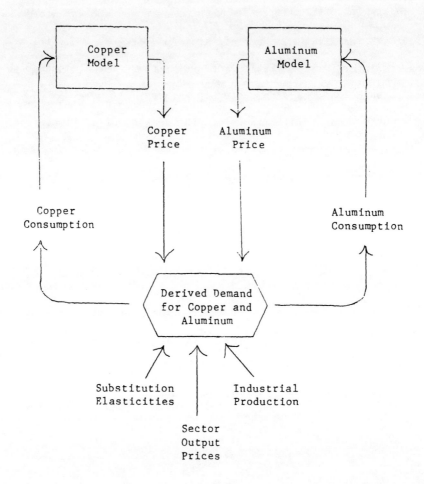

Figure I:3:1 Linkage of the Copper and Aluminum Models

8

Each industry model (a box in figure I:3:1) involves a complex set of relationships as shown in figure I:3:2. [4]   An industry is subdivided into a primary sector (where production is from metal ores) and a secondary sector (where production is from scrap metal). In figure I:3:2, the primary industry is shown at the top of the page; the principal primary-sector relationships are price and output. The secondary industry is shown at the bottom of the page, with two types of production -- production from new (industrial) and old (post-consumer) scrap -- as well as secondary metal price. The primary and secondary industries are linked through consumption and inventories (see the center of the page) with the three types of production -- primary, and secondary from new and old scrap -- adding to, and consumption subtracting from, inventories. The flow chart in figure I:3:2 is referred to, expanded, and clarified in later chapters.

---

[4]   In the flow chart, the symbols have the following inter-
pretations:

        The boxes represent stocks (tons).
        The ovals represent flows (tons/year).
        The circles represent not physical quantities, but
            information such as price or ore quality.
        Any variable that is not enclosed in a box, oval, or
            circle is exogenous to the model.
        The arrows do not represent physical flows; they in-
            dicate cause and effect (i.e., $X \rightarrow Y$ is equiva-
            lent to $Y = f(X)$).
        Roman numerals connect model relationships and chap-
            ters in the text.

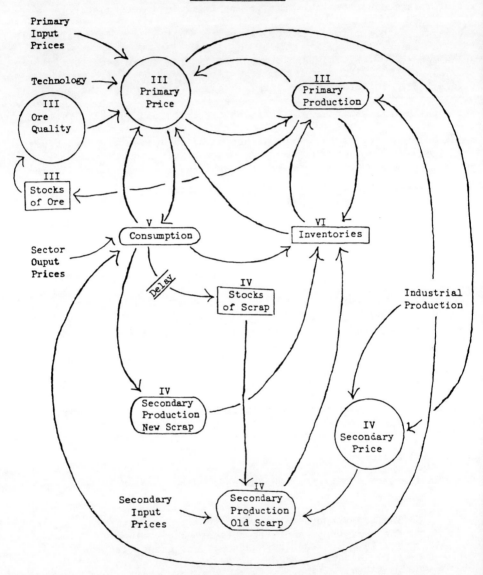

Primary Industry

Secondary Industry

Figure I:3:2 Flow Chart of an Industry Model

10

In the next chapter, econometric commodity models are reviewed, compared, and classified, and the differences between this study and previous commodity modeling efforts are discussed. The following four chapters (chapters III through VI) are devoted to detailed descriptions of different aspects of the copper and aluminum industries and the related model equations. Chapter III discusses the primary industries, chapter IV describes the secondary industries, and chapter V is devoted to metal consumption and substitution; inventories and imports are covered in chapter VI. The performance of the complete model over the historic (1962-1976) and forecast (1977-1986) periods is discussed in chapter VII, where different simulations are presented. Conclusions are drawn and policy implications analysed in the final chapter.

Because this is an economic study, it is organized according to economic relationships (price, production, consumption, etc.) rather than according to metal (copper and aluminum). The similarities between the domestic copper and aluminum industries with respect to structure and conduct make this economic organization both reasonable and tractable.

I:4 Limitations of the Analysis

The most important limitation of this analysis is its partial-equilibrium nature. For example, copper and aluminum are not just substitutes for one another, each is a substitute for other materials such as steel and plastic. The energy and other natural—resource costs of producing the principal substitutes for copper and aluminum are not explicitly considered here. Instead, the simplifying assumption is made that, if energy prices are high, there will be a shift away from using very energy-intensive materials such as copper and aluminum. It is not specified whether this shift will be accomplished through an increase in the use of substitutes for copper and aluminum that are less energy-intensive, or through a general decline in the demand for the products that are made with copper and aluminum as the prices of these products rise, if such substitutes are not available.

Another important limitation is that, although copper and aluminum are internationally traded, international factors are only cursorily treated in this study. Many events outside the United States (such as slow economic growth in the rest of the industrial world or political disruptions in the copper- or aluminum-producing developing nations) could influence domestic copper and aluminum markets. However, prediction of these events is difficult and well beyond the scope of this study. Changes in world metal markets are, however, treated exogenously in chapter VII.

A further limitation is the neglect of certain domestic cost factors, such as the higher capital requirements necessary to conform with U.S. government environmental regulations. The economic impact of federal air- and water-pollution-control legislation is too recent and uncertain to be analysed in the statistical framework developed here. Engineering estimates of future cost increases resulting from compliance with proposed environmental regulations could be constructed and used to adjust prices exogenously. This addition has not been made to the CAS model but is, however, a possible extension of the work reported here.

In spite of these limitations, the CAS model provides a very powerful tool for examinimg metal-market dynamics and for forecasting copper and aluminum prices, production, consumption, and recycling rates. Events that are outside the scope of the model (such as bauxite-producer country pricing policies) can be forecast exogenously, and the effects of such policies on domestic copper and aluminum markets can be analysed within the framework of the model. The direct linkage of the two markets means that, if an event occurs that seemingly affects only one market (such as a fall in the grade of copper ores mined or an increase in bauxite-producer-country royalties) the indirect effect on the other market (through substitution) can be analysed as well as the direct effect on the market of interest.

CHAPTER II   ECONOMETRIC COMMODITY MODELS

REVIEW AND COMPARISON

II:1   Econometric Non-Ferrous Metal-Market Models

Many econometric models of non-ferrous metal markets have been constructed and estimated. The basic variables are usually supply (or production), demand (or consumption), and price, but each modeler makes different assumptions about how these variables are determined. In this chapter, earlier econometric commodity models are reviewed, their evolution over time are described, and their differences from the CAS model are analysed. These models are then classified according to their treatment of certain key issues.

One of the earliest nonferrous-metal modeling attempts was Desai's (1966) model of the world tin industry. Desai was interested in the problem of price stabilization for primary commodities. Because he was principally concerned with softening the impact of demand fluctuations on the primary producers, his main focus was on the demand side of the market. Desai found neither supply nor demand to be sensitive to price, the former being principally a function of supply in previous years, the latter a function of aggregate economic activity. Desai's price equation is typical of many later price equations. In his model, price does not adjust instantaneously to equate supply and demand (as it would in a perfectly competitive industry with negligible adjustment costs), but it moves in the

direction of equating these two variables. In Desai's model,
price is a function of inventories (the cummulative difference between supply and demand) divided by consumption. The following is
a simplified version of Desai's model of the primary tin industry.

$$D_t = D(Y_t)$$
$$S_t = S(S_{t-1})$$
$$P_t = P(I_{t-1}/D_t)$$

where D_t is demand or consumption at time t

Y_t is the value of some aggregate economic activity
variable at time t

S_t is supply or production at time t

P_t is price at time t

and I_t is the level of inventories at time t.
$I_t = I_{t-1} + S_t - D_t$.

A somewhat later econometric commodity model is the Fisher-
Cootner-Baily (FCB) (1972) model of the world copper industry. The
focus of the FCB model is on geographic differences in the industry
and on the two-price system generally prevailing (where most copper
in the United States moves at the U.S. producer price while copper
in the rest of the world moves at the London Metal Exchange (LME)
price, which can be considerably different). FCB, unlike Desai, found
both supply and demand to be sensitive to the price of copper; demand
was found to be related to the price of a substitute (aluminum) as well.
The FCB U.S. producer-price equation includes the difference between

15

the U.S. and the LME copper prices as an explanatory variable; the U.S. price tends to move in the direction of the LME price if the two are very different. Like Desai's model, the FCB model is basically competitive; price responds to changes in inventories divided by changes in consumption. A difference between the Desai and FCB models is that distributed lags have been added to all equations in the FCB model. [1] The introduction of distributed lags captures the long-range effects of changes in the independent variables on the dependent variable.

A simplified version of the FCB model of the primary copper industry is

$$D_t = D(Y_t, P_{t-1}, Ps_{t-1}, D_{t-1})$$
$$S_t = S(P_t, S_{t-1})$$
$$P_t = P(\Delta I_{t-1}/\Delta D_{t-1}, (Pw_{t-1} - P_{t-1}), P_{t-1})$$

where P_t is the U.S. price at time t

Ps_t is the price of a substitute at time t

and Pw_t is the world price at time t. [2]

A diagram helps to explain the price adjustment mechanism in the FCB model. Supply is an upward sloping function of price as in

---

[1] Including the lagged value of the dependent variable as an explanatory variable results in a geometric distributed lag of the independent variables in the equation. (See Koyck, 1954).

[2] For a definition of the other variables in the equations, see page 15.

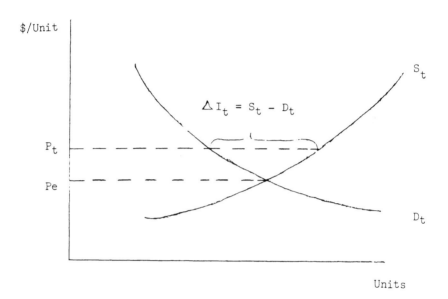

Figure II :1:1 Price Adjustment in the Fisher-
Cootner-Baily Copper Model

figure II:1:1; demand slopes downward. At price P_t, supply exceeds demand and changes in inventories are positive; this implyies a fall in price. Thus, P_{t+1} moves towards Pe, the price that equates supply and demand.

Charles River Associates (CRA) have estimated econometric models for nearly every important mineral industry. The CRA (1971) aluminum model will be discussed here because it represents a basic departure from the competitive price determination implied by Desai and FCB. The CRA aluminum model was designed for forecasting purposes and for testing the sensitivity of the aluminum market to sales from and purchases for the government stockpile. The CRA demand equation is very similar to the FCB demand equation.[3] The model differs from FCB in the absence of a primary aluminum supply equation.[4] And price, in contrast to the earlier models, is solely a function of cost, present and past. CRA constructed a cost variable from the prices of the principal inputs to primary-aluminum production and from a measure of the technology prevailing. They used engineering estimates of factor proportions to weight input prices before summing to obtain total cost. The pricing mechanism implied by the CRA price equation is a full-cost policy based on long-run average cost (which calls for a standard markup over the average cost of production when operating at the standard rate of output). The full-cost model is

---

3   CRA used a weighted average of past prices as explanatory
     variables in the demand equation. The weights were set in
     an ad hoc manner.

4   Presumably supply is determined as the intersection of the
     price and demand schedules.

a variant of an oligopoly model.

A diagram helps to explain price and output determination in the CRA aluminum model. Demand is a downward sloping function of price as in figure II:1:2. Price is a function of long-run average cost and is independent of the quantity produced (as in a constant-cost industry). Supply is obtained as the intersection of the price and demand schedules.

A simplified version of the CRA model of the primary aluminum industry is

$$D_t = D(Y_t, P_{t-i}, Ps_{t-i}) \qquad i = 0, \ldots, 3$$
$$P_t = P(LRAC_t, P_{t-1})$$

where $LRAC_t$ is long-run average cost at time t. [5]

The three commodity models just discussed by no means exhaust the subject of econometric non-ferrous metal-market models, but they serve to illustrate some important features of such models. In the third section of this chapter, nine econometric models of copper or aluminum markets are classified according to their treatment of price, production, consumption and substitution, and the natural-resource base. But first, the CAS model is described in greater detail and its differences from earlier models identified.

---

[5] For a definition of the other variables in the equations, see pages 15 and 16.

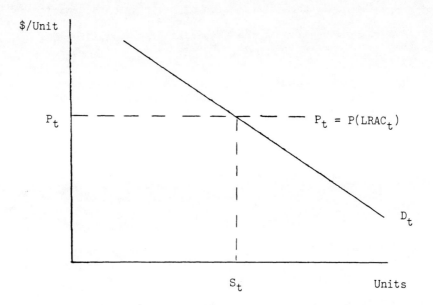

Figure II:1:2 Price and Quantity Determination in the
Charles River Associates Aluminum Model

II:2:1   The Primary Industries

The CAS model differs from earlier econometric models of non-ferrous-metal markets in several important ways. On the demand side there are two equations for each using sector, and each equation is derived from the production function of that sector.[6] The first equation determines the demand for copper and aluminum combined. The relevant price in this equation is a weighted average of copper and aluminum prices where weights are proportional to copper and aluminum usage in the sector. The second equation describes the division of the market between the two metals as determined by the elasticity of substitution in that sector.

There are thus two major departures here from previous models of demand for copper and aluminum. First, an explicit assumption about the using-sector production function is made, and all demand relationships are derived from this production function. And second, whereas in previous models, copper and aluminum markets have been connected only by an exogenous substitute price, here the two are linked directly and all variables are jointly determined. The markets are thus allowed to interact, and the structural relationships that connect them are explicitely stated. The demand equations are described in detail in chapter V.

---

6   Consumption is divided into five copper-aluminum-using sectors plus two sectors that use only aluminum.

On the primary supply and price-determination side, this model is oligopolistic. Unlike the producer in a competitive industry who is a price taker, the producer who has some market power has two decision variables -- price and output. In the CAS model, price is principally a function of long-run average cost, but cost is not determined by engineering-cost estimates as in the CRA aluminum model. The prices of the principal inputs to primary production and the measures of the state of technology and of ore quality are included as explanatory variables in the estimation of the price equations. Inventories are used as feedback to both price and output decisions in the model. When inventories accumulate, a producer can choose to cut price or to cut production. Therefore, the level of inventories is a determinant of production as well as of price in a concentrated industry. The aggregate economic-activity variable is also a determinant of production, because the producer can anticipate the demand for his product and produce accordingly.

Thus four major departures from previous models of primary supply and price determination are made here. First, the response of price to changes in cost variables is estimated statistically rather than being determined by engineering cost estimates. Second, in the simultaneous determination of price and output, the response of the producer to inventory accumulation -- whether to cut price or output -- is estimated, not assumed. Third, in the CAS model, price is determined principally by cost, as with a full-cost pricing policy, but demand considerations are not neglected in the price equations. The balance between the two possibilities -- pricing based on long-run average cost and pricing to equate supply and demand -- is empirically estimated, not assumed. And fourth, copper-ore-quality measures are included as cost determinants, allowing costs to rise as high-quality ore deposits are exhausted. Thus, the increasing costs incurred with cumulative production are made explicit. The primary price and production equations are discussed in detail in chapter III.

A simplified version of the CAS model of the primary industries is

$$\sum_j Dj_t = D_{c+a}(Y_t, Pc, a_t, \sum_j Dj_{t-1}) \qquad j = c, a$$

$$Dc_t/Da_t = Dc/a(Pa_{t-i}, Pc_{t-i}) \qquad i = 0, \ldots, 3$$

$$Sj_t = Sj(Pj_t, Y_t, Ij_t/Dj_t, Sj_{t-1}) \qquad j = c, a$$

$$Pj_t = Pj(Pi, j_t, Rj_t, Tj_t, Ij_t/Dj_t, Pj_{t-1}) \qquad j = c, a$$

where
Dj_t is demand for metal j at time t

Y_t is the value of some aggregate economic activity variable at time t

Pc, a_t is a weighted average of copper and aluminum prices at time t

Pj_t is the price of metal j at time t

Sj_t is primary supply of metal j at time t

Ij_t is the level of inventories of metal j at time t

Pi, j_t is the price of the i th input to primary production of metal j at time t

Rj_t is a measure of the quality of resource j at time t

and
Tj_t is a measure of the state of technology in the primary production of metal j at time t.

23

II:2:2   The Secondary Industries

Most metals are produced by a secondary industry (where production is from scrap) as well as a primary industry (where production
is from ores). Because refined secondary metal is virtually indistinguishable from refined primary metal, there is no separate demand for recycled metal. The determinants of supply, however, are
very different in the primary and secondary industries. The two
types of secondary production are: production from new (industrial)
scrap and production from old (post-consumer) scrap. Following FCB,
new scrap supply in the CAS model is a function of metal consumption
and is not sensitive to price. The treatment of old scrap supply
in this study is, however, significantly different from that in FCB.

In the FCB model, the assumption is that metal becomes available
for collection the moment it is consumed. The amount of old scrap
available for collection is therefore equal to cummulative consumption. The dependent variable in the FCB old-scrap-supply equation
is the fraction of the available scrap that is actually collected,
a function of price and of the previous year's fraction collected.
The FCB secondary supply equation from old scrap is thus

$$\mathrm{Sos}_t/CC_t = \mathrm{Sos}(P_t, \mathrm{Sos}_{t-1}/CC_{t-1})$$

where Sos_t is secondary supply from old scrap at time t

           CC_t is cummulative consumption at time t

and P_t is price at time t.

24

Because most metal products have very long average lifetimes, the assumption that a metal becomes available for recycling the moment it is consumed is very unrealistic. In the CAS model, consumption is divided into product types, each with a different average lifetime. The metal in the product becomes available for recycling only after the average lifetime of that product has elapsed. In addition, metal produced from old scrap is subtracted from the stock of scrap metal available for collection each year, because once the metal is recycled, it is again contained in a useful product.

In the CAS model, secondary price and output determination is competitive. The secondary producer is a price taker and produces to equate price and his short-run marginal cost (MC). Marginal cost is a function of the ratio of old scrap collected (Sos) to the stock of old scrap available for collection (SS) and of the prices of the inputs to secondary production (Pi). Figure II:2:1 illustrates the way in which output is determined by the secondary producer. Marginal cost is an upward sloping function of output, price is independent of output, and the quantity produced is determined by the intersection of the two.

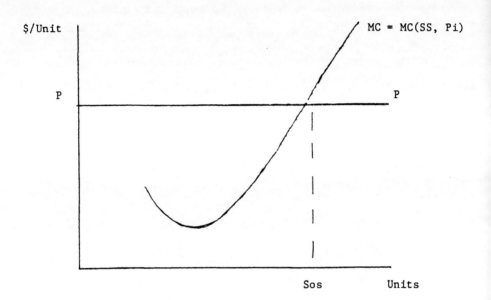

Figure II:2:1
The Determination of Secondary Production from Old Scrap
in the CAS Model

In algebraic notation, the secondary-supply equation from old scrap in the CAS model is [7]

$$Sos_t = Sos(P_t, SS_t, Pi_t)$$

where Sos_t is secondary supply from old scrap at time t

P_t is price at time t

SS_t is the stock of scrap available at time t

and Pi_t is the price of the i th input to secondary production at time t.

Thus, two important departures from previous models of secondary supply are made here. First, the stocks of scrap available for collection are computed with more accuracy. And second, the supply curve of the secondary producer is his short-run marginal cost curve, and the prices of the inputs to secondary production, as well as the stocks of scrap available, are determinants of this cost. The equations for the secondary industry are described in detail in chapter IV.

---

[7]   The secondary-industry supply curve is the horizontal sum of the marginal-cost curves for the individual producers.

II:3 A Classification of Econometric Models of Copper and Aluminum Markets

In section 1 of this chapter, three early econometric commodity models were discussed. The discussion of these models served to illustrate some basic concepts of commodity-market modeling and to show how these concepts have evolved over time. In this section, we look at a larger number of econometric models of copper and aluminum markets and classify them with respect to their treatment of price, production, consumption and substitution, and the natural-resource base. The models that are classified are:

		Year
Copper Models		
Fisher, Cootner, Baily	(FCB)	1972
Charles River Associates	(CRA-C)	1970
Synergy	(Synergy-C)	1977
Arthur D. Little	(ADL)	1978
Taylor	(Taylor)	1978
Slade	(Slade-C)	1979
Aluminum Models		
Charles River Associates	(CRA-A)	1971
Synergy	(Synergy-A)	1977
Slade	(Slade-A)	1979

The classification scheme is as follows:

Primary metal price

Primary-price behavioral relationships are classified according to whether they relate price principally to supply-demand imbalance (inventories) or to long-run average cost. The second type of relationship (price based on cost) can be further subdivided, depending on whether cost estimates are determined by means of engineering or statistical cost functions.

Consumption and substitution

Consumption and substitution behavioral relationships are classified according to whether they are based on demand equations that contain own and substitute prices (own-price and cross elasticities of demand are calculated) or on a specific form of production function (derived demand and elasticities of substitution are estimated).

Primary production

Primary production relationships are classified according to whether production is determined by flow adjustment (production is related to lagged values of price, economic activity, etc.) or by stock adjustment (investment, capacity, and capacity utilization relationships are estimated).[8]

---

8   More complete descriptions of stock and flow adjustment models are given, and the relative merits of each discussed, in chapter III:5.

The natural-resource base

The natural-resource base is classified according to whether the base is considered infinite (no measures of ore quality are considered) or finite (the effects of depletion due to cumulative production are explicitly specified).

A further subdivision of the above classes results from the fact that, in any model of supply, demand, and price, there are really only two independent relationships (if all three equations must intersect in a point). In some commodity models, a third equation is specified that shows how one of the variables (price or production) adjusts to the other two, and in other models, the third variable (price or production) is determined by the simultaneous solution of the two independent equations. In classifying models, the second method of price or output determination will be called "solution".

In table II:3:1, each of the nine econometric models listed earlier is classified according to its treatment of price, consumption and substitution, production, and the natural-resource base.

In the next chapters, all of the issues mentioned briefly here -- the determination of price, production, consumption and substitution, and ore quality in the copper and aluminum industries -- are discussed at greater length, when the treatment of each in the CAS model is analysed.

30

CLASSIFICATION OF ECONOMETRIC MODELS OF COPPER AND ALUMINUM
MARKETS ACCORDING TO BEHAVIORAL RELATIONSHIPS

Price based principally on

    Supply-demand imbalance   FCB, CRA-C, Taylor[9]

    Long-run average cost

        Engineering cost function   CRA-A, Synergy-C and A

        Statistical cost function   Slade-C and A

    Solution   ADL

Consumption and Substitution based on

    Demand equation   FCB, CRA-C and A, Synergy-C
                                  and A, ADL, Taylor

    Production function   Slade-C and A

Primary Production based on

    Flow adjustment   FCB, CRA-C, Synergy-C and A,
                                  Taylor, Slade-C and A

    Stock adjustment   ADL

    Solution   CRA-A

Natural-Resource Base considered

    Infinite   FCB, CRA-C and A, Synergy-C
                                  and A, ADL, Taylor, Slade-A

    Finite   Slade-C

---

9   The Taylor price equation doesn't fit neatly into any class.
    Of the eight independent variables in this price equation, six
    are price variables, one a demand, and one a cost variable (the
    wholesale-price index). I have included this model in the first
    price-determination category because its price equation does not
    include any specific copper cost variables.

II:4 The Assumptions Made in Modeling Such Markets

Econometric commodity models consist of a set of endogenous variables (such as metal price, production, and consumption), whose behavior is explained by the model, and a set of exogenous variables (such as GNP), whose behavior is explained outside the model. The data used to estimate the model-equation parameters usually consist of a set of observations on each variable (both endogenous and exogenous) at equally spaced intervals (e.g., monthly, quarterly, or yearly observations).

In the CAS model, the data consist of yearly time series for the period 1954 to 1976. There are twenty six estimated equations plus a number of identities that define the endogenous variables, as well as seventeen exogenous variables. The number of variables in the model is thus much greater than the number of observations, a situation that is commom in econometric model building. In constructing a model, we must make use of all of the available information and choose equations, variables, and parameters in a parsimonious fashion.

The design of an econometric model typically consists of five steps:

1) Identification of the important structural or causal relationships in each market [10]

2) Specification of the appropriate explanatory variables to include in each equation

---

10   This step is approximately equivalent to choosing the endogenous variables.

3) Determination of the functional form of each equation

4) Specification of the dynamic adjustment mechanism, if relevant

5) Choice of the appropriate estimation technique for each equation.

Step 1:

Focusing on only the most important structural or causal relationships in a market is a prerequisite to successful model building. For example, it may seem presumptuous to claim that twenty six estimated equations plus a few identities are sufficient to say anything meaningful about four industries (primary and secondary copper and aluminum) and how they interact. However, given the limitations of the data, adding complexity to a model often subtracts from the insights that can be gained from considering only the most important relationships. Therefore, the choice of equations (the choice of endogenous variables) is very important in determining the validity of a model. To identify the fundamental structural relationships, a knowledge of the industry to be modeled (the market structure, production process, etc.) as well as of economic theory is essential.

Step 2:

The appropriate variables to include in each equation are also determined by a knowledge of the industry and of economic theory. For example, we must be familiar with the market structure of an industry in order to be able to identify the way in which

33

prices are formed in such industries, and we must be familiar with
economic theory in order to be able to construct and test models
of price formation in industries that have a particular structure.
The model of price formation chosen will then determine the variables
to include in the price equation.

Step 3:

Once the variables to include in an equation have been determined, the way in which these variables are related must be specified. An equation typically consists of one endogenous variable (the
dependent variable or the variable to be "explained") on the left-
hand side and several current or lagged endogenous or exogenous variables (the variables that "explain" the dependent variable) on the
right-hand side. How these variables are related, that is, the
functional form of the relationship, is determined in one of
several ways.

In some cases, the functional form of the relationship can be
derived algebraically from another relationship. For example, the
derived demand equations in the CAS model (which are neoclassical
marginal productivity equations) were obtained by differentiating
the sector production functions. In these cases, the equation specification is exact (assuming that the choice of production function
was appropriate).

In other cases, engineering data must be used to determine
functional form. For example, while it is obvious that the
prices and quantities of the inputs to metal production determine

34

total cost, a knowledge of the production process is required to understand how the quantity of a particular input is related to the quantity of output produced. In these cases, the specification of an equation may be approximate (i.e., the relationship may be obviously nonlinear, but any simple algebraic representation may only approximate
the true relationship).

Step 4:

Typically, the equation that is specified by economic theory is
an equilibrium condition. For example, the equation might be a cost-
minimizing condition from the production function, where it is assumed
that the prices of all inputs are known with certainty and that there
are no costs incurred in changing factor proportions. However, in the
real world, markets are rarely in equilibrium and adjustments are costly.
Therefore, the equilibrium condition usually has to be modified, that
is, the dynamic adjustment mechanism has to be specified. In the above
example, the way in which purchasers of inputs adjust to changed relative factor prices must be made explicit.

35

Step 5:

When an equation has been specified as to the appropriate variables to include, the functional form of the relationship, and the dynamic adjustment process, it is necessary to estimate the equation parameters from the data. The form of the equation determines the statistical technique appropriate to its estimation. For example, if an equation includes current endogenous variables, it must be estimated by some simultaneous-equation technique in order to avoid the bias that results from simultaneity.

All of the models classified in the previous section were constructed using the same general principles. The common goal is to make maximum use of the information available and to minimize the limitations of the data by focusing only on the fundamental relationships and by choosing variables and parameters economically and wisely.

CHAPTER III   PRIMARY COPPER AND ALUMINUM

In this chapter, the primary copper and aluminum industries in the United States are described. The emphasis is on the pricing policies and output decisions of the firms in the industries. Because the structure of an industry, (its concentration, integration, barriers to entry, etc.), affects pricing and output behavior, the first section of this chapter discusses the structure of the primary copper and aluminum industries in the United States and the relationship of each to its world counterpart. Because pricing in these industries is based principally on mining and processing cost, section two of this chapter gives a brief description of primary industry technology and cost. In sections four and five, after a brief discussion of some of the statistical conventions used in estimating the industry model equations, models of industry pricing and output behavior are developed, and the results of estimating equations based on these models are presented.

III:1:1   The Relevant Market

Both the copper and the aluminum industries can be subdivided
into a primary industry (where production is from ores) and a secondary industry (where production is from scrap). For the purpose
of this study, the primary industry consists of mining, smelting,
and refining; semifabrication is ignored. The secondary industry
consists of scrap collection and, in some cases, smelting and refining. Because refined secondary metal is virtually indistinguishable from primary metal, there is no separate demand for secondary
material. Metal consumption in the United States (and therefore the
relevant market) consists of primary plus secondary production (including scrap used directly without re-refining) plus net imports.
However, in this chapter only the primary industries are described,
and concentration ratios given here (following the Bureau of the
Census) refer to the value of shipments for domestic primary metals
alone. These ratios thus overstate the true degree of concentration
in these markets.

In the historic period (1954-1976), the proportion of metal
supplied by primary, secondary, and foreign producers remained relatively constant. Table III:1:1 shows these proportions. [1] To

---

[1]   These figures refer to metal, not ores. The United States
        imports most of its bauxite.

38

obtain a more appropriate measure of concentration in these industries, we can multiply the concentration ratios given later by the
primary producers' market share from table III:1:1. This constant
division of the market, however, may not continue in the future, and,
in fact, in the simulations performed for the forecast period (1977-
1986), the shares of primary, secondary, and foreign producers vary
considerably, depending on the forecasts of the exogenous variables
used. The primary producers, therefore, can not ignore the secondary and foreign producers, and their pricing behavior reflects this
interdependence.

TABLE III:1:1
APPROXIMATE PROPORTION OF METAL SUPPLIED BY PRIMARY, SECONDARY,
AND FOREIGN PRODUCERS IN THE UNITED STATES   1954-1976

	Primary	Secondary	Foreign
Copper	60	40	0
Aluminum	75	20	5

39

III:1:2   Concentration

The primary copper and aluminum manufacturing industries in the United States are highly concentrated. [2] Table III:1:2 gives the number of firms in each industry, and the four- and eight-firm concentration ratios (CR4 and CR8 respectively) for 1972.

TABLE III:1:2
1972 CONCENTRATION RATIOS FOR PRIMARY COPPER AND ALUMINUM MANUFACTURING

	Number of Firms	CR4	CR8	SIC [4]
Copper	11	72	98 [3]	3331
Aluminum	12	79	92	3334

Source: Bureau of the Census (1975)

Industry concentration varies at each stage of the production process -- mining, refining, and smelting. For aluminum, the industry becomes less concentrated as you go down the vertical chain from mining to smelting. Table III:1:3 shows four-firm concentration ratios at various stages of primary aluminum production. Because

---

2   The term "manufacturing" refers to refining and smelting.

3   The Bureau of the Census does not give the 1972 eight-firm ratio for copper. The number shown is the ratio for 1970.

4   SIC stands for the U.S. government's standard industrial classification.

40

little bauxite is mined in the U.S., the ratios given are for the North-American continent (which includes the Caribbean Islands, major bauxite suppliers).

TABLE III:1:3
FOUR-FIRM CONCENTRATION RATIOS FOR ALUMINUM IN NORTH AMERICA
AT VARIOUS STAGES OF PRODUCTION

Stage	CR4	Year
Mining	93	1973
Refining	86	1974
Smelting	73	1974

Source: Council on Wage and Price Stability (1976)

The opposite is true for copper; concentration is less at the mining stage than at the smelting and refining stages. Because there are several independent copper mining companies that use custom or toll smelting and refining services, copper-market concentration increases as you go downstream. Table III:1:4 shows four- and eight-firm concentration ratios for copper mining and milling and for primary smelting and refining in the United States.

41

TABLE III:1:4

FOUR- AND EIGHT-FIRM CONCENTRATION RATIOS FOR U.S. COPPER
AT VARIOUS STAGES OF PRODUCTION

Stage	SIC	CR4	CR8	Year
Mining and Milling	1021	64	88	1974
Smelting and Refining	3331	72	98	1972

Source: Bureau of the Census (1975)
Arthur D. Little (1978)

Significant changes in concentration have taken place in these industries in the last three decades. The decrease in concentration in the aluminum industry in the U.S. was achieved principally through government intervention. For many years, Alcoa had a monopoly on U.S. aluminum production. Originally, Alcoa's monopoly position was due to possession of patents on the Hall and Bradley electrolytic reduction processes that change alumina into aluminum. However, Alcoa was able to maintain its monopoly position well beyond the expiration date of its patents because it had control over low-cost ore deposits and cheap hydroelectric-power sources. During World War II, the U.S. government constructed aluminum refineries and smelters, which it later sold to Kaiser and Reynolds. After the Korean War, the government again intervened in the aluminum market and induced the entry of three new producers -- Anaconda, Harvey (later acquired by Martin-Marietta), and Ormet -- by offering rapid amortization, guaranteed loans, and long-term supply contracts from the government stockpile. During the sixties and early seventies, six additional firms entered the industry, further reducing market concentration. Table III:1:5 shows the market share of the big three -- Alcoa, Kaiser, and Reynolds -- from 1950 to 1974. The decline in their market share is substantial, but, nevertheless, the domestic aluminum market remains much more concentrated than most industrial markets. Aluminum-market concentration is high even among metal markets.

TABLE III:1:5
U.S. ALUMINUM MARKET SHARE OF ALCOA, REYNOLDS, AND KAISER 1950-1974

	1950	1960	1970	1974
CR3	100	88	71	67

Source: Council on Wage and Price
Stability (1976)

The U.S. primary copper manufacturing industry has also experienced some decline in concentration over time, but, unlike the aluminum industry, this decline was achieved without direct government intervention. The market share of the four largest copper companies fell from 87% to 72% between 1958 and 1972.

The world copper and aluminum markets differ substantially with respect to concentration and, therefore, pricing. The non-communist-world aluminum market is dominated by six integrated, multi-national producers -- three American, one Canadian, one Swiss, and one French. [5] The proportion of the market controlled by these six

---

5   The firms are Alcoa, Reynolds, Kaiser, Alcan, Alsuisse, and Pechiney.

has declined as various producing governments have acquired capacity and new firms have entered the industry. However, the big six still have a noncommunist-world market share exceeding 65%, and the world aluminum market is definitely oligopolistic. Table III:1:6 shows how the market share of the six firms changed between 1953 and 1973.

TABLE III:1:6
NONCOMMUNIST-WORLD MARKET SHARE OF THE SIX LARGEST ALUMINUM FIRMS
1953-1973

	1953	1969	1973
Mining	NA	72	69
Primary Aluminum	87	76	70

Source: Council on Wage and Price Stability (1976)
Charles River Associates (1976)

Since World War II, significant changes have taken place in the world copper industry. New mines have been developed in Peru, the Philippines, the Republic of South Africa, and Papua-New Guinea that are not controlled by the major copper companies. In addition, many mines have been nationalized, causing a further decline in the role of the major copper-mining corporations. Table III:1:7 shows four- and eight-firm concentration ratios for the noncommunist-world copper industry from 1947 to 1974. The decline in concentration is very dramatic, and the world copper industry is now generally considered to be competitive.

44

TABLE III:1:7
CONCENTRATION IN THE NON-COMMUNIST-WORLD PRIMARY COPPER MANUFACTURING
INDUSTRY   1947-1974

	CR4	CR8
1947	60	77
1956	49	70
1974	17	28

Source: Herfindahl (1959)
         Arthur D. Little (1978)

45

III:1:3 Barriers to Entry

Such high concentration in the U.S. copper and aluminum industries is not achieved without barriers to entry into these industries.
In these markets, entry barriers consist principally of economies of
scale, vertical integration, high capital requirements, and absolute
cost advantages such as control over cheap natural resources.

Economies of scale are particularly important in the aluminum
industry. The Council on Wage and Price Stability (1976) estimated
that a new refinery of minimum efficient scale would produce between
600 and 1,000 thousand tons of alumina per year; a smelter of minimum efficient scale would produce between 150 and 300 thousand tons
of aluminum per year. Plants of these proportions would supply three
to eight percent of 1974 U.S. aluminum consumption. Economies of scale
are also very important in the copper industry. Arthur D. Little
(1978) estimated that an integrated mine-through-refinery operation
of minimum efficient scale would produce 100 thousand tons of copper
per year or three percent of U.S. copper consumption in 1974. However, the largest firms in both industries have more than one plant
at each stage of production. Therefore, economies of scale alone
can not account for the high concentration in these markets.

Vertical integration can be an important entry barrier because
capital requirements are much higher if a new firm must enter as an
integrated operation. Also, by integrating backwards into mining,
firms secure adequate sources of raw materials and may cut off ore
supplies from non-integrated producers. All of the largest copper

and aluminum companies are integrated backwards into mining (in the case of aluminum, mining may be exclusively abroad) and forwards into semifabricating, either directly or indirectly through subsidiaries.

High capital requirements can be a barrier to entry because, if initial investment must be substantial, only very large firms can raise the capital required to enter the industry. Capital requirements are extremely high in both the copper and the aluminum industries. A new integrated 100×10^3 TPY mine-through-refinery copper operation might require $500 - 700 million; [6] integrated aluminum facilities require similar investments. [7]

A company that owns a low-cost ore deposit has an absolute cost advantage over one that must mine lower-quality ores. This absolute cost advantage is most important in the copper industry, because mining and milling costs constitute a high percent of total production costs, and because unexploited high-quality ore deposits are rare. Bain (1956) argued that the major barrier to entering the copper industry was the cost of obtaining a sufficiently large ore body to maintain production over the lifetime of the smelting and refining facilities. The major copper companies in the United

---

[6]   Arthur D. Little (1978) estimated capital costs at $5000 - 6000 per ton of capacity. Metal's Week (1977) estimated these costs at $6500-7000 per ton.

[7]   Charles River Associates (1976) estimated the capital cost of an integrated aluminum operation to be minimally $150 - 250 million, and perhaps as high as $1 billion. Mikesell (1978) estimated capital costs to be $2400 per ton or $450 million for a 200×10^3 TPY facility.

States control most of the known U.S. copper reserves, and their holdings include most high-quality sources. Lack of possession of low-cost ore deposits, though important, is not as large a barrier for the aluminum industry as it is for the copper industry, because the cost of bauxite is only a small fraction of the total cost of producing aluminum [8] and because aluminum ores are more abundant than are copper ores. An additional absolute cost advantage at the aluminum smelting stage is control over a low-cost hydroelectric-power source.

The existence of the four types of entry barriers -- economies of scale, vertical integration, high capital requirements, and the absolute cost advantage of controlling scarce natural resources -- implies that the primary copper and aluminum industries in the United States will continue to be highly concentrated and that most firms in these industries will continue to be large, vertically integrated, multinational corporations.

---

[8] Charles River Associates (1976) estimates showed the cost of bauxite to be about 6% of the total before-tax cost of producing primary aluminum at 1974 prices.

III:2   Cost Trends in Primary Production

The costs of producing copper and aluminum from ores are
extremely important in determining the price and production of these
metals.   In this section, we will examine the technology of primary
copper and aluminum production, the principal inputs to the mining,
refining, and smelting processes, and how input prices, ore quality,
and the input quantities required to produce a ton of metal have been
changing with time.

III:2:1 The Technology of Primary Copper and Aluminum
Production

There is much to contrast in the histories of copper and aluminum production.   Copper, which occurs in metallic form ("native"
copper), was known to primitive man and used for hammered imple-
ments.   More surprising is the recent discovery of copper smelters
dating from 4000 B.C. in the Timna Valley of the Middle East.   Smelting, the art of extracting the metal from its ores, had been mastered
at this very early date.   In this valley, copper was mined, smelted,
and formed into a variety of products that were widely traded.   Thus,
in 4000 B.C. just as today, the industry was vertically integrated
and the metal was internationally traded.

Aluminum, in contrast, is a modern metal.   Though extremely
abundant, aluminum was unknown to primitive man because in nature
it occurs only in chemical combination with other elements.   In the

19th century, aluminum was considered a precious metal. In fact, the peak of the capstone of the George Washington Monument in Washington D.C. is made of aluminum because aluminum was both valuable and rare in 1884 when the monument was completed. Not until the late 1880's were economical methods of extracting aluminum from its ores discovered. In the last one hundred years, aluminum has changed from a rare and precious metal to one of the most inexpensive and widely used materials.

In spite of the rapid growth of aluminum consumption and the multiplicity of new uses for the metal, aluminum technology has changed little since the time of the development of economical recovery methods. The three major steps in the production of primary aluminum are: mining and drying of ores, refining the ores into alumina (Al_2O_3, the aluminum oxide), and smelting the alumina into pure aluminum.

Although many types of mineral deposits contain aluminum, most aluminum is produced from bauxite. Bauxite is found in tropical regions where it lies near the surface and can be mined by open-pit methods. Bauxite is mined in the United States, but domestic mine production accounts for only about 12% of U.S. bauxite consumption. The rest is imported from such countries as Jamaica, Surinam, the Dominican Republic, and Guinea. After mining, the bauxite is crushed, ground, and kiln dried to remove the excess moisture. Typically, the dried bauxite is transported to the U.S. at this stage, where it is shipped to the refinery.

The method used to refine the bauxite into alumina is the

Bayer process, invented in 1888. This process is still the only commercial method for producing alumina, though new techniques of refining non-bauxitic resources are being developed. In the Bayer process, the bauxite is mixed with a hot solution of caustic soda that, on reaction, leaves alumina in solution and a sludge of impurities which are filtered. Alumina, which precipitates from the solution on cooling, is dried and shipped to the smelter.

At the smelter, aluminum is produced by electrolysis, using the Hall-Heroult process developed in 1886. New smelting methods are often experimented with, but none has been demonstrated to be superior to the Hall-Heroult method. In this process, alumina is dissolved in an electrolyte of molten cryolite (sodium-aluminum flouride) in a reduction cell or "pot". An electrical current is passed through suspended carbon anodes and deposits aluminum on the bottom carbon lining, which, when covered with a molten layer of aluminum, acts as a cathode. The separated oxygen plates out on the anode. Because the Hall-Heroult process uses so much electricity, aluminum smelters are usually located near cheap hydro-electric-power sources, mainly in the Pacific Northwest.

Several conclusions can be drawn from an analysis of primary aluminum technology. First, no major technological breakthroughs have taken place in the last few decades. Almost all aluminum is produced by open-pit mining techniques, the Bayer refining process, and the Hall-Heroult smelting method. In fact, the production of primary aluminum approximates a fixed-coefficient production function (with fixed input quantities required to produce a

51

unit of output).

Second, because an individual potline can be turned on or off, variable costs in smelting are approximately proportional to the number of potlines in operation, and short-run average variable costs are nearly constant until capacity is reached (where they become almost vertical). Also, until capacity constraints are encountered, smelter output can respond rapidly to changes in price and demand.

Finally, the principal change in the cost of producing primary aluminum in the last two decades has been the increasing cost of obtaining electricity. Other costs have also increased. For example, in 1974, Jamaica raised its tax on bauxite eightfold, and many other members of the International Bauxite Association (IBA) followed suit. However, because the cost of bauxite is such a small fraction of the cost of producing aluminum, the effect of increased royalties on aluminum costs has been smaller than the effect of subsequent energy-price increases. The high price of electricity greatly affects the primary producers, even though most smelters purchase electricity under long-term contracts and are partially insulated from energy-cost increases. When these contracts expire, they will probably not be renewed on favorable terms. Also, when aluminum demand is high or hydroelectric-power supply is low (as during a drought), smelters are forced to purchase electricity at spot-market prices that are considerably higher than contract prices. High energy prices in the last few years have, therefore, been of considerable concern to the primary-aluminum industry.

Just as in the aluminum industry, where major technological progress was made in the 1880's, new developments in copper production technology between 1904 and 1912 completely revolutionized the industry. The advent of large earth-moving equipment, particularly the power shovel and the caterpillar tread, made the mining of extremely low-grade ore bodies possible, and the discovery, in 1920, of froth flotation made concentration of low-grade sulfide ores very economical. In a ten-year period, eight major mines were brought into production in the Southwestern U.S., including many of the largest mines producing today. Since 1912, no comparable improvements have been made in copper mining and milling technology.

In the copper industry, the production process varies with the type of ore deposit mined. Most commercially mined copper ores in the U.S. come from oxide or sulfide mineral deposits. [9] Native copper ores, in which the copper occurs in metallic form, contribute only a small fraction to total U.S. mine production. About fifteen percent of U.S. copper comes from oxide sources. After the oxide ore is mined, the copper is leached from the ore by applying a solution of sulfuric acid. Copper is then recovered from the acid solution by precipitation on scrap iron, to produce cement copper, or by electrowinning. The product of the electrowinning process may require further refining or may be of sufficient purity to be shipped directly to the fabricator.

---

[9]   In contrast to aluminum ores, most of the copper ores used by domestic smelters and refineries are mined in the country. Only about 15% of U.S. refinery output originated abroad.

By far the most commonly mined copper ore in the U.S. is the sulfide ore. Primary production from sulfide deposits consists of four major steps: mining, milling or beneficiation, smelting, and refining. Most copper-bearing sulfide ores are mined from near-surface deposits by open-pit methods. However, about 15% of copper sulfide ores mined in the U.S. come from deeper deposits which must be mined by underground methods. If the material removed from the mine is fairly high grade, it can go directly to the mill. However, the material often consists of very low-grade rock as well as of high-grade ores. The very low-grade parts of ore bodies are mined, taken to a dump, and leached with sulfuric acid to produce cement copper. The higher grade ore is sent to the mill for crushing, grinding, and flotation to separate sulfide minerals from rock particles. The output of the mill is a sulfide concentrate containing approximately 25% copper. This concentrate is sent to the smelter where it is mixed with the cement copper produced by the leaching and precipitation operations.

In the smelter, the mixture of concentrates and cement copper is sent to a reverberatory furnace where matte (approximately 50% copper) is produced. The liquid matte is transferred into converters that oxidize the iron and sulfur in the matte, leaving an impure blister containing about 98% copper. The last operation in the smelter is the fire refining of blister into anode copper and the casting of anodes which are shipped to the refinery. [10]

---

[10] Some fire-refined copper is cast directly into forms for industrial use.

The major operation in the refinery is the electrolytic refining of anode into cathode copper (99.9% pure) in an electrolyte of sulfuric acid. The cathodes are sold or melted and cast into commercial refinery shapes -- wirebars, ingots, cakes, slabs, and billets -- known collectively as "refined" copper.

Because ores generally contain less than 1% copper, beneficiation almost always takes place near the mine. Most smelters are located near mills for the same reason. However, because both blister and anode copper are nearly pure metal, transport costs are approximately the same whether blister, anode, or refined copper is shipped. Therefore, refineries can be located near smelters or near markets.

Several conclusions can be drawn from an analysis of primary copper technology. First, unlike the processing of aluminum, primary copper production does not approximate a fixed coefficient production function. The process used to convert copper ores into refined copper depends on many characteristics of the ore deposit mined, such as mineralogical and chemical properties (whether the ore is sulfide, oxide, or native copper, for example), ore grade (the proportion of metal contained in ore in the ground), and the stripping ratio (the ratio of waste rock to ore). These deposit characteristics vary from region to region; they also vary with time as near-surface or higher grade ore bodies are depleted. Therefore, the cost of producing copper will vary for many reasons, of which changing input prices is only one.

Second, because increasing the production of copper usually

implies changing the quality and characteristics of copper ores mined (even in the short run), we cannot expect the average variable cost of producing copper to be constant. Short-run average variable costs probably increase gradually until capacity constraints are approached and then rise sharply.

And finally, primary-copper production, though not as energy intensive as primary-aluminum production, requires many types of fuels at each stage of the production process. Natural gas, middle distillate, and residual fuel oil are used in large quantities in copper production, and the prices of these fuels have been rising faster than the price of electricity, which is also a major input. The increasing cost of fuel can therefore be expected to be a major concern for the copper industry as well as for the aluminum industry.

In the next section, the behavior of the prices of the principal inputs to primary copper and aluminum production are discussed and the effect of changing input prices on production cost is analysed.

III:2:2   The Prices of the Principal Inputs to Primary
          Production and Their Effect on Cost

Production costs are usually divided into fixed costs (which
are incurred by the firm whether it produces or not) and variable
costs (which increase with the quantity of output produced). Fixed
costs include capital costs, as well as taxes and insurance; variable costs include wages, energy, and other raw-material costs. In
this section, we focus on the behavior of the prices of the principal variable inputs to primary copper and aluminum production over
the historic period, 1954 to 1976, and how changing input prices
affect production cost. [11]

The principal variable inputs to primary copper and aluminum
production are labor, energy, and certain industrial chemicals. [12]
Yearly average prices for each major input in both industries have been
constructed. Wages in copper production are a weighted average of the
U.S. Bureau of Labor Statistics (BLS) average hourly earnings in copper
mining and average hourly earnings in primary metals. The weights are
proportional to the number of employees in each sector (copper mining
and primary copper production) in 1974. Because little aluminum ore
is mined in the United States, wages in aluminum production are the
BLS average hourly earnings in primary-aluminum manufacturing. [13]

---

[11]   As will be seen in section III:4, with the pricing model
       used, the only fixed-cost variable that enters the primary-
       price equations is the opportunity cost of capital.

[12]   Other variable inputs, such as explosives, are used in
       mining, but labor, energy, and chemicals are the most impor-
       tant factors.

Figures III:2:1 and 2 show plots of the prices of the principal variable inputs to copper and aluminum production respectively. All input prices were deflated by the BLS wholesale price
index, (1967=1), thus they are in 1967 constant dollars. Wages are
shown as solid lines in the top halves of the figures; they can be seen
to increase with time. However, wages are measured in dollars per
man. A more meaningful cost to the producer is wage cost per ton
of metal produced, which can be obtained by dividing the industry
wage ($/man) by labor productivity in the industry (tons/man).
Labor productivity in copper production was constructed as a weighted
average of the BLS labor productivity indices for copper mining and
primary-copper production with the same weights as were used in constructing copper wages. Labor productivity in aluminum production
is the BLS labor productivity index for primary-aluminum manufacturing. Deflated wages divided by labor productivity are shown as dashed
lines in the upper halves in figures III:2:1 and 2. Labor costs
per ton of metal produced have actually fallen in both industries,
but the decline has been more pronounced in the copper industry.

Energy- and chemical-input prices can be constructed from
indices produced by the BLS in tabulating the wholesale-price index
(WPI). The principal types of energy used in primary-copper production
are natural gas, electricity, [14] middle distillate, and residual

---

13   This series starts in 1963. To obtain earlier years, average
      hourly earnings in primary aluminum production was regressed on
      average hourly earnings in primary metals and backcasted.
      (See appendix C).

14   Because the WPI price index for electricity starts in 1958, the
      Edison Electric Institute price index was used in its stead.

fuel oil. To represent the price of energy to the copper produ-

cer, a weighted average of these energy prices was constructed

using weights proportional to the Btu value of the use of each type

of energy in the copper industry in 1972 (as reported by the U.S.

Department of Commerce, Office of Energy Programs). [15] The prin-

cipal type of energy consumed in primary-aluminum production is elec-

tricity, most of which is used in smelting. Natural gas is also

used, primarily in refining. Because electricity is such an impor-

tant input to aluminum production, and because the electrolytic pro-

cess requires electricity (whereas many fuels can generate steam at

the refinery), the electricity-price index was used to represent the

price of energy to the aluminum producer. Deflated energy prices

are shown by dashed lines in the bottom halves of figures III:2:1

and 2.

The principal chemicals used in primary copper production

are sulfuric acid (used in leaching and refining) [16] and

various chemical reagents (used in flotation). The principal

chemicals used in primary-aluminum production are hydrofluoric acid

(used in forming the molten cryolite electrolyte in the smelter

potline) and caustic soda (which dissolves the alumina in the Bayer

process). To represent the prices of chemicals to the primary

---

[15]   Of course, these weights change with time. However, 1976
       is the only other year for which weights are available. The
       1976 weights are not very different from those of 1972. In
       particular, the ranking of fuels according to usage remains
       unchanged.

[16]   Sulfuric acid is both an input (to leaching and refining)
       and an output (of the smelter). Often the sulfuric acid is
       recycled within the same establishment.

producers, it would be desirable to construct weighted averages of
chemical-price indices, with weights proportional to their usage
in the copper and aluminum industries. However, comprehensive figures on chemical usage were not available. Therefore, it was necessary to use one chemical for each industry -- sulfuric acid for
copper and hydrofluoric acid for aluminum [17] -- as proxies for more
general price indices. [18] Deflated chemical prices are plotted as
solid lines in the bottom halves of figures III:2:1 and 2. [19]

In the aluminum model, bauxite is considered a variable input.
Bauxite, unlike copper ore, is treated as an exogenous input for
two reasons. First, the cost of mining bauxite is only a small
fraction of the cost of producing aluminum. To treat copper
mining and milling costs, which constitute the principal costs
in primary-copper production, as exogenous would be very unrealistic,
but to view bauxite as just another raw material in the production
of aluminum does not seem unreasonable. Second, because most
bauxite is mined overseas and shipped to the U.S., the price of
bauxite depends on many factors, such as producer-country

---

17 The BLS hydrofluoric acid price index starts in 1959. To
    obtain earlier years, the hydrofluoric acid index was regressed
    on the price of flurospar (from the Bureau of Mines Minerals
    Yearbook) and backcasted. (See appendix C).

18 In estimating the price equations of section III:4, it would
    be possible to have the price index of each chemical used as
    a separate explanatory variable in the equation, but we run
    into problems with degrees of freedom.

19 Because no time-series data on energy and chemical usage per
    ton of metal exist, it is not possible to construct unit
    energy and chemical costs as was done for labor.

tax policies, whose prediction is beyond the scope of this study. However, changes in such variables as producer—country tax policies can be handled exogenously, and the effects of such changes on the domestic aluminum industry can be analysed within the framework of the CAS model. It is therefore necessary to construct a variable that represents the cost of bauxite to the aluminum producer. The variable used was the average value of crude undried domestic bauxite shipments as reported in the U.S. Bureau of Mines Minerals Yearbook. [20] This deflated price is the dotted line in figure III:2:2.

An examination of figure III:2:1 shows that the deflated prices of all three variable inputs to copper production have been rising. Wages rose steadily over the period. However, increased efficiency in the use of labor led to a decline in wage cost per ton of metal produced. Chemical prices were higher in the second half of the period than in the first, and energy prices rose dramatically after 1973. The data needed to construct unit energy and chemical costs for these industries do not exist. However, increased efficiency in the use of these inputs has probably not been comparable to the rise in labor productivity seen. If anything, the use of energy and chemicals has probably increased as production has become more capital intensive.

---

[20] Most bauxite is not sold; it is transferred within one integrated firm. In addition, only about 15% of the bauxite processed in the U.S. comes from domestic mines. However, the U.S. price should reflect mining, tax, and transport conditions abroad. The rational domestic mining concern will exploit lower quality deposits until marginal mining cost equals the delivered cost of the cheapest foreign source.

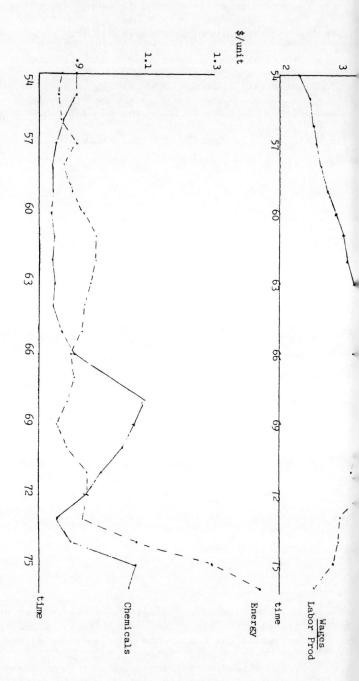

$/unit

1.3

1.1

.9

3

2

54   57   60   63   66   69   72   75   time

Wages
Labor Prod

Energy

Chemicals

54   57   60   63   66   69   72   75   time

62

Figure III:2:2 reveals that behavior for wages and wage cost per ton in the aluminum industry is similar to that in the copper industry. However, the deflated prices of the other variable inputs to aluminum production did not rise uniformly. Chemical prices oscillated but showed no marked trend; electricity prices fell until 1973 and rose thereafter (but not quite to their 1954 level), and deflated domestic bauxite prices rose until 1968 but fell after that year.

In section III:4, these input prices will be used in estimating the copper and aluminum primary-price equations.

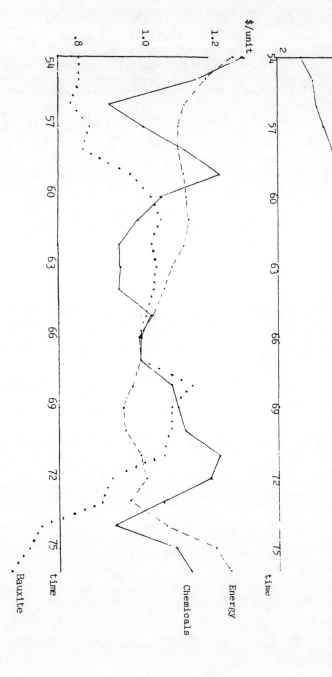

III:2:3   Natural-Resource Costs -- Ore Quality Measures

Many factors affect mineral industry costs -- the state
of technology, input prices, tax policies, and environmental
regulations -- to name a few. In the very long run, however,
geologic considerations will be the most important cost
determinants. Singer (1977) noted three geological factors that
affect metal availability and production cost: the amount of
metal in the earth's crust at each range of grades; its mineralogical form and chemical state; and its spatial distribution.
These three factors combined provide an index of metal-resource
quality.

Grade, the proportion of metal contained in ore in the ground,
determines the amount of rock that must be mined, crushed, ground,
and concentrated in the production process. As grade falls, costs
rise. Mineralogical and chemical properties determine the difficulty of liberating the metal from its ores. Generally, sulfide and
oxide ores are less costly to process than are the more abundant
but more refractory silicate minerals. Spatial properties such as
deposit size and shape and the thickness of overburden determine
the mining technique to be used; geographic location affects transport, labor, and other costs.

Though no single factor is a good indicator of ore quality, the average yield of ores mined is perhaps the best measure. Yield, defined as metal produced divided by ore mined, depends on deposit geometry and mineralogy as well as on grade; unfortunately, it also depends on the beneficiation technology. However, we concentrate on changes in yield as a measure of changes in ore quality in spite of this drawback.

An understanding of how copper-production costs vary as a function of the yield of copper ores mined is necessary. All mining and milling costs (capital, labor, chemical, and energy) vary with yield, but we will look only at energy cost per ton of metal as a function of yield because several people have attempted to measure this cost (Battelle, 1975, Bravard et al, 1972, Chapman, 1974, Page and Creasey, 1975). Other input requirements should change as yield changes in a manner similar to energy requirements. [21]

If we wish to determine energy usage in mineral processing as a function of time, we can look at the three components of this usage expressed in equations III:2:1 to III:2:3.

---

[21]   The argument used later to support the hyperbolic increase
        in energy use as ore grade falls applies to any input.

III:2:1 $E_T = E(Y_T)$

III:2:2 $Y_T = Y(\int_{T_0}^{T} Q_t \, dt)$

III:2:3 $O_T = Q(P_T, IP_T, O_{T-1})$

where E_T is energy usage per ton of metal at time T

            Y_T is average yield of ores mined at time T

            O_T is metal production at time T

            P_T is metal price at time T

and IP_T is industrial production at time T.

Equation III:2:1 states that energy usage per ton of metal produced at time T is a function of the yield of ores mined at that time. The second equation states that yield at time T is a function of cumulative production up to that point. And the last equation states that production at time T is a lagged function of metal price and of industrial production in the economy. [22] This last equation is the supply curve and will be discussed at length in section III:5. The other two relationships will be analysed here.

Perhaps the best study of energy use in mineral processing is the process analysis study made by Chapman (1974). He determined direct and indirect energy inputs to copper and aluminum production at each stage of the production process for the most commonly mined

---

[22] Q_{T-1} is included in equation III:2:3 as a proxy for the investment delay implicit in changes in supply. See III:5:3.

ore types, and summed over the processes to obtain total energy input per ton of metal produced. Next, Chapman noted that, as the grade of an ore falls, [23] energy use in mining and milling increases hyperbolically, because it is the tonnage of rock processed that determines the amount used. [24] In contrast, the energy cost of refining and smelting does not depend on the initial metal content of the ore. [25] Therefore, total energy cost per ton of metal (E_T) can be expressed as a simple function of ore grade (G_T)

III:2:4 $E_T = c_0 / G_T + c_1$

where c_0/G is energy cost per ton of contained metal mined and milled, for ore grade G (the grade used in the process analysis)

and c_1 is energy cost per ton of contained metal refined and smelted.

---

23   Chapman wrote his equation in terms of grade, not yield. However, because he assumed constant recovery rates for each process, yield and grade are constant multiples of one another.

24   This argument requires that the same mining and milling techniques be used as grade falls. The assumption may not be realistic, but the energy – ore grade relationship is employed here only as a heuristic device.

25   For example, most copper smelters are set up to handle a narrow range of mineral compositions, implying that energy requirements in smelting are fixed and are independent of the initial grade.

Figure III:2:3 shows plots of the energy-ore grade relationships obtained from Chapman's data. An examination of these curves
shows that, whereas in the U.S. copper industry, a fall in grade
would cause a large increase in energy usage, in the aluminum industry, a change in the grade of ores mined would have little effect.
This result is to be expected, because mining and initial processing
costs are only a small fraction of the cost of producing aluminum
but are the major outlays in copper production. The figure also shows
that primary-aluminum production requires about three times as much
energy per ton of metal as primary copper production, but this relative energy usage rate may not continue. A sharp decline in the grade
of copper ores mined would make copper extraction and processing almost as energy intensive in the future as aluminum production is today.

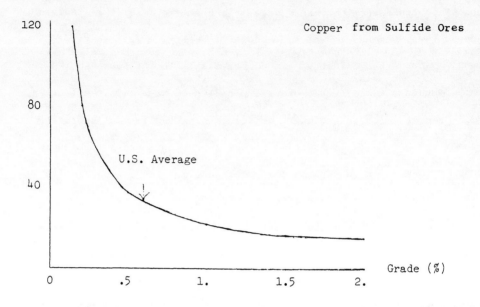

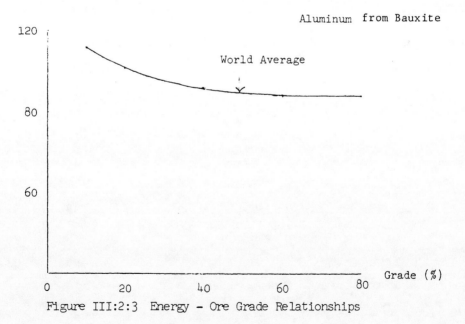

Figure III:2:3 Energy – Ore Grade Relationships

The relationship between yield and cumulative production of a metal (equation III:2:2) is much more complicated than is the energy - ore grade relationship. If the quality and quantity of metal reserves were known with certainty, and if high-quality ores were mined first, quantifying equation III:2:2 would be fairly straight-forward. However, the exploration process is constantly adding to the stock of reserves and determining their quality with greater accuracy. Because the results of investment in exploration are extremely difficult to predict, we cannot say much about reserves ten years hence. However, we can get a rough idea about the behavior of the yield - cumulative production relationship from examining the left-hand side of equation III:2:2 (yield as a function of time). Figure III:2:4 is a plot of the average yield of copper ores mined in the U.S. from 1953 to 1976. The fall in yield over the period has been dramatic, (.89 to .51), implying a change from 19 to 28 x 10^3 kWh per ton in energy usage, if we use Chapman's equation. In contrast, the average yield of aluminum ores mined during the same period remained relatively constant.

71

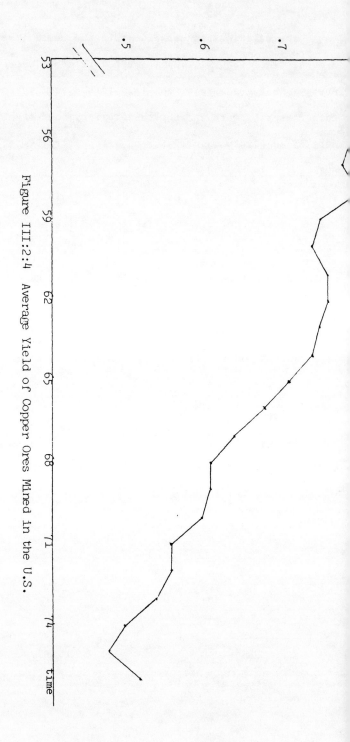

Figure III:2:4 Average Yield of Copper Ores Mined in the U.S.

72

The yield of copper ores mined is only one measure of copper-ore quality. Many other factors such as geographic location and deposit depth, geometry, and mineralogy influence mining cost. Unfortunately, because no time-series data on these variables are available, they cannot be analysed statistically. One variable, the annual production of primary copper in the U.S., was chosen as a proxy for all the other ore-quality measures. When the demand for copper is low, high-cost mines are closed first. Similarly, when demand is high, marginal deposits are worked. We can therefore expect that mining cost per ton of metal produced will be positively related to the level of output in any year. Figure III:2:5 lends credence to this statement. The figure was constructed from data in an article by Knight and Davies (1978) and shows how world refined-copper costs varied as a function of world output in 1976. The shape of the curve for U.S. copper production should be similar. [26] A considerable variation in production cost can be seen; refined copper from some deposits was produced for as little as twenty cents per pound, but copper from other deposits cost as much as ninety cents per pound. The U.S. price of copper that year was seventy cents per pound (and the world price was lower), implying that about fifteen percent of the copper produced in 1976 was produced at a loss.

---

[26] This curve, like the energy-ore grade relationship, is used
      only as a heuristic device. Therefore, its precise shape is
      not important.

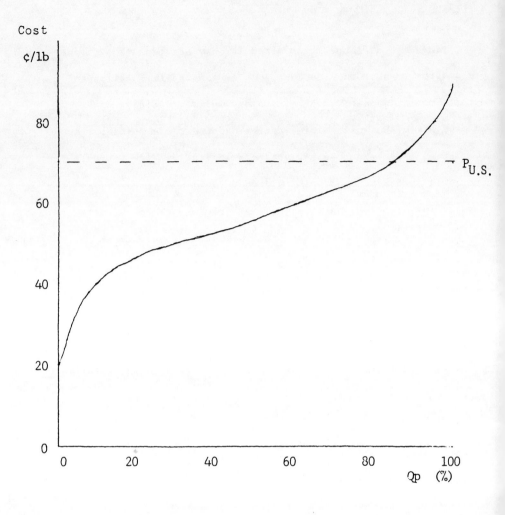

Figure III:2:5 World Refined Copper Cost in 1976
as a Function of Output

Figures III:2:3 and 5 indicate that primary-copper production costs vary considerably and that both the yield of copper ores mined and the level of copper production are important determinants of this variation. Therefore, when the price equations in section III:4:3 are specified, ore quality is a major factor in determining average costs in primary copper production. In contrast, ore quality does not enter into the calculation of aluminum costs in the model for two reasons. First, if the yield of aluminum ores were to decline, aluminum-cost changes would be small, and second, because aluminum ores are relatively abundant, significant quality deterioration is not apt to occur in the next decade.

Before looking at pricing in the primary copper and aluminum industries, we must examine one more cost item -- transport cost.

III:2:4 Transport Cost

Ores and metals are transported at many stages in the production of copper and aluminum. Therefore, any account of copper and aluminum industry costs would be incomplete without some discussion of transport costs.

If the production of aluminum took place within one country, it would be efficient to locate the refinery near the mine because shipping one ton of metal contained in alumina is cheaper than shipping its equivalent contained in bauxite. (The refinery reduces the volume of material by approximately a factor of two). However, because mines are often located in developing countries where capital costs are high and political policies uncertain, refineries are more apt to be built in industrial countries near smelters (which are in turn built near cheap sources of electricity). Therefore, the principal transport cost incurred in the production of domestic aluminum is the cost of shipping bauxite to the U.S. This cost accounts for from about one quarter to more than one half of the delivered cost of bauxite (Charles River Associates, 1976). However (as mentioned in section III:2:2), in the aluminum model, bauxite price is exogenous. Transport costs will be reflected in the price of bauxite, and there should be no need to consider these costs separately.

Transport costs in the copper industry are small. Dammert and Kendrick (1977) constructed a model of the world copper industry and

76

used linear programming to minimize total industry costs. In their
optimal solution, transportation accounted for only 1.5% of projected
world copper costs in 1980. As noted by Banks (1974), transport costs
in the U.S. copper industry are much less than those in the rest of the
world. Transportation should therefore account for considerably less
than 1.5% of the cost of producing domestic copper. It therefore
seems reasonable to neglect transportation-cost variables in the copper model as well as in the aluminum model. [27]

---

[27] A transportation-cost series based on shipping rates was
tested in both the copper and the aluminum price equations
and proved to be insignificant, as would be expected from
the arguments advanced above.

III:3 Estimating the Equations in the Copper and Aluminum Industry Models

In the next two sections of this chapter, the primary copper-
and aluminum-industry price and output equations are presented. But
first, the conventions used in the estimation process must be specified. A general discussion of these conventions is given here, and
more detailed descriptions of statistical techniques are given in
appendices following each chapter. The remarks of this section
apply to all of the model equations presented in this chapter and
in chapters IV and VI.

The data used to estimate most of the primary- and secondary-
copper- and aluminum-industry model equations consist of yearly time
series for the period 1954 to 1976. The series start in 1954 so that
disruptions due to the Korean War -- the closure of the London Metal
Exchange and price controls and rationing in the U.S. -- are avoided.
In the aluminum-price equations (both primary and secondary), data
problems were encountered with the early years of the 1954-1976
period (reflecting the aftermath of price controls and rationing).
Therefore, the first one or two years of the series were dropped
from the data used to estimate these equations. A listing of the
data used in the model, together with the data source for each
variable, is given in appendix C.

The equations presented form a simultaneous system that require
the use of instruments for the jointly dependent variables. The
instruments used for the endogenous explanatory variables appearing

78

in the aluminum-industry model equations consist of the predetermined variables in the aluminum model, [28] and those for the
endogenous explanatory variables in the copper-industry model
equations consist of the predetermined variables in the copper
model. [29] The simultaneous equations were estimated by two-stage
least squares.

All of the model equations were estimated in real (1967 constant) dollars. That is, all prices -- primary and secondary
metal, primary and secondary input, and sector output prices -- were
divided by the Bureau of Labor Statistics Wholesale-Price Index
(1967 = 1).

The variables to be included in each equation in the copper
and aluminum industry models were determined by a combination of
a knowledge of the industry and of economic theory. Therefore, if a
variable is dropped from an equation, the equation may be

---

[28]   The exogenous-variable instruments for the aluminum model
       were: the prices of the principal inputs to primary alumi-
       num production, the sector output prices, the index of
       industrial production, and a dummy variable for price con-
       trols in the aluminum industry. The lagged endogenous-
       variable instruments were: primary price, net imports, changes
       in inventories, and aluminum consumption. For both copper
       and aluminum, some lagged endogenous variables (such as
       primary production, whose lagged value was not very signi-
       ficant in either primary production equation) were not used
       as instruments. These predetermined variables were not used
       because it was necessary to reduce the number of instruments.

[29]   The exogenous-variable instruments for the copper model
       were: the prices of the principal inputs to primary copper
       production, the sector output prices, the index of indus-
       trial production, the yield of copper ores, changes in the
       government stockpile, and a dummy variable for strikes in
       the copper industry. The lagged endogenous-variable
       instruments were: copper consumption and private copper
       inventories.

misspecified, and bias in the coefficient estimates will result. On the other hand, when working with a small number of observations, increasing the degrees of freedom by dropping variables whose estimated coefficients are not significant may improve the accuracy of the estimates. There is always a trade-off between these two conflicting objectives -- better specification or more degrees of freedom. In the copper- and aluminum-industry model equations, a variable was usually dropped from an equation if the t-ratio of its estimated coefficient was less than one -- a compromise between the two conflicting objectives. This rule for retaining or dropping a variable leads to a maximum value of $\overline{R}^2$.

In the presentation of results, the numbers in parentheses under the estimated coefficients are the t-ratios of the corresponding coefficients (the ratios of the estimated coefficients to their asymptotic standard errors). Under each equation, the years of the data used to estimate the equation (usually 1954 - 1976), R^2 and the F statistic for the equation, the Durbin-Watson statistic (DW), and ρ, the estimated first-order autocorrelation coefficient for the error term (if applicable), are shown. A $\char`^$ over any variable in an equation implies that instruments were used for that variable in estimating the equation.

Each estimated equation is presented in the chapter where the related aspect of the industry is discussed. However, appendix A contains a summary of all of the variable names used in the model and appendix B lists all of the model equations, the number of the page where the equation appears, and the equation number in the text.

III:4 Primary Prices -- Mechanisms and Trends

In this section and the next, the principal primary-industry economic decisions -- what price to charge for a product and how much to produce at that price -- are discussed. Figure III:4:1, a flow chart of a primary industry econometric model, shows how price and output are jointly determined by cost and demand conditions in the econometric models. [31] In this section, a theoretical model of pricing in the primary industries is developed, and primary-price equations based on this model are estimated. But first, we define primary price behavioral mechanisms and analyse the behavior of primary prices over the historic period, 1954 to 1976, the period of the data used in estimating the model equations.

---

[31] For an explanation of the symbols used in the flow chart, see chapter I page 9.

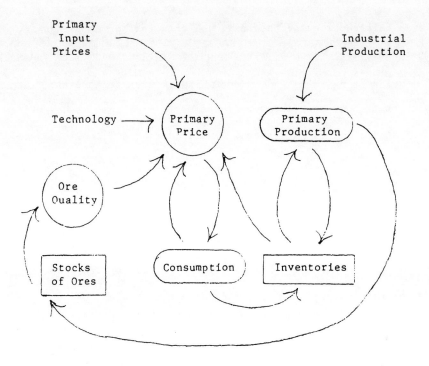

Figure III:4:1   Flow Chart of a Primary Industry
                 Econometric Model

82

III:4:1 Definition of Alternative Behavioral Pricing
Mechanisms

In both the copper and the aluminum industries, many products
are produced, each having a separate price. Copper production
starts with ore and goes on to concentrates, blister, and refined copper, but that is not the end. The refined copper goes to the brass and
wire mills, foundries, and powder plants. The products of the semifabricators go to the consuming sectors -- the construction, transportation, consumer-product, industrial-machinery, and electronic industries -- who in turn fashion new products. At some stages, metal is
sold in a market, whereas at other stages, it is transferred within the
same integrated firm. Aluminum production and pricing are equally complex. It is therefore difficult to say what the "price" of copper or
aluminum is.

In spite of this multiplicity of products and prices, there are
really only two methods of price determination in these industries,
determination by producers and by commodity exchanges. The two pricing
mechanisms are very different and result in dissimilar price behavior.

Producer prices are those set by the major firms in the industry. These prices change only at discrete intervals and have smaller
variances than exchange prices. In the copper industry, the producer price is that set by the major American and Canadian primary producers and is the price at which most domestic refineries sell copper
to affiliated and independent fabricators. About 75% of the refined
copper in the U.S. is sold at this price. The producer price represents
a common set of price quotations for delivery of refined copper to any
place in the nation. Some refinery shapes sell at slight discounts

and others at premiums, but the prices of all shapes are tied to a single price, the producer price. The data for the U.S. producer price of copper used in this study come from the U.S. Bureau of Mines Minerals Yearbook; it is an annual average of the daily weighted average of producers delivered price quotations for refined copper published in Metals Week. The producer price is based to a large extent on production costs and is moderately stable.

Commodity-exchange prices are related to price quotations on the major metal exchanges, the New York Commodity Exchange (COMEX) and the London Metal Exchange (LME). [32] The commodity exchanges are basically hedge and speculative markets, not physical markets. Prices are competitively determined in daily auctions where dealers make bids and offers and contracts are issued when the bids or offers are accepted. Some of the smaller U.S. primary copper producers sell at COMEX prices, and most of the refined copper sold outside of the U.S. and Canada, as well as copper imported into the U.S., moves at prices based on LME quotes. Secondary copper prices, though often not determined directly by the exchanges, are highly correlated with exchange prices. Commodity-exchange prices, unlike producer prices, fluctuate with short-run changes in supply and demand and are very unstable.

Copper product prices (the prices of sheet, tube, wire, castings, etc.) follow the price of refined copper closely and are not considered here.

---

[32] Not all metal sold at "exchange" prices is actually sold on an exchange. There are many complicated formulas relating copper prices to metal-exchange quotations.

Figure III:4:2 shows the behavior of the two types of copper prices. The U.S. producer price, plotted with a heavy solid line, changes only at discrete intervals. The exchange prices, LME, plotted with a heavy dashed line, and COMEX, plotted with a light solid line, fluctuate above and below the producer price; and the number two scrap price, plotted with a light dashed line, follows the movements of the exchange prices, but at a nearly constant discount.

In the aluminum industry, commodity exchanges play a very small role because the metal exchanges deal principally in copper, lead, zinc, tin, and silver. The world aluminum market, unlike the world copper market, is sufficiently concentrated so that world aluminum prices, as well as U.S. prices, are producer prices. Secondary-aluminum prices, however, are competitively determined.

The data for the U.S. producer price of aluminum used in this study comes from the U.S. Bureau of Mines Minerals Yearbook; it is an annual average of the f.o.b. list price of aluminum primary ingot published by the American Metal Market. Like the producer price of copper, the primary-aluminum price is based largely on production cost and is fairly stable. Scrap prices, however, which are competitively determined, fluctuate from day to day. Aluminum-product prices, like those of copper, are highly correlated with the primary-ingot price and are not considered here.

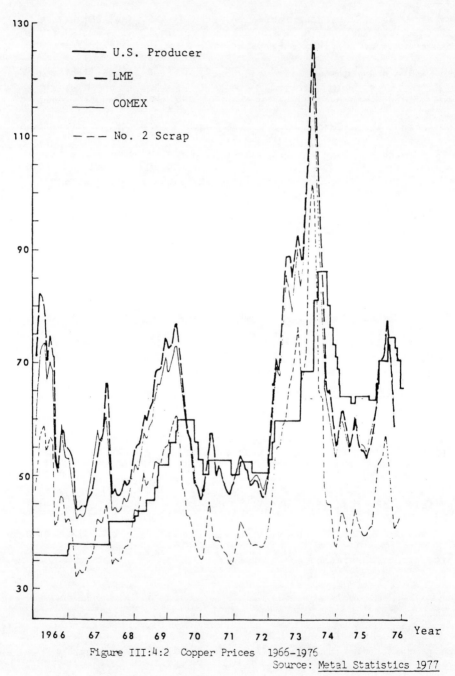

¢/lb.

Figure III:4:2 Copper Prices 1966-1976
Source: Metal Statistics 1977

86

Table III:4:1 summarizes the behavioral mechanisms that determine copper and aluminum prices in the U.S. and the world. In the U.S., most primary metal is sold at producer prices, and most secondary metal is sold at prices related to exchange prices. However, in the world industry, the pricing mechanisms for the two metals differ. Although most copper outside the U.S. is sold at prices related to exchange prices, most aluminum outside the U.S. is sold at producer prices.

TABLE III:4:1
COPPER AND ALUMINUM PRICING MECHANISMS

	World	U.S. Primary	U.S. Secondary
Copper	Exchange	Producer	Exchange
Aluminum	Producer	Producer	Exchange

In both the copper and the aluminum industries, when demand is low, producers offer discounts from list prices. There is therefore, at times, a separate transactions price for both metals. However, because the list price is a better indicator of long-run cost conditions and price trends than is the transactions price, it should provide a better signal to purchasers of the desirability of substitution. Because both copper and aluminum are intermediate inputs, substitution of one for the other is usually not possible without altering capital equipment. Purchasers will therefore make plans on the basis of long-run price trends, not short-run fluctuations. For this reason, no separate transactions price will be considered here.

87

III:4:2 Primary-Price History: 1954 to 1976

In spite of severely depressed conditions in the copper industry
between 1975 and 1978,[33] the long-term trend in the U.S. producer price
of copper in the post-Korean War period is positive. Figure III:4:3
shows a plot of the U.S. producer price of refined copper deflated
by the Bureau of Labor Statistics wholesale-price index. This
deflated price is subject to strong cyclical fluctuations, but
when the fluctuations are removed, it can be seen to increase with
time. The dashed line in figure III:4:3 shows the twenty-three-
year trend in copper price obtained by regressing deflated price
on time.

The increase in the price of copper in the post-Korean War
period is in sharp contrast to the findings of Herfindahl (1959)
and Barnett and Morse (1963) for the period from 1870 to 1957.
Herfindahl found that copper prices remained unchanged for long
periods of time. He noted a sharp decline in the deflated price
of copper after World War I, as technological progress lowered
costs, but found that, from the end of World War I to 1957, copper
prices remained very nearly constant. Barnett and Morse looked

---

33   In the 1975-78 period, copper prices were depressed (due to
      worldwide excess supply). By 1979, however, copper prices
      were again close to their long-run trend.

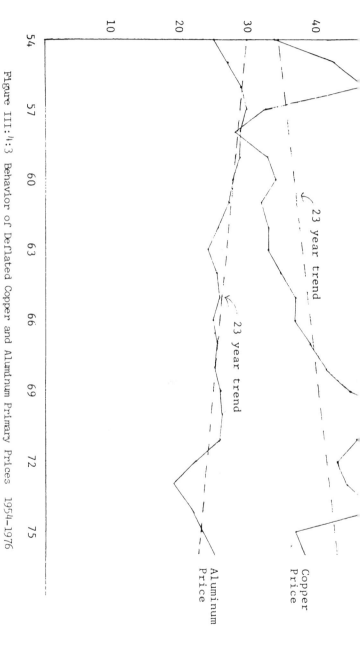

Figure III:4:3 Behavior of Deflated Copper and Aluminum Primary Prices 1954-1976

89

at real costs of production (capital and labor inputs per unit of output) in the mineral sector as a whole during the same period (1870-1957). They found a significant downward trend that became more pronounced in the later years.

There are many possible reasons why the pattern of constant or falling copper prices has not continued in recent years, but probably the most important contributors to higher copper prices have been cost considerations, such as the falling quality of ores mined and the rising prices of the principal inputs to copper production. (See sections III:2:2 and III:2:3.) It is informative to examine the significance of this upward trend in copper costs and prices. As Hotelling (1931) noted, the price of an exhaustible resource sold in a competitive market is equal to extraction and marketing cost plus scarcity rent (the value of the ore in the ground). Rising price may reflect either rising mining and processing cost or rising scarcity rent; [34] however, both phenomena indicate increasing metal scarcity. We consume copper, not copper ores, and copper production requires the use of many factors in addition to ores. If the cost of producing copper is rising because scarcity rents are earned in the energy industries, for example, metal production is consuming scarce energy resources. If, on the other hand, the price rise is due to new environmental regulations, these regulations only exist because copper production requires

---

34 A price increase could also be caused by a change from competitive to monopoly pricing in the industry, but there is no evidence of increased market power in either U.S. or world copper markets. (See section III:1.)

the use of valuable environmental resources -- air and water. In either of the above cases, as well as in the case where copper ores earn higher rents, copper, the metal, is becoming relatively scarce. The issue of scarcity rent in the copper industry is discussed at greater length in appendix III:2.

The adequacy of mineral materials to support continued growth of industrial economies without prohibitive costs is a much debated issue that gives rise to many divergent opinions. It is not the intent here to summarize or contribute further to this debate, but merely to point out that the factors leading to a rise in copper prices -- depletion of high-quality ore deposits and rising capital, labor, energy, and other raw material costs -- are phenomena that will be of continuing concern in the future. There are few grounds for optimism about the reversal of copper-cost trends in the U.S. in the next decade.

Aluminum price, in contrast to copper price, fell during the post-Korean War period. Figure III:4:3 shows plots of the deflated price of aluminum primary ingot, together with its twenty three-year trend. A downward trend in the price of primary aluminum is not surprising because the quality of aluminum ores mined has not deteriorated and primary-aluminum input prices have not all risen uniformly during the period of interest. (See sections III:2:2-3). Nonincreasing input prices, coupled with technological improvements, should imply falling aluminum prices. However, looking at the last four years of the period, 1973-1976, we see a sharp increase in the deflated price of aluminum. 1973, the turning point for aluminum price, coincides with the OPEC petroleum-price increases that have led to higher costs of purchasing all types of energy.

Because primary aluminum production is very energy intensive, a

rise in aluminum price when energy prices increase is to be

expected. It would, therefore, be foolish to predict the continua-

tion of the downward trend in aluminum prices that we see if we

look at the entire period. Instead, the upward trend that can be

noted after 1973 is more likely to prevail in future years.

In the next section, a model is developed that explains the

movements in the primary prices of copper and aluminum that we have

observed here.

III:4:3   Specification of a Primary Price Equation

The theory of price formation in manufacturing industries has
focused on the role of market structure in determining price behavior. In a series of interview studies of actual pricing practices
in large companies, Lanzillotti (1958) found that the most commonly
stressed pricing goals were

  1)   pricing to achieve a target return on investment

  2)   stabilization of price and margin

  3)   pricing to realize a target market share

and   4)   pricing to meet or prevent competition.

The difference between strategies one and two is difficult to define,
because it is not stated how the target return or the markup over
cost is determined. For example, the markup of strategy two may be
set to achieve the target-rate of return on capital of strategy one.

The Council on Wage and Price Stability (1976) found that, in
the aluminum industry, price leaders use a full-cost approach for
setting list prices. To determine price, firms add a profit margin to
the long-run average cost of producing an item, where long-run average
cost is calculated at some standard rate of output (or capacity utilization). Followers then choose to adopt the leaders' price.

To see that full-cost pricing is compatible with long-run profit
maximization, we can use the following formula from microeconomics.

$$MR = P(1 - 1/\mu)$$

where MR is marginal revenue, P is price, and μ is the leader's price

93

elasticity of demand. [35] To maximize profits, marginal revenue is equated to marginal cost (MC).

$$MR = MC.$$

If long-run average cost is constant, then, in the long-run, average and marginal costs are equal and

$$MR = P(1 - 1/\mu) = LRAC$$

which, after algebraic simplification, becomes

$$P = \left[1 + \frac{1}{\mu - 1} \right] LRAC. \text{[36]}$$

Therefore, to maximize profits in the long-run, price is set equal to a markup over long-run average cost, where the markup depends on the long-run elasticity of demand (the more elastic the demand, the smaller the markup).

---

[35] Full-cost pricing is also compatible with industry profit maximization in a collusive oligopoly, but in this case, μ would be the industry's elasticity of demand.

[36] For profit maximization, μ must be greater than one. That is, if MR = MC, marginal revenue must be positive, implying that μ is greater than one and $1/(\mu - 1)$ is greater than zero.

A full-cost pricing policy is not possible for a firm in a competitive industry because it implies some degree of market power -- some control over the rate of return earned. In an oligopoly, the markup chosen will lie somewhere between the short-run profit-maximizing (monopoly) rate and the competitive rate (which is zero). It may be set as the highest rate that will limit the entry of new firms into the industry or will keep substitutes and imports from eroding the size of the market (Lanzillotti's strategy three).

Equation III:4:1 shows the full-cost pricing model

III:4:1 $\qquad P_t = (1+\pi)[r_t K/\overline{Q} + w_t L(\overline{Q})/\overline{Q} + m_t M(\overline{Q})/\overline{Q}]$

where
$\quad P_t \quad$ is price at time t

$\qquad \pi \quad$ is the markup over cost

$\qquad r_t \quad$ is the rental rate of capital at time t

$\qquad K \quad$ is the capital stock

$\qquad \overline{Q} \quad$ is the standard rate of output

$\qquad w_t \quad$ is the wage at time t

$\qquad L \quad$ is the labor force

$\qquad m_t \quad$ is the price of materials at time t [37]

and $\quad M \quad$ are materials used.

---

[37] Because unit material cost includes some capital costs, in section III:4:4, where the model is quantified, m will be replaced by the prices of the principal nonlabor variable inputs.

Even in industries where full-cost or target-return pricing prevails, demand can not be totally ignored. As Eckstein notes

> "The empirical question is not whether prices are determined by target-return pricing or by supply and demand, but rather: what is the actual combination of the two mechanisms in any particular industry?" (1964, p. 270)

A summary measure of the imbalance between supply and demand is the level of stocks or inventories. If there is some desired ratio of inventories to consumption, then long-run deviations from this level will cause price changes. The price equation, III:4:1, modified to include inventories, is

III:4:2 $\qquad P_t = (1+\pi)[r_t K/\overline{Q} + w_t L(\overline{Q})/\overline{Q} + m_t M(\overline{Q})/\overline{Q}] + c1\ In_t/C_t$

where c1   measures the sensitivity of price to changes in the ratio of inventories to consumption

      In_t is the level of inventories at time t

and C_t is consumption at time t.

In both the copper and the aluminum industries, which are highly concentrated, we might expect a full-cost-pricing objective to play a major role. Short-run fluctuations in supply and demand can be absorbed by changes in inventories, but long-run accumulations or depletions of inventories can be expected to cause price changes. [38] Equation III:4:2 should therefore provide a good model for the behavior of copper and aluminum producer prices.

---

[38]   The distributed lag introduced later in this section implies that it is a weighted average of present and past inventory levels that determines price.

The pricing policy implied by equation III:4:2 can be thought
of as an iterative process of determining the long-run elasticity of
demand μ for domestic primary copper or aluminum. Figure III:4:4
helps illustrate this process. Let D_T be the total demand schedule
for copper in the U.S. and D_P be the demand for the primary producers.
D_P is obtained by subtracting the supply curves of secondary and
foreign producers from D_T. Primary producers have two decision variables: price (or equivalently the markup over cost) and output. They
will set a price P based on long-run average cost. At the price P,
they hope that the quantity demanded will be equal to the standard rate
of output Q_P, as it does with demand curve D_P. But, if the long-run
supply of imports and secondary metal is more price elastic than believed
by the primary producers (as illustrated by demand curve D_P' which is
more elastic than D_P), the quantity sold, Q_P', will be less than $\overline{Q_P}$, and
production will fall or inventories will accumulate. If the primary
producers are not willing to accept a permanent erosion of their
market, they will have to lower price (and therefore the desired markup
over cost) until supply and demand are in long-run equilibrium. [39]
If the errosion of the market is caused by increased use of substitutes
such as aluminum instead of by imports and secondary copper, then

---

[39]   Whether the producers choose the lower price P' (which main-
       tains the size of the market), the higher price P (with
       subsequent inroads by secondary and foreign producers), or
       a price somewhere in between is an empirical issue.

D_T is more price elastic than believed, and a similar result occurs. In either case, price falls. Price formation is thus an iterative process -- finding the markup over cost that will produce long-run equilibrium in supply and demand, or equivalently, determining the long-run elasticity of demand μ for primary metal.

In the copper industry, there is a world price as well as a U.S. price, and though the two are often different for long periods of time, one cannot remain above the other indefinitely. Figure III:4:4 can also be used to illustrate what eventually happens to the U.S. price of copper when the world price falls. Suppose initially that both the U.S. and the world prices are equal to P, and the U.S. primary producers' demand curve is D_P. If the world price falls to P', the primary producers find that imports increase and that their demand curve shifts to D_P'. At price P, the U.S. is producing more than it is selling, and inventories accumulate. Eventually, either the world price moves back toward P as the U.S. demands more imports, or U.S. producers lower price to stop inventory accumulation (or some combination of the two). In the new long-run equilibrium, the two prices must be equal. The resulting price, say P', is lower than P, but is still based on domestic production costs. Domestic costs, however, are for a lower level of output, Q_P', because some high-cost operations have been forced to close.

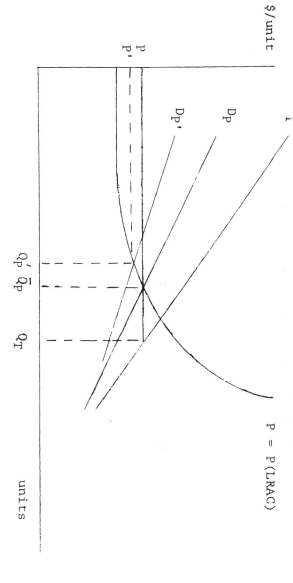

Figure III:4: 4 An Iterative Solution to the Pricing Problem

Two factors not included in equation III:4:2 have been important determinants of metal prices: technological progress and
depletion. Technological progress occurs whenever the same output
can be produced from fewer inputs (the capital-output, labor-output,
and materials-output ratios decline). [40] Technological progress
can be included in equation III:4:2 by making these ratios functions of time. Depletion occurs when lower-cost ores are used up.
Measures of ore quality can be included in the price equation directly
Equation III:4:2, modified to include technological change and depletion, becomes

III:4:3 $P_t = (1+\pi)[r_t(K/\overline{Q})_t + w_t(L(\overline{Q})/\overline{Q})_t + m_t(M(\overline{Q})/\overline{Q})_t$
$+ c2\ OO_t] + c1\ In_t/C_t$

where   c2   measures the sensitivity of price to the quality
                         of ores mined

and OO_t is an index of ore quality at time t.

Equation III:4:3 defines the equilibrium level of producer
prices (i.e., the price of metal when all input prices and the quality of ores are known with certainty and when inventories are at
their desired level). However, markets are rarely in equilibrium
and it is necessary to specify how producers respond to changed
conditions. Suppose that producers make their plans on the basis

---

40   Technological progress can also cause factor prices to fall.
      However, in equation III:4:2, factor prices are already
      functions of time.

of their expectations about input prices, ore quality, and the level

of inventories. Then III:4:3 becomes

III:4:4 $P_t = (1+\pi)[r_t*(K/\bar{Q})_t + w_t*(L(\bar{Q})/\bar{Q})_t + m_t*(M(\bar{Q})/\bar{Q})_t$

$$+ c2\ OQ_t*] + c1\ (In_t/C_t)* + u_t$$

$$u_t \sim N(0, \sigma_\mu^2)$$

where the *'s denote expectations and u is a disturbance term that

indicates that there may be uncertainties in setting prices. If

expectations are updated each period by a fraction δ, of the dis-

crepancy between the current observed variables (prices, invento-

ries, etc.) and their previous expected values, [41] then III:4:4

becomes

III:4:5 $P_t = (1+\pi)[r_t(1-\lambda)(K/\bar{Q})_t + w_t(1-\lambda)(L(\bar{Q})/\bar{Q})_t + m_t(1-\lambda)$

$$(M(\bar{Q})/\bar{Q})_t + c2(1-\lambda)OQ_t] + c1(1-\lambda)(In_t/C_t) + \lambda P_{t-1}$$

$$+ u_t - \lambda u_{t-1} \qquad 0 < \lambda = 1-\delta < 1.$$

In the next section, equation III:4:5 will be quantified and

estimated for primary copper and aluminum prices.

---

[41] This is an "adaptive expectations" model. To see that equation III:4:5 results from III:4:4 combined with an adaptive
expectations dynamic adjustment, see Johnston (1972, pp. 301-
302). We have made the simplifying assumption that the declining geometric weight, $\lambda = 1-\delta$, is the same for all variables.

III:4:4 Estimation of the U.S. Producer-Price Equations

III:4:4:1 The data

Copper- and aluminum-producer-price data were discussed in section III:4:1, and variable input prices (the prices of labor, energy, industrial chemicals, and bauxite) were discussed in section III:2:2. The ratio of after-tax profits to stockholders equity for all manufacturing was used as a measure of the opportunity cost of capital (r in equation III:4:5). This ratio is computed by the Federal Trade Commission. [42]

---

[42] Capital costs may be treated in two possible ways. We can look at the opportunity cost of capital or at actual capital costs. Both methods were tested in the price equations. Data on the costs of the principal types of capital used in mining, refining, and smelting were collected and used as explanatory variables in the price equations, but the opportunity-cost measure gave better results.

Copper and aluminum inventories were obtained by summing primary and secondary inventories as reported in Copper Development Association's (CDA) Annual Data and the Aluminum Association's (AA) Aluminum Statistical Review. [43]   Copper and aluminum consumption were computed as primary and secondary production minus changes in inventories plus net imports. Changes in primary and secondary inventories and secondary production figures are from CDA and AA; primary production and import and export figures are from the Bureau of Mines.

Technological change is measured by changes in the quantity of inputs required to produce a unit of output. The Bureau of Labor Statistics reports yearly average labor productivity figures for copper mining and for copper and aluminum primary production. These productivity figures (using a weighted average for copper as described in section III:4:2) give the best measures of technological progress in copper and aluminum primary production. Because time-series data on the input-output ratios for the other inputs were not available, time was used as a proxy for changes in these ratios.

---

[43]   Ideally we should look only at private inventories, and this was done with copper. However, sometimes the U.S. government stockpile has been used as an economic, not a strategic, stockpile. This happened in 1973-74; the aluminum stockpile was virtually depleted at a time that coincided with worldwide excess demand for most commodities. The price of aluminum did not rise in this period because there were price controls in the U.S. Without stockpile sales, there would have been rationing in the industry, but no rationing occurred. The building and depleting of the stockpile has helped to level out price and production behavior, therefore, the government stockpile has been included in the aluminum-inventory variable.

As was noted in section III:2:3, ore quality can be measured
in many ways. However, yield (metal produced/ore mined) was sin-
gled out as perhaps the best, and the one for which the most complete data exist. The average yield of copper ores mined in the
U.S. each year (published by the Bureau of Mines) was used in the
copper-price equation as the principal measure of ore quality.
Annual production of primary refined copper in the U.S. (also from
the Bureau of Mines) was used as a proxy for other copper-ore quality measures (because high-cost operations close first when production is low, and marginal deposits are mined when production
is high). No ore-quality measures were used in the aluminum price
equation. (See section III:2:3).

III:4:4:2 The price equations

The final specification for the U.S. producer price of copper

equation, based on III:4:5, was a log-log functional form.

III:4:6 $\ln \text{Ppc}_t = -2.1 + .46 \ln \pi /E_t + 1.7 \ln \text{Wc}_t/\text{LPc}_t + .46 \ln \text{Pcc}_t$
             $\qquad\qquad\quad (7.8) \qquad\qquad (7.3) \qquad\qquad (6.2)$

$\qquad\qquad + .11 \ln \text{Pec}_t - .14 \ln \text{Inpc}_t/\hat{\text{Cc}}_t - .17 \ln t$
$\qquad\qquad\quad (.95) \qquad\quad (-2.8) \qquad\qquad\quad (-2.4)$

$\qquad\qquad - 1.4 \ln Y_t + .31 \ln \hat{\text{Qpc}}_t$
$\qquad\qquad\quad (-22) \qquad\quad (5.7)$

$R^2 = .98 \qquad\quad \text{D.W.} = 2.5 \qquad\quad F = 52 \qquad \begin{matrix} \rho_1 = -1.2 \\ \rho_2 = -.44 \end{matrix}$

Years: 1954-69 1971-76

where   Ppc   is the U.S. producer price of refined copper

π /E is the ratio of after-tax profits to stockholders
           equity for all manufacturing

Wc   is the wage in primary copper production

LPc   is a labor productivity index for primary copper

Pcc   is an industrial chemical price index for copper

Pec   is an energy price index for primary copper

Inpc is private copper inventories

Cc   is consumption of copper

Y   is the average yield of copper ores mined

Qpc   is production of primary refined copper

and   t   is time measured in years (1950 = 1).

All prices (copper, labor, chemical, and energy) were defla-

ted by the wholesale-price index.

105

A log-log functional form was chosen to reflect the increasing costs of expanding copper production. Because expanding the production of primary copper involves changing the quality and composition of copper ores mined, average cost is a nonlinear function of output, and because mining and milling costs are inversely proportional to yield, industry costs increase in a nonlinear fashion when yield falls. Figure III:4:5 shows plots of fitted copper price versus yield and price versus primary-copper production obtained from equation III:4:6 by holding all other variables in the equation constant at their 1974 values. By comparing figures III:2:3 and 5 to figure III:4:5 we can see that a log-log functional form reproduces the price behavior expected from an engineering analysis of copper production costs very well. [44]

The year 1970 was omitted from the estimation period because, in that year, producers raised price in spite of falling demand, high inventories, and declining world prices. Dropping the year 1970 improves the fit considerably. The copper-price equation that includes 1970 is the first equation in table III:4:2.

Instruments were used for the ratio of inventories to consumption and for annual production because these variables must be considered jointly dependent. (See section III:3).

The lagged value of copper price was dropped because, when the lagged dependent variable was included in the equation, its

---

[44] It is possible to make statistical tests of the appropriate functional form to use. (See Tukey, 1957 and Box and Cox, 1962). However, these tests assume no a priori information. Instead of estimating the functional form, the a priori information obtained from the earlier analysis of the production process and costs was used.

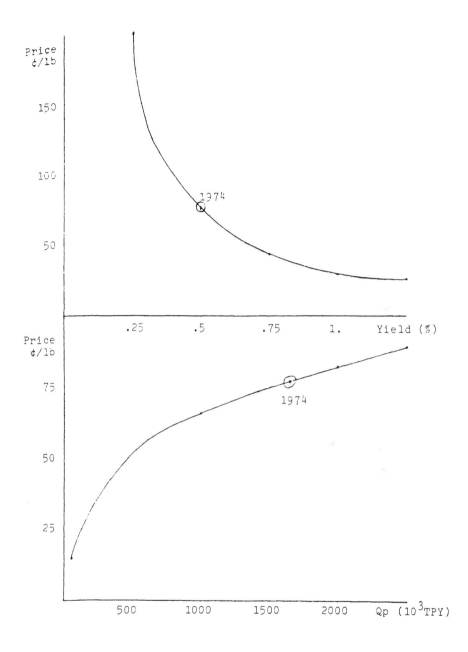

Figure III:4:5   Fitted Copper Primary Price as a Function
of Yield and Primary Production

coefficient was very small and not statistically significant, implying that copper price responds promptly to changed underlying conditions. The trend in copper costs over the period has been steadily upwards. Therefore, it is possible that producers see short-run cost changes as likely to persist, accounting for their prompt response to these changes. The copper-price equation with a geometric distributed lag is the second equation in table III:4:2.

All the coefficients have the expected signs. Copper price rises with increases in input prices; it falls with improvements in technology (as measured by labor productivity and time); and it rises when ore quality falls (as measured by falling yield and higher production). Inventory buildup also causes price to fall, implying that demand considerations are not neglected (as would be the case with a pure full-cost pricing policy). In the equation, only the coefficient of energy price has a t-ratio less than two. It is unlikely that an increase in the price of energy has very little effect on the price of copper. Rather, the small elasticity with respect to energy price and small t-ratio are probably caused by the coincidence of high energy prices and depressed conditions in the copper industry (due to worldwide excess supply) in the last two years of the estimation period. The elasticity with respect to yield is greater than one in absolute value and has the largest t-ratio in the equation, implying that lower ore quality may be a major cause of cost increases in the copper industry. The strong response of price to cost conditions is obvious; the mitigating effects of technology are also clear.

TABLE III:4:2

ALTERNATIVE SPECIFICATION FOR COPPER PRIMARY PRICE

Change	c	In/C	π /E	W/LP	Pe	Pc	t	Y	Qp	Pp-1
1970 Added	-10.9	.15 (1.0)	.43 (2.1)	1.8 (2.2)	-.67 (-2.1)	.64 (2.7)	.01 (.04)	-1.2 (-5.9)	.59 (3.8)	
Pp-1 Added	-5.9	-.11 (-1.2)	.47 (6.6)	1.7 (6.6)	.034 (.15)	.44 (4.2)	-.13 (-1.1)	-1.3 (-16)	.31 (5.4)	-.003 (-.38)

109

The final specification for the U.S. producer price of aluminum equation, also based on III:4:5, was a linear functional form. The resulting equation is

III:4:7 $\hat{Ppa}_t = -49.5 + .64 \ \pi/E_t + 4.4 \ Wa_t/LPa_t + 12.2 \ Pca_t$
                      (3.7)   (7.0)   (5.7)

$+ 11.6 \ Pea_t + .65 \ Pb_t - .007 \ \Delta \hat{Ina}_{t-1}$
   (3.5)   (2.7)   (-7.6)

$-.004 \ (\hat{Ma-Xa})_{t-1} \quad -3.1 \ DPC_t + .83 \ \hat{Ppa}_t$
  (-2.9)   (-4.5)   (6.5)

$R^2 = .96 \qquad D.W. = 2.8 \qquad F = 31 \qquad \rho = -.70$

Years: 1955–1976

where   Ppa   is the U.S. producer price of primary aluminum ingot

π/E is the ratio of after-tax profits to stockholders equity for all manufacturing

Wa   is the wage in primary aluminum production

LPa   is a labor productivity index for primary aluminum

Pca   is an industrial chemical price index for aluminum

Pea   is an energy price index for primary aluminum

Pb   is the price of bauxite

Δ Ina is the change in aluminum inventories

Ma   is aluminum imports

Xa   is aluminum exports

DPC   is a dummy variable for price controls

and   t   is time measured in years (1950 = 1).

All prices (aluminum, labor, chemical, energy, and bauxite) were deflated by the wholesale-price index.

110

A linear functional form was chosen to reflect the fact that average costs for the primary-aluminum industry are probably constant in the long run. The arguments advanced for the nonlinearity of copper-industry average costs do not apply to aluminum production. To test if the aluminum industry is characterized by increasing or decreasing costs, primary production and primary production squared were added to the equation, but proved insignificant. A linear form, therefore, seemed the best choice and corresponds to a fixed coefficient production function, for which there is some evidence. (See section III:2:1). The aluminum-price equation with output as an explanatory variable is the first equation in table III:4:3. [45]

In the aluminum-price equation, unlike the copper-price equation, the lagged value of price proved very significant. The response of aluminum price to changes in cost and demand conditions is strong, but there is a considerable lag between the occurrence of a change and the full price response to it. Because the prices of the principal inputs to primary-aluminum production have been oscillating for the last twenty five years and have shown no marked trend (see figure III:2:2), producers probably consider cost changes to be temporary until they persist for long periods of time.

The lagged endogenous variables in the equation introduce estimation problems. Appendix III:1 discusses the method used to estimate equations with lagged endogenous variables and serially correlated errors.

---

[45]   When primary production alone (without primary production squared) was added, its coefficient was negative but not significant.

In the copper primary-price equation, the ratio of the level of inventories to consumption was used as a measure of the imbalance between supply and demand. In the aluminum price equation, a different measure proved more successful. The difference between domestic consumption and production is filled by net imports minus changes in inventories, and these variables were used in the price equation. In the aluminum-price equation, the response of price to an increase in imports was estimated directly (high imports $\rightarrow$ lower price), while in the copper-price equation the response was estimated indirectly (high imports $\rightarrow$ high inventories $\rightarrow$ lower price).

Several variables appear in the copper-price equation that are not found in the aluminum equation. The reasons for not including ore-quality measures were discussed in section III:2:3. Time was not used as a measure of technological progress in aluminum production because its coefficient was not significant. We cannot conclude, however, that there has been no improvement in aluminum production technology. If aluminum price is a function of time (as specified by equation III:4:5),

$$Pp = a_0 + a_1 t,$$

then $\qquad dPp/dt = a_1,$

the rate of change of aluminum price is a constant. Because the coefficient of lagged price in equation III:4:7 is large, the aluminum price equation is essentially a first difference equation, and the effects of improved technology may be reflected in the constant term. Aluminum price with time as an explanatory variable is the second equation in table III:4:3.

A dummy variable for price controls was included in equation

112

TABLE III:4:3

ALTERNATIVE SPECIFICATION FOR ALUMINUM PRIMARY PRICE

Change	c	Pp_{-1}	ΔIn_{-1}	$(M-X)_{-1}$	π/E	W/LP	Pe	Pb	Pc	Dpc	Qp	Qp^2	t
Primary Production Added	-33	.65 (2.9)	-.007 (-7.7)	-.003 (-1.9)	.61 (3.4)	3.6 (3.4)	9.1 (2.0)	.69 (2.4)	12.4 (4.6)	-4.9 (-2.3)	-.004 (-.9)	10^{-6} (.8)	
Time Added	-46	.78 (2.9)	-.007 (-7.1)	-.004 (-3.7)	.63 (3.0)	4.3 (5.9)	10.2 (2.7)	.58 (2.3)	12.6 (4.9)	-3.2 (-4.2)			-.024 (-.27)

III:4:7. In August 1971, the Cost of Living Council proposed a price freeze under Phase I of its attempt to halt inflation. Controls of one sort or another (Phases I-IV) existed until August 1974, at which time the industry was totally decontrolled. However, in the early years of the freeze, there was excess capacity in the industry, and the controls were not binding. For this reason, the dummy variable is equal to one only in 1973 and 1974, when the controls were binding; it is equal to zero elsewhere.

All the coefficients in the aluminum-price equation have the expected signs, and all the t-ratios are larger than two. Aluminum price rises with increases in the prices of inputs (capital, labor, energy, chemicals, and bauxite); it falls with technological improvements (as measured by higher labor productivity); and it falls when inventories build up or when net imports increase (implying that demand considerations are not ignored). Price controls in 1973-1974 kept the price of one pound of primary-aluminum ingot approximately three cents below what it would have been without them.

This completes the analysis of copper and aluminum primary prices. We will consider the second important economic decision -- how much to produce at a given price -- in the final section of this chapter.

III:5 Primary Production

In a concentrated industry, price and output decisions are
made simultaneously, and the individual producer has some control
over both. In the primary copper and aluminum industries, the price
set and the quantity produced depend jointly on cost and demand
conditions, as shown in the primary-industry flowchart of the previous section (figure III:4:1). The determinants of primary price
were discussed in the last section. Here, we develop a theoretical
model of output determination and present the results from estimating
primary-production equations based on this model. First, however,
the sources of copper and aluminum primary supply are discussed
and domestic production trends for both metals are analysed.

III:5:1 The Sources of Primary Supply

Mineral-resource occurences are classified into two categories: reserves and resources. The term "reserves" generally refers to economically recoverable material in identifiable deposits, and the term "resources" denotes reserves, as well as deposits that are either uneconomic, undiscovered, or both. Primary production is always from reserves. Therefore, a knowledge of reserves is essential to any analysis of potential metal supply. However, the boundary between reserves and resources is determined by changing economic and technological conditions and is constantly shifting. Thus any discussion of supply would be incomplete without an analysis of resources as well. The dividing line between reserves and resources depends principally on metal price, production cost, and exploration effort. An increase in price, without a comparable increase in cost, makes previously uneconomic deposits potentially minable. New mining, smelting, and refining techniques that lower costs also shift resources from the uneconomic into the recoverable category, and geologic exploration shifts resources from the undiscovered into the identified class.

Table III:5:1 shows U.S. and world reserve and resource estimates for copper and aluminum in 10^6 short tons of recoverable metal. Because commercial production of primary aluminum has been almost exclusively from bauxite, the estimates given in the table are for aluminum in bauxite only. Adding non-bauxitic deposits would substantially increase aluminum resource estimates, but would have a negligible effect on reserve estimates. This table shows that the U.S.

116

possesses about one-fifth of world copper reserves and resources
but only a tiny fraction of world bauxite resources.

The second table (III:5:2) shows the ratio of U.S. and world reserve and resource estimates to U.S. and world consumption of copper
and aluminum in 1974. [46] This ratio indicates the number of years that
reserves and resources would last if produced at 1974 consumption rates. [47]
U.S. bauxite deposits are obviously inadequate to supply domestic
consumption. However, because world bauxite reserves are very large,
no major technical problems are foreseen in obtaining bauxite supplies
in the near future.

The U.S. copper reserves to consumption ratio suggests that our
copper would last thirty three years at present consumption rates.
However, we cannot conclude that we will run out of copper in thirty
three years (or sooner if there is any growth in copper consumption).
The U.S. copper reserves to consumption ratio has remained virtually
constant in the last few decades in spite of growth in copper usage.
Improved technology and greater exploration effort have led to
increases in copper reserves comparable to those in consumption. [48]
The real problem for the domestic copper industry in the future will
not be the lack of minable deposits; the problem will be the lack of
deposits minable at costs competitive with those of foreign countries.

---

[46]   World consumption statistics used here are from Metal Statistics.

[47]   Production at constant rates is not a realistic assumption, but
        it does provide a useful comparison between metals.

[48]   Mining companies have little incentive to explore if the reserve
        to consumption ratio is greater than thirty. Therefore, the
        near constancy of this ratio is not surprising.

TABLE III:5:1
U.S. AND WORLD RESERVE AND RESOURCE ESTIMATES
FOR COPPER AND ALUMINUM (10^6 SHORT TONS)

	U.S.		World	
	Reserves	Resources	Reserves	Resources
Copper	107	427	610	1800
Aluminum	10	50	5600	8000

Source: U.S. Bureau of Mines, 1978
Mineral Commodity Profiles

TABLE III:5:2
U.S. AND WORLD COPPER AND ALUMINUM RESERVES AND RESOURCES
AS A FRACTION OF 1974 CONSUMPTION (YEARS)

	U.S.		World	
	$\dfrac{\text{Reserves}}{\text{Consumption}}$	$\dfrac{\text{Resources}}{\text{Consumption}}$	$\dfrac{\text{Reserves}}{\text{Consumption}}$	$\dfrac{\text{Resources}}{\text{Consumption}}$
Copper	33	131	66	196
Aluminum	1.6	7.8	365	522

Domestic mine production of copper is approximately four-fifths from open pits and one-fifth from underground mines. Most copper ores mined are sulfides, but oxide ores are contributing an increasing fraction to domestic production. Five states -- Arizona, Utah, New Mexico, Montana, and Michigan -- account for more than 90% of U.S. copper reserves, and almost all the reserves are in deposits where copper is the dominant value. The area where the potential for expanding domestic copper production is greatest is the porphyry copper-bearing Basin and Range province of the Southwest.

Domestic mine production of bauxite accounts for only 12% of U.S. aluminum consumption, with Arkansas producing about 90% of the total and the remainder mined in Alabama and Georgia. The U.S. imports most of its bauxite from countries in the Western Hemisphere -- Jamaica, Surinam, The Dominican Republic, and Guyana. However, there are major producers outside this hemisphere, such as Australia and Guinea, that can supply bauxite to us at somewhat higher transport costs, and there are countries within the hemisphere, such as Brazil, with large reserves that will begin bauxite production in the near future. Large world bauxite reserves distributed in many countries with governments having greatly varying political persuasions make it unlikely that the U.S. will suffer from severe supply restrictions in years to come. There may be increases in the price of bauxite in the next decade, but, in the long run, increases are unlikely to go beyond the point where the cost of bauxite delivered to the U.S. from different sources is equalized. The U.S. is, therefore, relatively secure and can expect to obtain its bauxite supplies at

moderate cost. [49]

---

49   If all producers agreed on a common tax policy, bauxite
      prices could go as high as the cost of producing aluminum
      from non-bauxitic deposits in the U.S., but, because there
      are so many potential and actual producers, such a cohe-
      sive policy is not apt to be feasible. The more likely
      possibility is that, in the long run, producers will only
      be able to exploit their cost advantages (in both mining
      and transportation). However, the possibility that foreign
      producers will raise bauxite prices substantially beyond
      present levels is considered in chapter VII, where the
      effects of such a policy on domestic production and consump-
      tion of aluminum are analysed.

III:5:2   Trends in Primary Production

Figure III:5:1 shows plots of primary production of copper
(the dashed line) and aluminum (the solid line) in the U.S. between
1954 and 1976. The dotted line represents the index of industrial
production for the same period. Aluminum production follows industrial
production rather closely. However, the rate of growth of aluminum
production has been greater than the rate of growth of the economy
as a whole, and fluctuations in industrial production have been
magnified in primary-aluminum production.

Primary-copper production has grown less than the economy as
a whole, but has followed the same general cyclical pattern. However, noticable drops in primary copper production took place in
the years of major strikes in the mining industry (denoted by the
circles on the graph).

In the next section, a theoretical model of primary supply
that attempts to explain the observed fluctuations in production
will be developed.

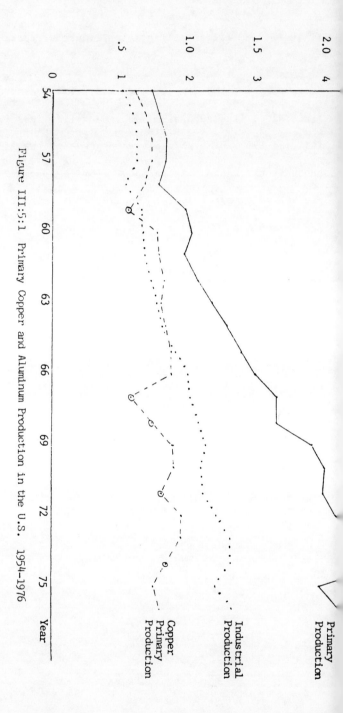

Figure III:5:1 Primary Copper and Aluminum Production in the U.S. 1954-1976

Primary
Production

Industrial
Production

Copper
Primary
Production

122

III:5:3   Specification of a Primary-Production Equation

Any market model (supply-demand-price), contains only two
independent relationships. In the standard competitive model,
there is a supply curve, S (a function of marginal cost, MC) and
a demand curve, D (a function of economic activity, Y). Price, P,
and output, Q, are determined by the intersection of the two, as
illustrated in figure III:5:2. The competitive model contains no
independent price equation.

Many oligopoly models contain no independent supply relationship. In the model that we have been discussing -- the full-cost
pricing model, a variant of an oligopoly model -- price, P, is a
function of long-run average cost, LRAC. Price is either independent of the quantity produced, as illustrated in figure III:5:3 A
(which corresponds to the aluminum industry) or it is an upward-
sloping function of quantity (figure III:5:3 B, which corresponds to
the copper industry). At any point in time, the price charged and
the quantity produced are determined by the intersection of the price
and demand relationships.

Because, in reality, price and output do not adjust instantly
to changes in cost and demand, it is customary to specify a third
equation (price in the competitive model and output in the oligopoly model) that shows how price or output adjusts (what the adjustment mechanism is and whether adjustment to changed conditions is
rapid or slow). For example, in both the Desai (1966) and the
Fisher-Cootner-Baily (1972) models discussed in chapter II, there

123

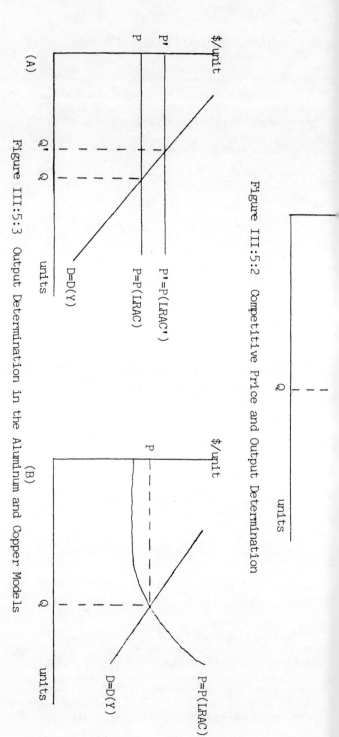

Figure III:5:2 Competitive Price and Output Determination

Figure III:5:3 Output Determination in the Aluminum and Copper Models

is a separate equation that shows how price adjusts to changes in inventories. In the CAS model, there is a separate primary-production equation for each metal that shows how output adjusts.

The two methods of explaining fluctuations in output are: stock adjustment and flow adjustment. A typical stock-adjustment model explains investment in new capacity as a function of the rate of return to capital, capacity as a function of investment, and capacity utilization as a function of price, inventories, and economic activity. Equations III:5:1-3 provide an example of a simple stock-adjustment model.

III:5:1 $\quad I = I(\pi/K)$

III:5:2 $\quad K = K(I, K_{-1})$

III:5:3 $\quad Q/K = Q/K(P, In/C, Y)$

where
$\quad I \quad$ is investment

$\quad \pi \quad$ is profit

$\quad K \quad$ is capacity

$\quad Q \quad$ is output

$\quad P \quad$ is price

$\quad In/C \quad$ is the ratio of inventories to consumption

and
$\quad Y \quad$ is economic activity.

In a typical flow-adjustment model, output is a function of price, inventories, and economic activity. Output adjusts with a lag because capacities change slowly; therefore, a lagged dependent variable is used as a proxy for the investment delay implicit in capacity expansion. Equation III:5:4 provides an example of a simple flow-adjustment model.

III:5:4 $\quad Q = Q(P, In/C, Y, Q_{-1})$

The stock-adjustment model is much more complicated than the flow-adjustment model, but the behavior of the two is virtually identical until capacity constraints are reached ($Q \simeq K$). Normally, when an exogenous increase in demand takes place, the higher demand is met by a combination of price and output adjustments. Therefore, capacity constraints are most apt to be limiting when price cannot adjust, either because price controls are in effect or because producers choose to ration output instead of raising price. In either case, (price controls or rationing), the flow-adjustment model may predict output levels that are too high. Both price controls and rationing have been present in one form or another in the primary copper and aluminum industries. Price controls existed in the U.S. in the early seventies. Rationing in the copper industry is a much discussed issue for which no completely satisfactory explanation has been forthcoming. (See McNicol, 1975). However, an analysis of the residuals of the primary production equations should tell whether output levels predicted by the model were too high during periods when price could not adjust. Appendix III:3, where price controls and rationing are discussed, gives the details of such an analysis.

In the CAS model, flow adjustment was used to explain fluctuations in output because I believe that, for the purposes of this study, the simple model works just as well as the more complicated one. Therefore, no investment equation was estimated. Of course, for other purposes (examining investment dynamics, for example), the flow-adjustment model would be totally inadequate.

The preceeding discussion centered on investment in new capacity. However, capacity expansion is only one type of investment. Funds are invested in research and development and in mineral exploration as well. In the history of copper and aluminum production, it has been the discovery of new techniques (the Bayer and Hall-Heroult processes for aluminum; large earth-moving equipment and the froth-flotation process for copper) that have revolutionized the industry, not the discovery of new deposits. These techniques enabled known, but previously uneconomic deposits to be mined and processed at low cost, thus changing low-quality resources into high-quality reserves. However, in the last sixty years, there have been no fundamental changes in copper and aluminum production technology. The technological improvements that have occurred since World War I have been gradual and marginal, the sort of changes that can easily be handled by the measures of technological progress used in the primary-

127

price equations. For very long-term forecasting, probabilistic models of the exploration process and of technological innovation are important, but, because of the long lags involved, they are unnecessary for short- to mid-term forecasting. [50]

To specify a primary-production equation for the CAS model, we must consider how output adjusts to changes in the desired level. If desired output is a function of price, economic activity, and the ratio of inventories to consumption

III:5:5 $Qp^* = a_0 + a_1Pp + a_2Y + a_3In/C$

where Qp^* is the desired level of primary production

           Pp is the U.S. producer price

           Y is economic activity

and In/C is the ratio of inventories to consumption,

and if, in the current period, output can adjust only a fraction, Y, of the difference between the previous level, Qp_{-1}, and the desired level, Qp^*, (due to investment delay), then equation III:5:5 becomes [51]

---

50   Capacity expansions take about three years to implement. However, the time required to bring totally new facilities into operation is much greater, often as long as ten to fifteen years. The implementation of radically different mining, refining, and smelting techniques requires investment in new facilities, and is therefore beyond the time frame of this study.

51   This is a "partial-adjustment" model. To see that equation III:5:5 combined with a partial adjustment mechanism results in III:5:6, see Johnston (1972, pp. 300-301).

III:5:6　　　$QP_t = a_0 \gamma + a_1 \gamma Pp_t + a_2 \gamma Y_t + a_3 \gamma In/C_t + (1-\gamma)QP_{t-1}$

　　　　　　　　$+ u_t$　　　　　　　　$0 < \gamma < 1$

where u_t, a disturbance term, was added because the level of output can not be controlled completely. Equation III:5:6 is the flow-adjustment equation for primary metal production used in the CAS model. Primary production is determined primarily by price (Pp) and demand (Y). However, the coefficient a_3 of the ratio of inventories to consumption captures the magnitude of output adjustments to short-run supply-demand imbalance, and the coefficient γ of the lagged value of production measures the speed of adjustment to long-term changes in cost and demand conditions.

It should be noted that in equation III:5:6, unlike the typical supply equation, the sign of the coefficient of price is indeterminate, as can be illustrated by figure III:5:3 (page 124). If price is independent of the quantity produced (figure III:5:3 A), then changes in price occur only with shifts in LRAC. When P moves upward to P', the new quantity produced, Q', is less than Q, implying that price and quantity are negatively related. If, on the other hand, industry costs increase as output expands (figure III:5:3 B), price and quantity are positively related when moving along the industry cost curve.

In the next section, the results of estimating primary-production equations based on III:5:6 are presented.

III:5:4   The Econometric Estimates

III:5:4:1   The data

The data for primary price, output, inventories, and consumption were discussed in the last chapter. The only new variable needed to estimate the primary-production equations is a
measure of the level of aggregate economic activity. Because
most metal is used as an industrial input, not as a consumer
good, the index of industrial production was chosen to represent
economic activity. The index of industrial production is computed
by the Board of Governors of the Federal Reserve System.

The primary-production equations for both copper and aluminum include a lagged dependent variable, which introduces estimation problems if the error term u_t is serially correlated. [52]
Appendix III:1 describes the method used to test for serial correlation in the presence of a lagged dependent variable and the
estimation technique used if serial correlation was found to be
present.

---

[52]   Note that the partial-adjustment model, unlike the adaptive
expectations model, does not introduce serial correlation
if none was present originally.

III:5:4:2 The primary production equations

The final specification for U.S. primary copper production, based on III:5:6, was

III:5:7 $\hat{Q}pc_t = 1163 + 6.9 \; \hat{P}pc_t - 1271 \; Inpc_t\hat{/}Cc_t + 3.0 \; IP_t$
$\phantom{III:5:7 \quad \hat{Q}pc_t = 1163 + } (2.1) (-3.5) (2.5)$

$ - .62 \; Dcs_t \; Qpc_t + .064 \; \hat{Q}pc_{t-1}$
$ (-10.7) (.72)$

$R^2 = .92 \qquad D.W. = 2.4 \qquad F = 36 \qquad \rho = .49$

Years: 1954 - 1976

where   Qpc   is U.S. production of primary refined copper

           Ppc   is the U.S. producer price of refined copper

           Inpc   is private copper inventories

           Cc   is consumption of copper

           IP   is the index of industrial production

and   Dcs   is a dummy variable indicating strikes in the
                  copper industry.

Instruments were used for two variables -- primary price and the ratio of inventories to consumption -- because these variables are jointly dependent.

A dummy variable was included in the equation to correct for the fall in production that occurred in years when there were industry-wide strikes. This variable is equal to the fraction of each year that was affected by the strike (i.e., if the strike lasted for six months of the year, the dummy variable for that year is equal

to one-half). Because the amount of output lost during a strike
depends on the amount of output normally produced, the dummy variable was multiplied by the previous year's output. One strike lasted for parts of two years (1967-1968). Therefore, the dummy variable for 1968 was multiplied by the quantity produced two years
previously.

The coefficient of the lagged dependent variable (which measures the speed of adjustment to changes in desired output) is very
small. [53] Output can respond very quickly to changed conditions if
such changes can be met by changing capacity utilization. Because
the copper industry did not grow rapidly during the 1954-1976
period, most fluctuations in demand were met by changing utilization
rates. If the demand for copper were to grow more rapidly in the
future, the primary-production equation might forecast expansion
rates that are too high to be met in practice. However, in all
simulations considered in chapter VII, the domestic copper industry
does not grow more rapidly in the forecast period than it did in
the historic period.

In an oligopoly, there is no short-run supply curve. Therefore, it is not possible to compute a short-run elasticity of supply.
However, if industry pricing corresponds to a full-cost model (where
we assume that the markup over cost has been chosen to maximize profits
in the long run), then it is possible to compute a long-run elasticity
of supply (i.e., the long-run supply curve is the markup over long-run
average cost curve). There is, however, a difficulty in computing

---

53   The t-ratio of this variable (and of lagged production in the
     aluminum equation) is less than one. However, the variable was
     not dropped because it is certain that there must be some
     investment delay.

this elasticity from equation III:5:7. With a linear relationship, the value of any elasticity varies at each point on the curve. It is customary to compute elasticities for linear relationships at the point of means. However, the choice of the point of means is somewhat arbitrary, especially if the means for the historic period are not equal to the means for the forecast period (as is apt to be the case with time-series data). To avoid this problem, the primary production equation was reestimated in log-log form. If the new equation is

$$\text{III:5:8} \qquad \ln Opc = c_0 + c_1 \ln Ppc + \sum_{i=2}^{n} c_i \ln X_i + \lambda \ln Qpc_{-1},$$

where the X_i represent all variables in the equation other than price and output, then the long-run supply elasticity, η_ℓ, is

$$\text{III:5:9} \qquad \eta_\ell = c_1/(1-\lambda).$$

The long-run elasticity of supply of U.S. primary copper, computed from III:5:9 (using the coefficients from the primary production equation in log-log form), is .21. Supply is very inelastic, even in the long-run. This small supply elasticity is very different from that computed by Fisher-Cootner-Baily (1972). FCB found supply to be fairly elastic in the long-run (η_ℓ = 1.67). Because FCB used the traditional short-run supply-curve approach, the two results are not directly comparable. However, it is possible that the U.S. copper industry is now operating at a point where costs increase sharply as output expands. The last year of the data used for the FCB estimates was 1966. In the ten years between 1966 and 1976, there have been two important contributors to higher costs for capacity expansions in the domestic copper industry. First, in copper mining, most of the very large, high-quality porphyry-copper deposits have been fully developed. Because newly discovered deposits tend to be smaller, of lower grade, or more deeply buried, costs for new mines are higher than are costs for existing ones. And second, in copper smelting, new air-pollution-control regulations limiting emissions of sulfur dioxide (SO_2) and particulates have led to increased capital costs. Because new smelters have to meet New-Source Performance Standards, substantial price increases are required to bring new smelting capacity on line. Even though the econometric estimates of long-run supply elasticities may be fairly imprecise, with such a large difference between the two estimates, it seems reasonable to conclude that the long-run supply of copper in the U.S. is substantially less elastic now than it was ten years ago.

The final specification for U.S. primary aluminum production, also based on III:5:6, was

III:5:10 $\quad \ln\hat{Q}pa_t = 2.8 - .25 \ln\hat{P}pa_t + .97 \ln IP_t + .20 \ln\hat{Q}pa_{t-1}$
$$\quad\quad\quad\quad\quad\quad\quad (-1.4) \quad\quad\quad (4.9) \quad\quad\quad (1.46)$$

$\quad\quad\quad\quad R^2 = .98 \quad\quad F = 407 \quad\quad D.W. = 1.9$

$\quad\quad\quad\quad\quad\quad\quad\quad\quad\quad\quad\quad\quad\quad$ Years: 1954–1976

where $\quad\quad$ Qpa $\quad$ is U.S. primary production of aluminum

$\quad\quad\quad\quad\quad$ Ppa $\quad$ is the U.S. price of primary aluminum ingot

and $\quad\quad\quad$ IP $\quad\quad$ is the index of industrial production.

Natural logarithms were taken of all of the variables before estimation because, with a linear relationship, the variance of the residuals was heteroscedastic. Instruments were used for primary price because this variable is jointly dependent. The inventory variable was dropped from the equation because its estimated coefficient was small and was not significant at any reasonable level of confidence (t-ratio = .15).

Because the primary-aluminum industry is a constant-cost industry (see section III:4:4), the long-run supply of primary aluminum in the U.S. is infinitely elastic. In the long run, at least until high-quality aluminum ores are depleted, shifts in demand should be fully met by increases in supply.

This completes the analysis of the primary copper and aluminum industries. In the next chapter, the secondary industries will be discussed.

<u>Appendix III:1 Estimating Equations with Lagged Endogenous Vari-
ables and First-Order Serially Correlated Errors</u>

Many of the equations in the CAS model have lagged endogenous variables and autoregressive errors, which introduce two
sorts of problems. First, the Durbin-Watson statistic cannot be
used to test for serial correlation, and second, ordinary least
squares results in inconsistent estimates of the equation coefficients. These two problems will be discussed in sequence, but first,
some notation must be introduced.

Suppose that there are at least two endogenous variables,
yl and y2, and that

A:III:1:1 $y1 = a0 + a1\ y1_{-1} + a2\ y2 + \alpha\ X1 + u$

$u = \rho_1\ u_{-1} + \varepsilon_1$ $\varepsilon_1 \sim N(0, \sigma_1^2)$

A:III:1:2 $y2 = b0 + b1\ y2_{-1} + b2\ y1 + \beta\ X2 + v$

$v = \rho_2\ v_{-1} + \varepsilon_2$ $\varepsilon_2 \sim N(0, \sigma_2^2)$

where y1 and y2 are Tx1 vectors of observations on the endogenous
variables; $y1_{-1}$ and $y2_{-1}$ are y1 and y2 respectively, lagged once;
X1 and X2 are Txn_1 and Txn_2 matrices of observations on the predetermined variables other than $y1_{-1}$ and $y2_{-1}$ (X1 and X2 are subsets
of the set of all predetermined variables, $X = X1 \cup X2$, with X1 containing those variables in the first equation and X2 those in the
second).

The first problem arises when testing to see if u and v are

136

first-order autoregressive. There are several large-sample tests

for autocorrelation in the presence of lagged endogenous variables

(Durbin, 1957, Guilkey, 1975, Godfrey, 1976) that are asymptoti-

cally valid. However, we are dealing with small samples. Kenkel

(1975), in looking at the small-sample properties of Durbin's test,

found that in many cases, the Durbin-Watson statistic performed

better than Durbin's large-sample test. A test with the desired

asymptotic properties may therefore not be an improvement over the

standard Durbin-Watson statistic if the sample is not large.

Instead of testing for autocorrelation in the presence of

lagged endogenous variables, a different procedure was adopted here.

In the price and demand equations, the lagged dependent variables

result from adaptive-expectations models. Because the adaptive-

expectations model causes serial correlation in the error term, in

the equations resulting from such a model, the presence of auto-

correlation was assumed. [1] However, after estimating a price or

demand equation of the form A:III:1:1 (by the method to be described

shortly), if the estimated value of ρ_1 ($\hat{\rho}_1$) turned out to be

less than .1, the equation was reestimated without the correction

procedure. The re-estimation was performed because, with a very

small value of ρ_1, the estimated coefficients of equation A:III:1:1

are hardly changed by the correction procedure. It was decided that

---

[1]   Serial correlation would be absent in the extremely unlikely
        case that the error term of the equation, prior to perform-
        ing the Koyck transformation, were first-order autoregressive
        with parameter ρ, and ρ were equal to the parameter λ of
        the adaptive expectations model. In that case, the two would
        cancel each other out.

the loss of two degrees of freedom (one to estimate ρ_1, and one
for the loss of the first observation) was too much to pay for the
only slight gain in consistency that results when ρ_1 is very small.

In contrast, the lagged dependent variable in the production
equations results from a partial-adjustment model, which does not
introduce autocorrelation into the error term. The production equations were estimated with and without the correction for autocorrelation (also by the method to be described shortly), and the correction was kept if the t-statistic of $\hat{\rho}_1$ was greater than one.

The second problem arises in estimating the coefficients of
equation A:III:1:1. Sargan (1961) proposed an iterative procedure
for dealing with such an equation that is both consistent and asymptotically efficient. Fair (1970) modified Sargan's procedure in
order to reduce the number of instruments required and make it more
useful in practical applications. Hatanaka (1976) reduced Fair's
method to a two-step procedure without loosing the asymptotic efficiency, and Dhrymes and Taylor (1976) independently obtained results
that are very similar to Hatanaka's.

Recent work has thus concentrated on two aspects of the problem: 1- reducing the number of required instruments and 2- introdu-
cing computational efficiency. In many practical applications, it
is the first aspect (reducing the number of instruments) that is of
greatest importance. For example, in the most extreme case, if the
number of instruments is equal to the number of observations then the
estimates of the endogenous variables obtained by using instruments $(\hat{y})$
will be identical to the original variables (y), and no correction

138

will have been performed.

Unfortunately, none of the above methods can be applied to estimate many of the equations in the CAS model. For example, with the copper primary-production equation, Fair's small-sample method (which is asymptotically less efficient than others proposed) calls for twenty two instruments plus a constant term, and there are only twenty three observations. With the demand equations the situation is worse, because these equations link the copper and aluminum models and thus require predetermined variables from both models. It is therefore obvious that even Fair's small-sample method can not be used.

It was decided that it was more important to correct for the small-sample bias introduced by the lagged dependent variable than to concentrate on asymptotic properties. [2] Therefore, the following procedure was used:

Step 1:

Regress all endogenous variables (both current and lagged but not $y1_{-1}$) in equation A:III:1:1 on X, the set of predetermined variables (these are the varaibles listed in section three of this chapter). Define $\tilde{X}1 = X1 \cup \hat{y}2$ (where, if X1 contains any lagged endogenous variables, they have been regressed on instruments).

---

[2] Fair's method, which concentrates on asymptotic properties, does not correct for the small-sample bias introduced by the lagged dependent variable.

Equation A:III:1:1 then becomes

A:III:1:1′ $y1 = a0 + a1\ y1_{-1} + \gamma\ \tilde{X}1 + u$

Step 2:

Regress $y1_{-1}$ on $\tilde{X}1 \cup \tilde{X}1_{-1}$ to obtain $\hat{y1}_{-1}$.[3]

Step 3:

Apply the Cochrane-Orcutt iterative procedure to estimate

A:III:1:1′′ $y1 = a0 + a1\ \hat{y1}_{-1} + \gamma\tilde{X}1 + u$

$$u = \rho_1\ u_{-1} + \varepsilon_1.$$

---

[3]   Note that X1 contains only variables that are included in equation A:III:1:1, and thus $\tilde{X}1 \cup \tilde{X}1_{-1}$ should not be very large

Appendix III:2 An Attempt to Measure Scarcity Rent in the Copper
                Industry

In section four of this chapter, a model of price formation
in the U.S. copper industry, with price based principally on long-
run average cost, was presented. However, as noted earlier, copper
is geochemically scarce. If scarcity rent is an important determinant of copper price, then a model of price formation that ignores
scarcity rent will be inadequate. In this appendix, we attempt to
see if there has been an increasing deviation of price from cost in
the U.S. copper industry that can be attributed to rising scarcity
rent. Scarcity rent is extremely difficult to measure (for discussions of the difficulties, see Smith, 1978 and Brown and Field, 1978),
and the test performed here is at best limited. However, an imper-
fect test is better than no test at all.

The basic literature of exhaustible resources is well known.
Hotelling (1931) showed that a profit—maximizing owner of a deplet-
able resource will choose an extraction rate such that rent, or
price net of extraction and marketing cost, will increase exponen-
tially at a rate equal to the rate of interest. [1] Hotelling
derived his result as a condition of flow equilibrium in the market
for ore, but Solow (1974) deduced the same principle as a condition of stock equilibrium in the asset market (an ore deposit being
a capital asset). Herfindahl (1967) showed that with more than

---

[1]   If the resource owner is a monopolist, it will be marginal
        revenue minus marginal cost that will grow exponentially.

one quality of deposit, use will be sequential, the high-quality

deposits will be used first, and rent for the grade currently

extracted will rise at a rate equal to the rate of interest, though

rent increases for the resource as a whole will no longer be expo-

nential. [2] Gordon (1967) demonstrated that, with increasing costs

to cummulative output, the exponential growth of rent rule no longer

holds, but the qualitative behavior of prices remains unchanged.

The upward trend in deflated copper price that has occurred

over the last two decades is possibly due to a deviation of price

from cost that reflects scarcity rent. To test this hypothesis,

we can examine the behavior of price versus cost for a single

uniform-quality copper deposit over time. The behavior of rent

for the resource as a whole is more difficult to treat because

quality differences must be considered. Even for a single deposit,

the exact functional form of rent increases is difficult to pre-

dict, but, if scarcity rent is important, price deflated by cost

should rise with time.

The best cost figures come from the the annual reports of

primary-copper producers, but, because most copper companies are large

diversified multinationals, their cost figures are useless for

testing the scarcity-rent hypothesis. However, one company, Copper

Range, has no overseas activities and produces copper from a single

---

2   Schultze (1974) showed that with a continuum of deposit quali-
      ties and sequential usage, rent for the grade currently
      extracted will rise at a rate less than the rate of interest,
      reflecting the increasing cost of extraction.

deposit, the White Pine mine, mill, and smelter on the Upper Michigan Peninsula. [3] A crude measure of cost per unit of production,
Ccr, can be obtained by dividing Copper Range's total cost [4] for
a given year by its annual production for that year. [5]

The price chosen to test the scarcity-rent hypothesis was not
the U.S. producer price, which is set by the primary producers, it
was the number-two scrap price, P2s, a competitively determined
price. [6] Figure AIII:2:1 shows the behavior of the scrap price
deflated by average cost for Copper Range. The dotted line shows
the twenty-one year trend in this ratio; [7] it was obtained by

---

3   Copper Range has some rolling mills outside Michigan and some
     logging activities, but it is principally engaged in primary
     copper production. About 65% of its revenues come from sales
     of refined copper and 30% from copper products. Less than 5%
     of revenues come from non-copper related activities.

4   Any examination of cost data is complicated by such issues
     as the treatment of old, undervalued assets. Therefore, the
     following test is at best highly approximate.

5   In recent years, Copper Range shows figures for the cost per
     pound of refined copper (which does not include its other acti-
     vities). However, the better cost figures go back only as
     far as 1963. The cost figures used here are uniformly higher
     than the true cost per pound, but the two series show similar
     behavior. In particular, using only the years 1963-1976 we
     find a downward trend in P/C with either series.

6   Using the scrap price, a competitively determined price,
     makes it easier to separate the the scarcity rent hypothesis
     from the hypothesis of increased market power. The scrap
     price is highly correlated with the world price of copper,
     and neither one is simply a reflection of U.S. primary pro-
     ducers' pricing decisions. However, the scrap price is pre-
     ferred to the LME price for this test, because the world price
     is subject to speculative pressures.

7   Data on cost was not available prior to 1956.

regressing P2s/Ccr on time. [8] The resulting equation is

A:III:2:1 $P2s_t/Ccr_t = .478 + .0038\ t$ Years: 1956-1976
                            (.35)

            $R^2 = .23$ DW = 1.5   F = 5 $\rho = .46$

It can be seen, either by observing the nearly horizontal trend
line in figure A:III:2:1 or the t-statistic of the coefficient
of time in equation A:III:2:1, that there has been no significant
rise in the price-cost ratio, a result that is consistent with
the theory of exhaustible resources if the rent component of
copper price is small. A small rent component is quite likely
for copper, because price increases still elicit significant
supply responses in the world (if not the U.S.) copper industry.
Certainly the test performed here is not conclusive, but it
indicates that scarcity rent is not a major factor in explaining
the behavior of copper price.

---

8   When nonlinear versions of the equation were tested, the
     fitted trend turned downwards, not upwards as would be ex-
     pected if scarcity rent were important.

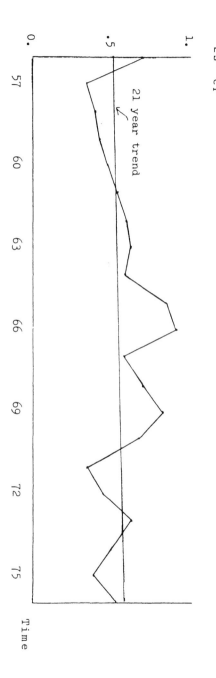

Figure A:III:2:1   # 2 scrap price / Average cost   (Copper Range)

145

Appendix III:3 Non-Market Mechanisms -- Price Controls and
                Rationing

The primary copper and aluminum industries in the U.S. were
subject to various forms of price controls from the middle of 1971
to the middle of 1974 (Phases I-IV of the Cost of Living Council's
attempt to halt inflation). However, in the early years of the
freeze, which were years of low overall economic activity, there
was excess capacity in these industries, and the controls were not
binding. In contrast, during the 1973-74 period, price controls
kept primary-metal prices in the U.S. below what they would have
otherwise been. A dummy variable equal to one in 1973-74 and zero
elsewhere was used in the primary copper and aluminim price equations of the CAS model to correct for the existence of controls.
However, this variable proved significant only in the aluminum
price equation, where controls kept the price of primary-aluminum
ingot approximately three cents per pound below what the uncon-
trolled price might have been. [1]

The issue of rationing in the U.S. copper and aluminum
industries is much more complex than is the issue of controls.
Rationing of one form or another has been used in both industries,
but, because little rationing occurred in the aluminum industry
in the post-Korean War period, we will concentrate on rationing
in the copper industry.

In the period between 1955 and 1956 and again between 1964

---

[1]   The very high prices experienced both in the U.S. and in the
      world copper industries occurred in the Spring of 1974 and
      coincided with decontrol of the U.S. industry.

and 1970, the major copper producers kept their price below the level that would have cleared the market, and rationed their supplies. During parts of these periods, the U.S. copper-scrap price, which is normally considerably below the the U.S. producer price, rose above the producer price. [2] (See figure III:4:2). It is not the intention here to discuss the reasons why producers choose to ration instead of raising price (for various explanations, see McNicol, 1975); it is merely the intention to describe copper-market dynamics during periods of rationing and to analyse how the CAS model performs when rationing occurs.

When producers ration, copper is not rationed; only domestic primary copper is rationed. Purchasers can always buy secondary and imported copper, but at higher prices. Therefore, secondary copper and imports absorb the difference between the demand for and the supply of primary copper. Rationing occurs only when the demand for copper is high; therefore, we should expect the price of secondary copper to be very sensitive to the level of economic activity. This expectation is confirmed by the size of the estimated elasticity of secondary copper price with respect to the index of industrial production (which is 1.8 -- see equation IV:3:2). The high secondary price that occurs during periods of rationing stimulates secondary supply; the remainder of the gap is filled by imports. (Imports can always be purchased at the world price, which will also be above the U.S. producer price in periods of high demand).

_____

[2]   During the 1973-74 period of controls, the scrap price also
       rose above the producer price in the U.S.

If rationing in the primary-copper industry had occurred in some periods of high demand but not in others, the CAS model primary-price equation would probably predict price levels that were too high in the years of rationing. Figure A:III:3:1 shows plots of the residuals from the CAS model primary-copper price and production equations. The preidcted price was not unusually high during the rationing periods. In other words, keeping price down in periods of high demand can be considered "normal" behavior in an industry where price is based principally on long-run average cost.

Rationing will not occur if excess capacity exists in the primary industry. However, primary production in the CAS model is based on flow adjustment, and there are no capacity constraints in the model. It is therefore possible that, with high demand and sticky prices, the primary production equation will predict output levels that are too high to be met in practice. However, figure A:III:3:1 shows that predicted output levels during the periods of rationing were also not abnormally high. Copper secondary price, secondary production, and net imports were above their long-term trend over most of the rationing period, and the CAS model, in the simulation of the historic period, reproduces this behavior very well.

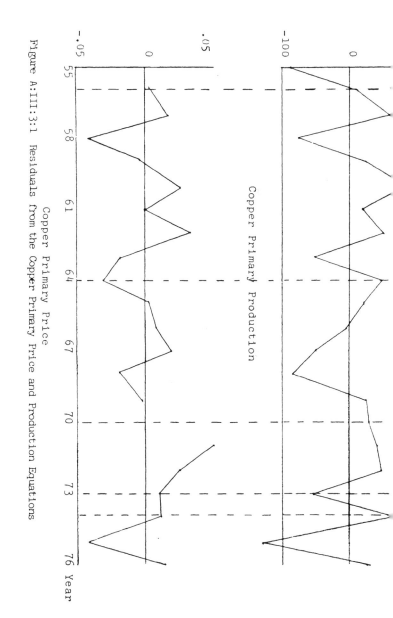

Copper Primary Production

Copper Primary Price

Figure A:III:3:1 Residuals from the Copper Primary Price and Production Equations

149

CHAPTER IV   SECONDARY COPPER AND ALUMINUM

This chapter is devoted to the secondary copper and aluminum industries -- the industries that reclaim and reprocess scrap metal. As with the primary industries, the emphasis here is on the pricing policies and output decisions of the firms in the industries.   The first two sections of the chapter describe industry structure, tech-nology, and costs, in preparation for sections three and four, where models of industry pricing and output behavior are developed and econometric estimates of equations based on these models are presented.

IV:1 The Structure of the Secondary Industries

IV:1:1 Industry Description

In the secondary industries, metal production is from scrap, not ores. The three types of scrap are new, home, and old. New scrap is industrial scrap and is generated at various stages of the production process by primary producers, semifabricators, and the manufacturers of end products. Home (or run-around) scrap, a subset of new scrap, is recycled by the same company that generated it. Because home scrap never leaves the company and is never marketed, it is generally not included in new-scrap statistics. [1] Old scrap is recovered from worn-out and discarded products. Whereas new scrap is recycled almost immediately, the metal that becomes old scrap may be contained in a product for several decades before it is reused.

Scrap can be virtually pure metal or it can be one of many types of metal alloys containing as little as 30% copper or aluminum. Refinery slags, dross, skimmings, and ash, though not technically scrap, are also treated by the secondary industries.

Some scrap is used directly by the primary refineries, mills, foundries, and chemical plants. Other scrap goes through the scrap dealers to the secondary refiners, smelters, and alloy-ingot makers.

---

[1]   The figures for new scrap used in this study do not include home scrap.

Figure IV:1:1 shows the complicated flow of metal from the primary producers to the semifabricators, end-product manufacturers, and ultimate consumers. [2] Scrap is generated at each stage and is returned, either directly or via the secondary producers, to each stage of the production process.

The secondary-metal industry can be broadly or narrowly defined. The term "secondary producer" commonly refers to the secondary refiners, smelters, and alloy-ingot makers. The term "secondary industry" may refer only to the secondary producers, or it may include the scrap dealers and collectors as well. In this study, the secondary industry is broadly defined to include the scrap dealers, and all scrap statistics used here include scrap used directly as well as scrap that is treated by the secondary producers.

---

[2]   In this flow chart, unlike the other flow charts in this study, the arrows represent physical flows, not causality.

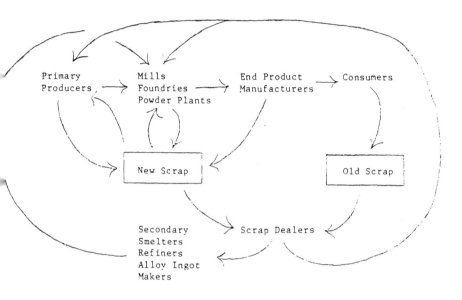

Figure IV:1:1   The Flow of Metal Through Primary and
Secondary Production and Consumption

IV:1:2 Concentration and Barriers to Entry

Unlike the primary-metal industries, which are highly concentrated, the secondary industries range from extremely to moderately
unconcentrated, depending on how the industry is defined. There
are thousands of scrap dealers and collectors and fifty to one
hundred secondary producers in each industry. [3] However, actual
concentration may be somewhat higher if regional markets exist.

The Bureau of the Census publishes concentration ratios in
secondary copper and aluminum production, computed on the basis
of value of shipments. [4] These ratios are given in table IV:1:1.
Concentration in these industries is somewhat lower than average
market concentration in the U.S.; if the scrap dealers were
included in the definition of the industry, concentration would
be considerably less. [5] Industry concentration has fluctuated
from year to year; no definite trend can be seen in the secondary-
copper industry, but, in the secondary-aluminum industry, concentration seems to be increasing.

---

3   McMahon (1965) noted eighty ingot makers and smelters in the
     secondary-copper industry. The Council on Wage and Price Sta-
     bility (1976) noted sixty two reclycling firms operating ninety
     one plants in the secondary-aluminum industry.

4   Secondary production is defined by the Bureau of the Census
     to include secondary refined metal and alloys but not unpro-
     cessed scrap.

5   The average four-firm concentration ratio for four-digit in-
     dustries in the U.S. is 34. The four-firm concentration ratio
     for SIC 3341, secondary nonferrous metals, is 24.

TABLE IV:1:1

SHARE OF VALUE OF SHIPMENTS ACCOUNTED FOR BY THE FOUR
AND EIGHT LARGEST SECONDARY PRODUCERS   1958-1972

| | Secondary Copper | | Secondary Aluminum Ingot | |
| | SIC 33412 | | SIC 33417 | |
	CR4	CR8	CR4	CR8
1972	39	62	50	69
1967	40	60	44	64
1963	42	62	44	62
1958	45	60	--	--

TABLE IV:1:2

1972 STATISTICS FOR SIC 3341 (SECONDARY NONFERROUS METALS)

CR4	CR8	Number of Companies	Specialization Ratio	Coverage Ratio
24	40	324	98	28

155

For the four-digit industry, secondary nonferrous metals, specialization and coverage ratios are published in addition to concentration ratios. [6] These ratios are shown in table IV:1:2. The specialization ratio which is 98 implyies that plants that are classfied as being in the industry specialize almost completely in the production of secondary nonferrous metals. However, the coverage ratio which is 28 implyies that only 28% of secondary nonferrous metal production comes from plants in the industry. Concentration is thus much lower than that implied by the concentration ratios. In contrast, in the primary industries, both specialization and coverage ratios are very high.

Barriers to entry into the secondary industries vary with the type of potential entrant. Barriers to entry are almost nonexistent for scrap collectors, and scrap markets are highly competitive. For secondary producers, barriers are higher than for the scrap dealers, but not nearly as high as for the primary producers. Because much secondary processing consists simply of melting and diluting lower grade scrap with higher grade metal, a much simpler process than primary refining and smelting, secondary smelters tend to be smaller than primary smelters and to cost less per ton of capacity. [7] Barriers are thus fairly low, but there is some concern that environmental regulations will increase capital requirements and the minimum

---

6   SIC 3341, secondary nonferrous metals, consists primarily of
     secondary copper, aluminum, lead, and zinc.

7   Metals Week (1968) estimated the cost (per ton of capacity)
     of a secondary aluminum smelter to be one tenth that of a
     primary smelter. In addition, secondary smelters tend to be
     smaller than primary smelters because economies of scale are
     less prevalent.

efficient scale of plant in the secondary industries, causing small firms to exit and increasing industry concentration.

IV:2 Cost Trends in Secondary Production

IV:2:1 Secondary-Production Technology

Some aluminum scrap is of sufficient purity to be reused directly. The rest is sold to the secondary-aluminum smelters, where it is processed into secondary-aluminum ingot. Secondary-smelter production is heavily concentrated in those alloys used by the casting industry.

At the smelter, the degree of prior preparation of scrap material depends on the form of scrap used. Clippings are only sorted, borings and turnings are shredded and dried, residues are run through a milling machine to separate aluminum concentrates from nonmetallics and oxides, and castings and sheet are crushed and magnetically separated before they can be smelted in a reverberatory furnace. When the scrap in the furnace has melted, it is analysed and mixed with metal of known composition until the molten alloy meets product specification. Next, the melt is fluxed with reactive salts or chlorine gas and filtered. And, finally, the finished alloy is poured into molds to cool and harden.

Like aluminum scrap, much copper scrap can be reused directly without further processing. The remainder goes either to the secondary-ingot makers or to the secondary refiners. The ingot makers adjust the composition of the scrap material to specification by melting and then diluting the molten alloy with higher grade scrap or primary metal. If substantial impurities are present, a fluxing agent must be added to the melt. The secondary refiners need only melt high-grade scrap before refining, but lower grade material requires prior smelting in a blast furnace. Refining of secondary copper, like that of primary copper, consists of fire refining, if the precious-metal content is low, or electrolytic refining, if additional by-products are to be recovered.

The principal conclusion that can be drawn from this analysis of secondary copper- and aluminum-production technology is that production cost varies greatly and depends on the form in which the scrap material is recovered. We can, therefore, expect that industry costs will increase in a nonlinear fashion as output (or recovery efficiency) expands.

IV:2:2   Energy Usage in Secondary Production

In chapter III, we saw that primary–metal production cost
varies with the quality of ore mined, and that, at least for copper,
increasing primary production means that higher cost ore bodies
are mined. The same is true for secondary–metal production. The
cost of reclaiming scrap depends on the form in which the scrap metal
is found, and increasing secondary-metal production means reclaiming
scrap material of lower quality.

Marginal cost in secondary-metal production increases with
recovery efficiency (defined as the fraction of the stock of scrap
available for collection that is actually reclaimed). We would
like to know the shape of the marginal-cost function; however,
good data exist only for energy usage in secondary-metal production as a function of recovery efficiency. We will, therefore, have
to be content with an analysis of marginal energy costs.

Several process-analysis studies of the energy costs of
reclycling metals have been made (Bravard and Portal, 1972, Chapman,
1974, Penner and Spek, 1976). The general conclusion is that, on
the average, secondary-aluminum production uses 1/25 to 1/30 as
much energy per ton of metal as primary-aluminum production, and
secondary-copper production uses 1/5 to 1/10 as much energy per ton
as primary-copper production.

Of the studies just mentioned, only Chapman looked at energy
usage in secondary–metal production as a function of the fraction
of the stocks of scrap available for collection that are actually

reclaimed. Therefore, in the discussion that follows, we will use Chapman's data. If we wish to determine energy usage in secondary metal production, we can look at the two constituent parts expressed in equations IV:2:1 and IV:2:2.

IV:2:1 $\quad Es = Es(RE)$

IV:2:2 $\quad RE \equiv Qs/SS = RE(Ps, Pi, C)$

where
- Es is energy usage per net ton of metal reclaimed
- RE is recovery efficiency
- Qs is secondary metal production
- SS is stocks of scrap
- Ps is secondary-metal price
- Pi is the price of the ith input to secondary-metal production

and
- C is metal consumption.

These equations state that energy usage in secondary-metal production is a function of recovery efficiency, and that recovery efficiency is a function of secondary-metal price, cost, and total metal consumption. Equation IV:2:2 is the supply curve of secondary metal and is examined in detail in section IV:4. In this section, we look only at equation IV:2:1, the energy - recovery efficiency relationship.

Chapman used process analysis to determine the energy required to reclaim three types of new scrap -- clippings and trimmings, borings and turnings, and skimmings and runners from castings -- and three

160

types of old scrap -- sheet, tube, and castings; wire and cable; and "irony" scrap -- for both copper and aluminum. [8] He also estimated the relative proportions of each type of scrap available for collection. If we assume that scrap requiring less energy per net ton of metal is reclaimed first, then Chapman's estimates can be used to construct the marginal energy cost of secondary copper and aluminum production as a function of recovery efficiency. Figure IV:2:1 shows the marginal energy cost relationships for both metals (smooth curves drawn through the six points). Chapman also estimated 1974 U.S. copper- and aluminum-recovery efficiency to be 45% and 20% respectively. These points are marked on the graph.

We can see from the curves that marginal energy cost in secondary-aluminum production increases only gradually with increases in recovery efficiency, whereas, in secondary-copper production, marginal cost increases very steeply after about 45%, the present U.S. recovery-efficiency rate. We might predict from these curves that small increases in aluminum prices would lead to improvements in secondary-aluminum recovery efficiency, and that much larger copper-price increases would be needed to improve the efficiency of secondary-copper recovery. Some evidence tends to confirm this prediction. Table IV:2:1 shows aluminum-can-reclamation data compiled by the Aluminum Association (1976). As noted in chapter III,

---

8   These six types of scrap include most of the nondissipative
     uses of the two metals.

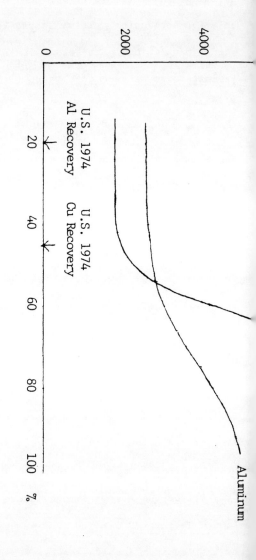

Figure IV:2:1 Marginal Energy Cost per Ton of Metal
as a Function of Recovery Efficiency

deflated primary-aluminum price has been rising since 1973,
when higher energy prices led to greater primary-aluminum-production
costs. Aluminum cans reclaimed as a fraction of aluminum cans
used doubled in the three-year period between 1972 and 1975, as
shown in the table. In contrast, little change in secondary-copper
recovery efficiency took place over the same period. [9]

TABLE IV:2:1
ALUMINUM CAN RECLAMATION DATA   1972-1975

	Number of Cans Reclaimed (10^6 Cans)	$\dfrac{\text{Cans Reclaimed}}{\text{Cans Used}}$ (%)
1972	1.2	12.9
1973	1.6	14.7
1974	2.3	16.9
1975	4.0	25.4

Source: The Aluminum Association

In the next two sections, models of pricing and output in
the secondary industries are developed from the discussions of
industry structure and production cost just presented.

---

9   Copper prices were depressed in the last year of the 1972 -
1975 period. However, the long-run increase in copper prices
since the mid-fifties has not led to improved secondary-
recovery efficiency for copper.

163

IV:3 Secondary Prices -- Mechanisms and Trends

In this section, secondary prices are defined, the behavior of secondary prices over the historic period is discussed, a theoretical model of secondary-metal price determination is developed, and econometric estimates of secondary-price equations based on this model are presented. Figure IV:3:1, a flow chart of a secondary industry econometric model, [10] shows how secondary-metal prices are determined in the CAS model and how these prices are related to secondary-industry output -- the subject of the final section of this chapter.

---

10   For a definition of the symbols used in the flow chart, see chapter I, page 9.

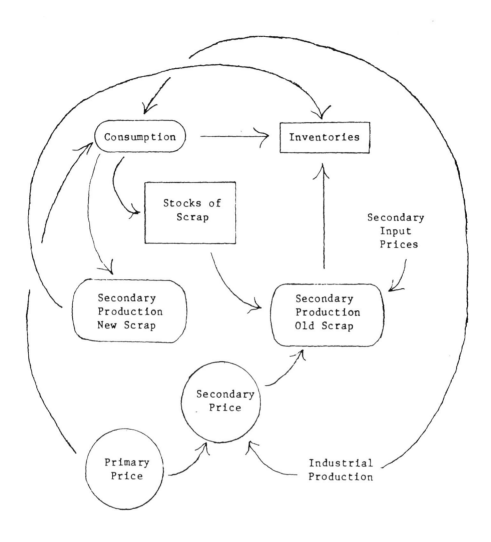

Figure IV:3:1 Flow Chart of a Secondary
Industry Econometric Model

IV:3:1 Definition and Historic Behavior of Secondary-
Metal Prices

In chapter III, we noted that no single, well defined "price"
of a primary metal exists. The same is true for a secondary metal.
Secondary "price" may refer to one of the prices of the different
types of scrap, to one of the prices of the various secondary alloys,
or it may refer to the price of unalloyed, secondary-refined metal.
However, for simplicity in modeling (and because all secondary
prices are highly correlated), we must choose a single, representative secondary price. The two possible choices are a scrap
price or the price of secondary refined metal, each with different
advantages.

In equilibrium, we should expect the following relationship
to hold

$$Psr = Ps + Cr$$

where   Psr   is the price of secondary-refined metal

          Ps   is the scrap price

and   Cr   is the cost of refining (including a competitive
                return to capital).

The difference between the two prices, therefore, depends on the degree of processing required.

Because it is refined secondary metal that competes most directly with primary metal, Psr might be the better secondary price to choose. However, much scrap is used directly without reprocessing and is sold at scrap prices. The choice between the two prices, therefore, depends on three factors: (1) the size of Cr (the smaller Cr, the less the spread between the two prices); (2) the volume of metal sold at each price; and (3) the data available.

In the aluminum model, the number 380 secondary-aluminum-ingot price is used to represent secondary "price". This price is a yearly average of remelt-aluminum-ingot prices compiled from quotations published daily in American Metal Market; the yearly average price is published in Metal Statistics. The secondary-ingot price was chosen because most secondary aluminum is sold in ingot form. In addition, the large spread between the secondary ingot and the scrap price (they differ by roughly a factor of three) implyies that processing cost is a large proportion of total cost for secondary aluminum.

In the copper model, the dealer's number-two heavy copper-scrap price is used to represent secondary "price". [12] This price is a yearly average of dealer's buying prices at New York, compiled from quotations published daily in American Metal Market; the yearly average price appears in Metal Statistics. The small spread between

<hr />

12   Because data on the number-two-scrap price goes back only as far as 1956, the number-one-scrap price was used in earlier years.

the scrap price and the price of refined copper implyies that processing cost is a small proportion of total cost in secondary-copper production. In addition, a large volume of copper is sold directly at the scrap price. However, the principal reason for choosing the scrap price in preference to the price of secondary-refined copper is that better data exist for the former.

Figure IV:3:2 shows plots of copper and aluminum secondary prices, deflated by the wholesale-price index. Copper prices show a slight upward trend, and aluminum prices show a slight downward trend. However, neither trend is significant. Secondary-copper prices are much more volatile than are secondary-aluminum prices. Stable primary-aluminum prices tend to encourage steady investment in new capacity. Therefore, fluctuations in secondary-aluminum prices are most apt to be caused by fluctuations in the demand for aluminum. In contrast, primary-copper prices show much more variation than do primary-aluminum prices. This variation gives rise to cyclical investment in the primary-copper industry, which in turn leads to fluctuating secondary-copper prices. For example, the low secondary-copper price observed in 1976 was a consequence of the excess supply of primary copper that was triggered by unusually high primary-copper prices in 1973-74. Therefore, fluctuations in supply as well as in demand are important contributors to unstable secondary-copper prices.

In the next section, a model is developed that attempts to explain the fluctuations in secondary prices observed here.

168

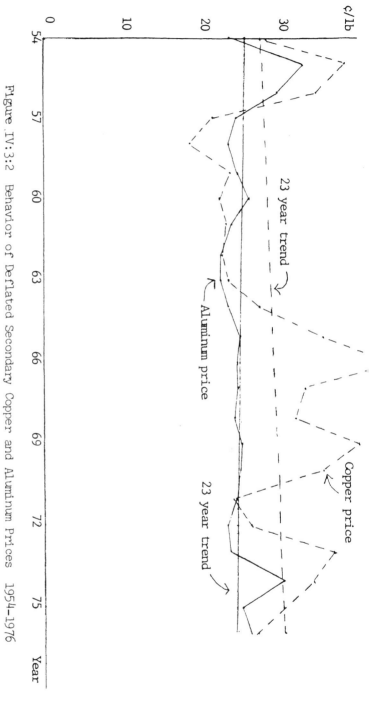

Figure IV:3:2   Behavior of Deflated Secondary Copper and Aluminum Prices   1954-1976

169

IV:3:2 Specification of a Secondary-Price Equation

In the standard, perfectly competitive industry model, price
is determined by the intersection of the industry supply and demand
curves, as illustrated in figure IV:3:3 A. Supply (S) is an upward
sloping function of price (P); demand (D) is a downward sloping
function of P; and price (Pc) is competitively determined by the
intersection of the two curves. Even though the secondary-metal
industries are fairly unconcentrated and no one secondary producer
can affect price by his actions, price determination in these
industries does not correspond to the perfectly competitive industry
model. The principal difference between price determination in the
secondary-metal industries and in the perfectly competitive industry
model is that the secondary-metal industries as a whole (not just
the individual producers) are price takers. Secondary price (Ps)
is given to the secondary industry; it is primarily a function of
primary price (Pp), but it also fluctuates with changes in economic
activity (Y). Because there is no separate demand for secondary
metal, secondary firms can produce all they want at the price given
to them (i.e., the demand for secondary metal is infinitely elastic).
Figure IV:3:3 B illustrates price and output determination in the
secondary-metal industries. Secondary supply (Ss) is an upward
sloping function of price (Ps), as in the perfectly competitive
model, but secondary demand (Ds) is infinitely elastic at Ps.

170

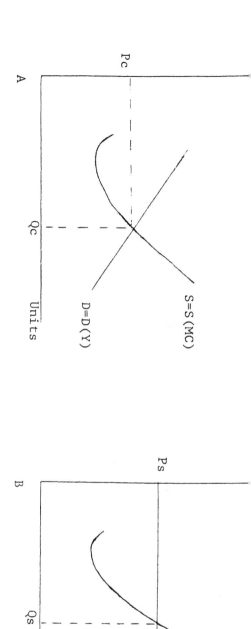

Figure IV:3:3 Price and Output Determination in the
A: Perfectly Competitive Industry
B: Secondary Metal Industries

171

The claim that the secondary copper and aluminum industries are price takers needs some justification. Table IV:3:1 shows that, in 1976, secondary-copper production provided 44% of total domestic copper supply and that secondary-aluminum production provided 24%. Such large proportions might indicate that the secondary industries have a great deal more price power than was just claimed. However, as is shown in section IV:4, the supply of metal from new scrap (which is a by-product of the production process) is proportional to the amount of metal consumed and does not depend on price (i.e., the price elasticity of new-scrap supply is equal to zero). Therefore, only metal produced from old scrap responds to changes in price. Old scrap accounted for only 18% of domestic copper supply in 1976 and for only 6% of domestic-aluminum supply. These proportions are small enough so that the secondary producers as a whole can ignore their effect on the prices of their products.

TABLE IV:3:1
1976 PRIMARY AND SECONDARY COPPER AND ALUMINUM PRODUCTION
AS A PERCENT OF TOTAL DOMESTIC SUPPLY

	Primary Supply (%)	Secondary Supply (%)	New Scrap (%)	Old Scrap (%)
Copper	56	44	27	18
Aluminum	76	24	18	6

172

Because refined primary and secondary metals are virtually indistinguishable in many applications, secondary price is primarily a function of primary price. However, because the primary-producer price is not very sensitive to short-run shifts in demand, secondary price (especially secondary-copper price) shows larger fluctuations than does primary price. These fluctuations can be seen in figure III:4:2 of the previous chapter. The number-two-scrap price for copper is highly correlated with both primary exchange prices (LME and COMEX) but is always below them. This scrap price, which fluctuates much more than the U.S. producer price, is usually below the producer price, but, in periods of high demand, it may remain above the producer price for some time. The scrap price thus fluctuates to absorb some of the excess supply and demand caused by sluggish primary prices. We can, therefore, expect secondary price to be a function of economic activity as well as of primary price.

Equation IV:3:1 is the secondary-metal-price-formation model from which secondary-price equations will be estimated.

IV:3:1 $Ps = a_0 + a_1 Pc + a_2 Y + a_3 Ps_{-1}$

where Ps is secondary-metal price

             Pp is primary-metal price

and Y is aggregate economic activity.

The lagged value of secondary price (Ps_{-1}) was included in the equation to test the hypothesis that secondary prices are damped (i.e.,

173

that prices respond slowly to changed conditions -- $a_3 > 0$) or that
secondary prices are overly responsively (i.e., that the immediate
response to changed conditions is larger than the equilibrium response -- $a_3 < 0$).

In the next section, secondary-price equations based on IV:3:1
are presented.

IV:3:3 Estimation of the Secondary-Price Equations

The final specification for the secondary price of copper equation, based on IV:3:1, was

IV:3:2 $\ln \hat{Psc}_t = -8.8 + 1.15 \ln Ppc_t + 1.7 \ln IP_t + .23 D66_t$
$\phantom{IV:3:2 \ln \hat{Psc}_t = -8.8 + } (4.0) (2.6) (2.5)$

$\phantom{IV:3:2 \ln \hat{Psc}_t = } - .30 \ln \hat{Psc}_{t-1}$
$\phantom{IV:3:2 \ln \hat{Psc}_t = } (-2.1)$

$R^2 = .79 \qquad F = 16 \qquad D.W. = 2.1 \qquad \rho = .94$

Years: 1954 - 1976

where   Psc   is the number-two price of copper scrap
                 deflated by the wholesale-price index

           Ppc   is the U.S. producer price of primary copper
                 deflated by the wholesale-price index

           IP   is the index of industrial production

and   D66   is a dummy variable equal to one in 1966
                 and zero otherwise.

Natural logarithms were taken of all of the variables before estimating the equation because, with the scrap price ordinarily considerably below the producer price, it seems more sensible to relate percent changes in the scrap price to percent changes in the producer price than to relate absolute changes in the two prices. The estimated coefficient of primary price is greater than one, implying that fluctuations in the producer price are magnified in the scrap price. The estimated coefficient of the index of industrial production is

175

even larger than that of primary price, implying that the scrap price is very sensitive to fluctuations in economic activity. A dummy variable, equal to one in 1966 and zero otherwise, was included in the equation because, in 1966, uncertain copper supplies in Zambia led to unusually high copper prices world wide. As would be expected, the estimated coefficient of the dummy variable is positive. Finally, the estimated coefficient of the lagged value of secondary price is negative, implying that secondary price is overly responsive to changed conditions (i.e., that the immediate response is greater than the equilibrium response). The signs and magnitudes of the estimated coefficients of all four variables in equation IV:3:2 reinforce the conclusion that secondary-copper prices are very volatile and that they take up some of the slack caused by more sluggish primary prices.

The final specification for the secondary price of aluminum, also based on IV:3:1, was

IV:3:3 $\quad \hat{Psa}_t = 5.4 + .56\ Ppa_t + .052\ IP_t + 7.0\ D74_t$
$$\quad\quad\quad\quad (4.2) \quad\quad\quad (3.7) \quad\quad\quad (9.7)$$

$$R^2 = .88 \quad\quad F = 38 \quad\quad D.W. = 1.7 \quad\quad \rho = .33$$

$$\text{Years: } 1957 - 1976$$

where $\quad$ Psa $\quad$ is the price of number 380 secondary-aluminum ingot deflated by the wholesale-price index

$\quad\quad\quad\quad$ Ppa $\quad$ is the U.S. producer price of primary aluminum deflated by the wholesale-price index

176

IP   is the index of industrial production

and   D74   is a dummy variable equal to one in 1974 and zero otherwise.

The coefficients of all of the variables have the expected signs, and all t-ratios are greater than three. A dummy variable equal to one in 1974 and zero elsewhere was included in the equation because, in that year, price controls in the primary industry kept primary prices low and caused unusual pressure on secondary prices. The lagged value of secondary price was dropped from the equation because it was not significant, indicating that secondary-aluminum prices adjust fully to changed conditions within a year. A linear functional form was chosen because the series that represents secondary-aluminum price is not a scrap price; it is the price of secondary-aluminum ingot which is usually close to the price of primary ingot. It therefore seems reasonable to relate absolute changes in the two prices to one another.

In the next section, the output response of the secondary producers to the secondary prices discussed here is analysed.

IV:4   Secondary Supply -- Recycling

The two types of secondary-metal supply are metal produced
from new and from old scrap. New, or industrial scrap, is generated by the production process itself, while old, or post-consumer
scrap, is recovered from discarded and worn-out products. Because
the determinants of the supply of metal from the two sources are
very different, the two types of secondary-metal supply will be
discussed separately.

IV:4:1 Production from New Scrap

New-scrap supply is from waste material generated by primary producers, mills, foundries, powder plants, and end-product manufacturers and returned to be reused, either directly or after processing by the secondary establishments. New scrap consists primarily of clippings and plate trimmings, borings and turnings, and skimmings and runners from castings. Most new scrap is fairly high quality and is recycled to the production cycle almost immediately after it is generated. The metal produced from new scrap is not an addition to supply. However, if we define consumption as shipments of metal to the semifabricators, then the metal produced from new scrap is an addition to consumption.

Figure IV:4:1 shows plots of the production of copper and aluminum from new scrap over the historic period (1954 - 1976). The supply of aluminum from new scrap grew faster than that of copper, as would be expected because aluminum consumption grew faster than copper consumption during the period.

The determinants of the supply of metal from new scrap are technological, not economic. The quantity of metal produced from new scrap depends on the quantity of metal consumed and is independent of price. [13] A model for the supply of metal from new scrap is thus

179

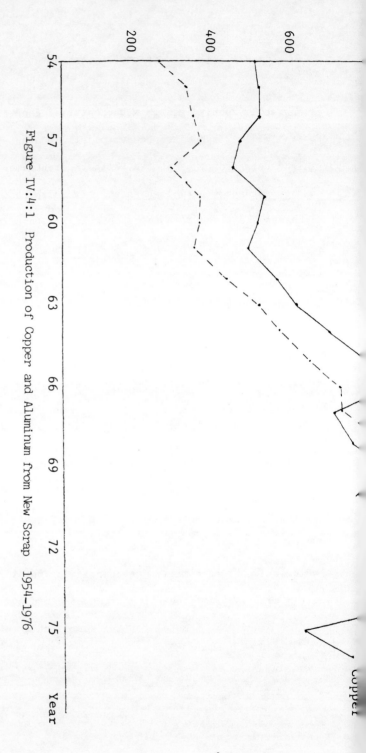

600

400

200

54   57   60   63   66   69   72   75   Year

Figure IV:4:1 Production of Copper and Aluminum from New Scrap 1954-1976

Copper

180

IV:4:1 $Qns = \alpha C$

where   Qns   is the supply of metal from new scrap

and   C   is metal consumed.

The data for metal production from new scrap come from the

trade associations, Copper Development Association and The Aluminum

Association (1954 - 1976). Metal consumption was computed as pri-

mary production plus secondary production minus changes in inven-

tories plus net imports.

The final specification for the supply of copper from new

scrap was

IV:4:2 $\hat{Qnsc}_t = .25\ Cc_t$
                         (25)

           $R^2 = .97$ D.W. = 2.0 $\rho = .83$

                                      Years: 1954 - 1976

where   Qnsc is the supply of copper from new scrap

and   Cc   is copper consumption.

---

13   The hypothesis that new scrap supply is independent of price
      is testable. Equations of the form

           $Qns/C = a_0 + a_1\ Ps$

      were estimated for both metals, but were not found signifi-
      cant by any standard test (t-ratio of a_1, F statistic, or
      R^2). In addition, new-scrap recovery was found to be insen-
      sitive to primary price.

181

The final specification for the supply of aluminum from new scrap was

IV:4:3 $\ln \hat{Qnsa}_t = -1.9 + 1.01 \ln Ca_t$
                      (-5.6) (24)

          $R^2 = .97$ $F = 585$ $D.W. = 1.5$

                                      Years: 1954 – 1976

where   Qnsa is the supply of aluminum from new scrap
and   Ca   is aluminum consumption.

Natural logarithms were taken of the variables in the aluminum equation before estimation because, without logarithms, the variance of the residuals was heteroskedastic. $e^{-1.9}$ is .15; therefore, equation IV:4:3 is approximately equivalent to

$$\hat{Qnsa}_t = .15 \ Ca_t. \quad [14]$$

---

[14] The coefficient of Ca in equation IV:4:3 is not significantly different from one.

IV:4:2   Production from Old Scrap

Old-scrap supply is from material that becomes available
when products reach the end of their useful lifetimes. Old scrap
consists primarily of sheet, tube, and castings, which are fairly
clean, wire and cable, which are free of metalic impurities but
require processing to remove insulation, and scrap that is conta-
minated with extraneous metals. In contrast to new scrap, the
metal produced from old scrap is an addition to supply as well
as to consumption.

Figure IV:4:2 shows plots of the production of copper and
aluminum from old scrap for the historic period (1954-1976).
The recovery of copper from old scrap remained virtually constant over the entire period, but aluminum recovery showed a
steady increase that accelerated in the later years.

Unlike the determinants of new-scrap supply, which are purely
technological, the determinants of the supply of metal from old
scrap are economic as well as technological. The old-scrap-supply
curve for the individual producer is his marginal-cost curve, and
the secondary producer, who is a price taker, equates his marginal
cost to price. The industry old-scrap-supply curve is the horizontal sum of the producer marginal-cost curves. Figure IV:3:3 B of
the previous section illustrates the determination of the supply of
metal from old scrap. The quantity of metal produced from old scrap

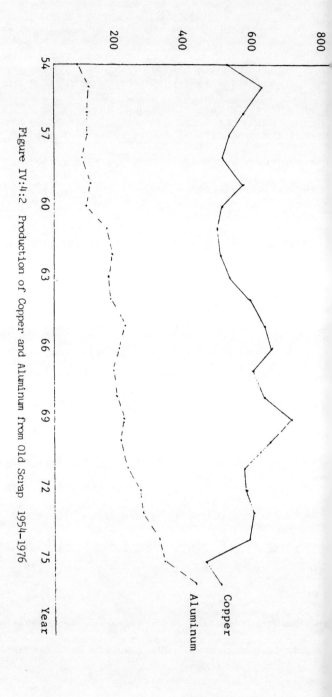

Figure IV:4:2 Production of Copper and Aluminum from Old Scrap 1954-1976

184

(Qos) is determined by the intersetion of marginal cost (MC) and the price of secondary metal (Ps),

IV:4:4 $Ps = MC.$

   Because the quality of old scrap reclaimed varies with output, marginal cost is a nonlinear function of recovery efficiency (RE) as well as a function of the prices of the principal inputs to secondary metal production (where RE is defined as metal reclaimed (Qos) divided by the stocks of old scrap available for collection (SS)).

IV:4:5 $MC = MC(RE, Ps_i)$ where $RE = Qos/SS.$

   Suppose that the marginal-cost function is multiplicative,

IV:4:6 $MC = \alpha_0 RE^{\alpha 1} \prod_i Ps_i^{a_i}$

and IV:4:4 becomes

IV:4:7 $Ps = MC = \alpha_0 RE^{\alpha 1} \prod_i Ps_i^{a_i}.$

Substituting Qos/SS for RE in IV:4:7, we obtain

IV:4:8 $Ps = \alpha_0 \left(\dfrac{Qos}{SS}\right)^{\alpha 1} \prod_i Ps_i^{a_i}.$

Taking logarithms of both sides and solving for Qos results in

185

$$\ln Qos = -\frac{\alpha_0}{\alpha_1} + \ln SS + \frac{1}{\alpha_1} \ln Ps - \sum_i \frac{a_i}{\alpha_0} \ln Ps_i$$

or

IV:4:9 $\ln Qos = c_0 + c_1 \ln SS + c_2 \ln Ps + \sum_i b_i \ln Ps_i$

with $c_1, c_2 > 0$ and $b_i < 0$ $i = 1,\ldots,n$

where   Qos   is the supply of metal from old scrap

SS   is stocks of old scrap

Ps   is the price of secondary metal

and Ps_i are the prices of inputs to secondary production.

IV:4:9 is the model that will be used to estimate equations for the supply of copper and aluminum from old scrap. First, however, we must have a method of calculating SS, the stocks of old scrap available for collection. In contrast to new scrap, which is recycled almost immediately after it is generated, the metal that becomes old scrap may be embodied in a product for thirty years or more before it can be reused. In any year, net additions to the stocks of scrap are equal to the metal that becomes available for collection in that year minus the metal produced from old scrap. The metal that becomes available for collection in a given year is the sum of the metal contained in all products whose useful lifetime has just expired. In mathematical notation, ΔSS_t is

IV:4:10 $\Delta SS_t = \sum_i f_i C_{t-t_i} - Qos_t$

where ΔSS are net additions to the stocks of old scrap

f_i is the fraction of metal consumption that goes into product type i

186

C   is metal consumption

t_i is the average lifetime of product type i

and   Qos   is the production of metal from old scrap.

The stocks of scrap at time T are then equal to

$$IV:4:11 \qquad SS_T = SS_{T-1} + \Delta SS_T = SS_{t_0} + \sum_{t=t_0+1}^{T} \Delta SS_t$$

where t_0 is some base year. If the stock of scrap at time $t = t_0$, the f_i, and the t_i were known, IV:4:10 and 11 could be used to calculate the stock of scrap in any year.

Table IV:4:1 shows the values of the parameters of equations IV:4:10 and 11 used in calculating the stocks of old scrap of copper and aluminum. The fraction of metal consumption going into each type of product (the f_i) were chosen to equal their 1976 proportions. Several people (Brown and Butler, 1969, Brubaker, 1967, Farin and Reibsamen, 1969) have made rough estimates of product average lifetimes (the t_i). The estimates from the various sources do not differ greatly and an average is used here. The base year was chosen to be 1942, and very rough estimates of the stocks of scrap available in that year were made. [14]

---

14   The estimates used are approximately two times total consumption of metal in that year. Fortunately, the estimates of the coefficients of the supply equation are not sensitive to the choice of SS_{t_0}, a result to be expected because metal that has been scrapped for twelve years or more is not very apt to be reclaimed.

PARAMETERS USED IN CALCULATING THE STOCKS OF OLD SCRAP OF COPPER
AND ALUMINUM

ALUMINUM

	Percent of Consumption (%)	Average Lifetime of Product (Years)
Building and Construction	25	30
Transportation	20	17 [16]
Consumer Durables	9	5
Electrical and Electronic	11	30
Industrial Machinery	8	20
Containers and Packaging	21	2
Other	6	(1/2) 20 (1/2) lost

$t_0 = 1942$ $\qquad$ $SS_{t_0} = 1500 \times 10^3$ tons

COPPER

	Percent of Consumption (%)	Average Lifetime of Product (Years)
Building and Construction	24	30
Transportation	14	17 [16]
Consumer Durables	22	5
Electrical and Electronic	23	30
Industrial Machinery	16	20

$t_0 = 1942$ $\qquad$ $SS_{t_0} = 4000 \times 10^3$ tons

---

[16] An average lifetime of 17 years was computed by assuming that three-fourths of metal consumed in transportation goes into automobiles, that have an average lifetime of ten years, while the rest goes into products that have an average lifetime of forty years.

The parameters of table IV:4:1 imply old-scrap-generation

cycles for copper and aluminum. A scrap-generation cycle is

defined as the proportion of metal consumed today that becomes scrap

t years from now. [17] Smooth curves representing these cycles are

plotted in Figure IV:4:3. The aluminum-scrap cycle is strongly

bimodal, with a large volume of short-lived products, such as cans

and foil, combined with a large volume of much longer-lived pro-

ducts. The copper-scrap cycle shows very little scrap being

generated until five years after consumption, and the majority of

products having fairly long average lifetimes.

Having quantified equations IV:4:10 and 11, we can now esti-

mate old-scrap-supply equations for copper and aluminum based on

IV:4:9. The data used for the price of secondary metal were dis-

cussed in section IV:3. The data for the production of metal from

old scrap come from the trade associations, Copper Development

Association and The Aluminum Association (1954 - 1976).

The principal inputs to secondary-metal production are capi-

tal, labor, energy, and transportation. Unfortunately, time-series

data on the prices of these inputs were not always available. The

Bureau of Labor Statistics (BLS) does not publish wage data for

secondary-metal production, and an attempt to use wage data for

---

17   If old-scrap generation is a function of past consumption,
      then the scrap-generation cycle is the distributed lag on
      consumption in the function that relates scrap generation
      to consumption.

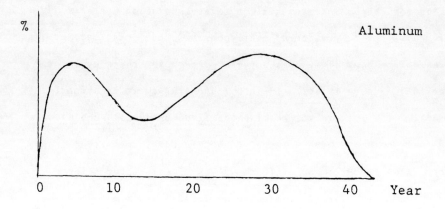

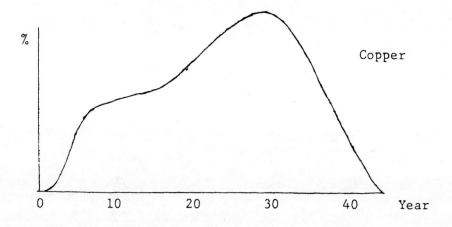

Figure IV:4:3   Old Scrap Generation Cycles
for Copper and Aluminum

primary-metal production in the old-scrap-supply equations proved

unsuccessful. BLS data on freight rates go back only as far as

1969, and attempts to use other measures of transport cost were not

successful. Therefore, only energy-cost and capital-cost data

are included in the old-scrap-supply equations. Price indices

for various energy sources are compiled by the BLS, but no data

were available on the proportion of total energy usage in secon-

dary-copper and secondary-aluminum production that each energy source

contributes. Energy-use proportions were therefore chosen to be

the same in the secondary-metal industries as those computed for

the primary industries. The AAA corporate bond yield from Moody's

Bond Survey was chosen to measure the opportunity cost of capital

to the secondary producers.

The final specification for the supply of aluminum from old

scrap, based on IV:4:9, was

IV:4:12 $$\ln \hat{Q}osa_t = -6.3 + 1.3 \ln SSa_t + .24 \ln Psa_t + .47 \ln Pea_t$$
$$\qquad\qquad\quad (9.5) \qquad\quad (1.01) \qquad\quad (1.74)$$

$$- .99 \ln CBY_t$$
$$(-4.1) \qquad\qquad\qquad\qquad \text{Years: } 1954 - 1976$$

$$R^2 = .95 \qquad F = 87 \qquad D.W. = 2.1 \qquad \rho = -.22$$

where   Qosa   is the supply of aluminum from old scrap

              SSa   is stocks of old aluminum scrap

              Psa   is the price of number 380 secondary aluminum ingot deflated by the wholesale-price index

              Pea   is an index of energy prices for aluminum production deflated by the wholesale-price index

and   CBY   is Moody's AAA corporate bond yield.

The supply of aluminum from old scrap is fairly inelastic with respect to price (estimated price elasticity of supply = .24), a result that is in keeping with earlier estimates. For example, Charles River Associates (1976) found the price elasticity of aluminum supply from old scrap to be .22.

The sign of the coefficient of energy price deserves further discussion. Because energy is an input to secondary-aluminum production, the estimated coefficient of energy price might be expected to be negative. However, the weights used in computing Pea were those relevant to primary aluminum production. Therefore, Pea measures the price of electricity. When the price of electricity goes up, the secondary producer (unlike the primary producer who must use electricity) can substitute other energy sources for electricity. Therefore, with an increase in the price of electricity, secondary aluminum becomes cheap relative to primary aluminum and more secondary metal is produced.

The estimated coefficients of all of the other variables in equation IV:4:12 have the expected signs.

The final specification for the supply of copper from old scrap, also based on IV:4:9, was

IV:4:13 $\ln \hat{Q}osc_t = 4.1 + .11 \ln SSc_t + .29 \ln Psc_t - .46 \ln Pec_t$
$\qquad\qquad\qquad\quad (3.3) \qquad\quad (7.0) \qquad\quad (-4.9)$

$\qquad R^2 = .88 \qquad F = 47 \qquad D.W. = 2.0$

$\qquad\qquad\qquad\qquad\qquad\qquad$ Years: 1954 - 1976

where   Qosc is the supply of copper from old scrap

              SSc   is stocks of old copper scrap

              Psc   is the price of number-two-copper scrap
                      deflated by the wholesale-price index

and   Pec   is an index of energy prices for copper production
                      deflated by the wholesale-price index.

The supply of copper from old scrap is also fairly inelastic with respect to price (estimated price elasticity of supply = .29), a result that is also in keeping with earlier estimates. For example, Fisher et.al. (1972) found the price elasticity of supply of copper from old scrap to be .31.

The estimated coefficients of all of the variables in equation IV:4:13 have the expected signs. The corporate-bond-yield variable was dropped from the equation because it was not significant.

This completes the analysis of the secondary industries. In the next chapter, the consuming sectors will be discussed.

CHAPTER V: THE USING SECTORS

Up to this point, we have been discussing the supply side
of the copper and aluminum markets. We now consider the major
uses of copper and aluminum, how usage is determined, and the
facility with which one metal can be substituted for the other.

V:1   The Pattern of Consumption

It is difficult to say exactly when a metal is "consumed".
Is it consumed by the mills and foundries, by the manufacturers
of end products, or by the purchasers of these products? In
chapters III and IV, consumption was defined as shipments to the
semifabricators (consumption equaled primary and secondary
production plus net imports minus changes in inventories).
This definition was chosen of necessity because, before 1960,
the data on copper and aluminum usage are poor. However, a
different definition of consumption is used in this chapter
because the emphasis here is on substitution between copper
and aluminum. It is the end-product manufacturers, not the
semifabricators, who substitute. Therefore, consumption is
defined in this chapter as shipments to the major markets.

An example may make this distinction clearer. The purchaser
of an automobile is indifferent as to whether his car radiator
was made with copper or aluminum. It is the manufacturer of the
automobile who minimizes cost by choosing the appropriate material.
At the other end, the semifabricator produces because the end-
product manufacturer (the automobile maker in the above example)
wants his products (that is, the demand for the products of the
semifabricator -- wire, sheet, tube, etc. -- is derived), but substitution is not possible at the stage of semifabrication because
most mills produce either copper or aluminum products but not
both.

When we must distinguish between the two types of consumption,
we will call the first "apparent consumption" and the second
"consumption by sector". The equations discussed in chapters
III and IV use "apparent consumption" as an explanatory variable,
but the equations that are presented here explain "consumption
by sector". Fortunately, this difference presents no problem
for the simulations performed later. The average difference
between the two variables is less than two percent of total
consumption for both metals, and the difference shows no systematic
pattern. Therefore, no attempt was made to correct for the different definitions of consumption used.

In section V:1:1, we will discuss the historic (1954-1976)
behavior of "apparent consumption". After section V:1:1, however,
all references to consumption are to "consumption by sector".

195

V:1:1 Copper and Aluminum Apparent Consumption 1954-1976

The semifabricators include the mills, which produce sheet, plate, tube, rod, and wire, the foundries, which produce castings and molds, and the powder plants. Copper and aluminum are also used by other industries such as those that manufacture chemicals and steel. Table V:1:1 shows the destination of copper and aluminum shipments in 1976.

TABLE V:1:1
COPPER AND ALUMINUM CONSUMPTION BY THE SEMIFABRICATORS
IN 1976 (%)

	Mills	Foundries	Powder Plants	Other
Copper	86	10	1	3
Aluminum	76	15	1	8

Figure V:1:1 shows plots of copper and aluminum apparent domestic consumption between 1954 and 1976 together with the index of industrial production. [1] Consumption of both metals follows the same general cyclical pattern as does overall economic activity, but cyclical swings are more pronounced in metal usage than in the

---

1   Apparent domestic consumption was computed as primary and secondary production plus net imports minus changes in inventories (private and government). As will be seen in chapter VI, there is a problem in obtaining data on private aluminum inventories prior to 1967. In earlier years, changes in private aluminum inventories were calculated as primary production minus primary shipments (changes in secondary inventories were ignored).

rest of the economy. Aluminum consumption grew faster than the economy as a whole, whereas growth in copper consumption was slower.

In the next section, we examine the uses that are made of the products of the semifabricators.

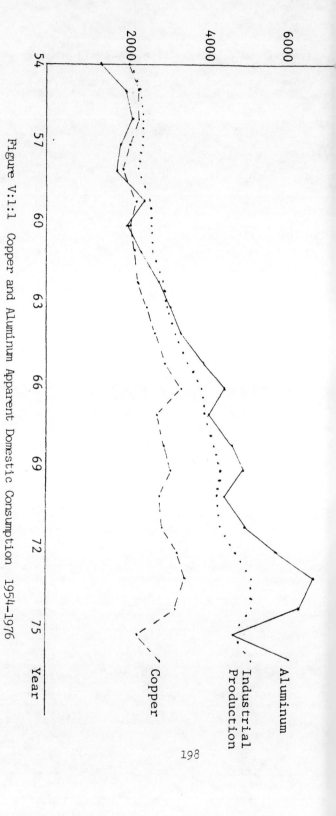

Figure V:1:1 Copper and Aluminum Apparent Domestic Consumption 1954-1976

198

V:1:2   The Major Markets

The major consuming markets for copper semifabricated products are: building and construction, transportation, electrical
and electronic products, industrial machinery, and consumer
durables. The markets for aluminum semifabricated products are
those listed above as well as containers and packaging. In addition, both metals have miscellaneous uses such as in military
and chemical applications. Tables V:1:2 and 3 list the percentages
of copper and aluminum shipments in 1976 that went to each major
market as well as the principal uses of the metals in each of
these markets. [2]

Figures V:1:2 and 3 show plots of copper and aluminum shipments to each of the major markets between 1960 and 1976.
Growth in copper consumption was not very significant in any
of the markets during the seventeen-year period. [3] In contrast, aluminum consumption grew rapidly in most of its markets.
The fastest growing sector was the container and packaging market, where average growth rate was 13% per year.

---

[2]   Most of the information condensed into tables V:1:2 and 3
      comes from the U.S. Bureau of Mines Mineral Commodity Profiles.

[3]   Regressions of copper consumption in each sector versus time
      were performed. Only in the transport market was the t-ratio
      of the estimated coefficient of time greater than two.
      Similar regressions for aluminum consumption were performed.
      t-ratios of the estimated coefficients of time were greater
      than two in all markets except electrical and "other".

TABLE V:1:2

COPPER USAGE IN THE MAJOR MARKETS (PERCENTS FOR 1976)

Market	Percent	Usage
Construction	24	Wiring, roofing, plumbing, decorative items
Transportation	15	Radiators, heaters, defrosters, wiring, bearings, carburators, brakes, air conditioners, switching and signal devices
Electrical	23	Transformers, busbars, switchgear, lighting and wiring equipment, cable transmission lines
Industrial	16	Air conditioners, farm machinery, distillation plants
Consumer	22	Refrigerators, air conditioners, decorative items
Other		Ordnance, chemicals, pigments, coinage

ALUMINUM USAGE IN THE MAJOR MARKETS   (PERCENTS FOR 1976)

Market	Percent	Usage
Construction	25	Wiring, doors and windows, siding, roofing, awnings and canopies, heating and ventillating
Transport	21	Pistons, automotive transmission parts, air conditioners, wiring, brakes, steering, airplane bodies
Electrical	11	Transmission and distribution lines, telephone cable, lighting fixtures, electric lamps, capacitors
Industrial	8	Materials handling equipment, irrigation pipe
Consumer	9	Refrigerators, air conditioners, washing machines, furniture, utensils
Containers	22	Foil, cans, semi-rigid food containers, caps, closures
Other	5	Ordnance, steel, chemicals

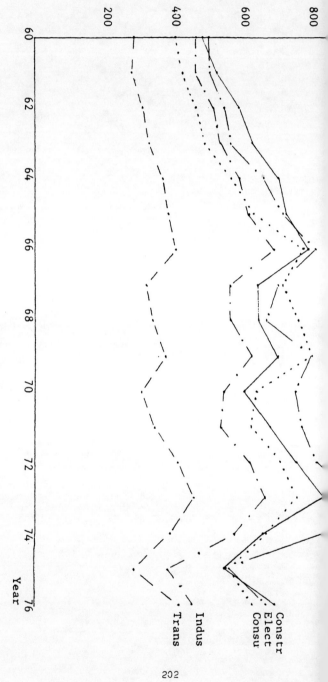

Figure V:1:2 Copper Consumption by Sector 1960-1976

202

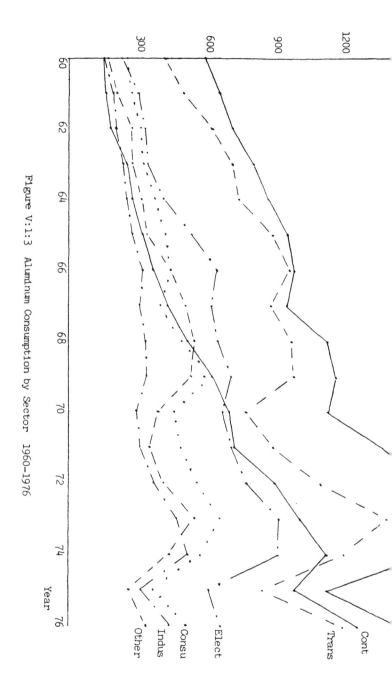

Figure V:1:3 Aluminum Consumption by Sector 1960-1976

203

V:2 Substitution Between Copper and Aluminum

V:2:1 Areas of Potential Substitution

In some applications, special properties of copper or aluminum are required, and no substitution can take place. However,
in a broad number of applications, one material can serve as an
alternative to the other. In this section, we summarize the areas
where substitution between copper and aluminum is possible.

Both copper and aluminum are good conductors of electricity,
and the prime area for substitution between the two is in electrical conductor applications. Table V:2:1 shows two properties of copper and aluminum that make this substitution possible.
For equal units of conductivity, copper weighs about twice as
much as aluminum but aluminum is nearly twice as voluminous.
Tradeoffs exist and usage depends on the application. For example,
in overhead power-transmission wires, where weight is a factor,
aluminum is preferred. In contrast, in wiring in small electronic
devices, where size is important, copper is more suitable.

TABLE V:2:1
SOME PROPERTIES OF COPPER AND ALUMINUM

	Relative Conductivity (on an equal volume basis)	Weight lb/ft^3
Copper	100	550
Aluminum	59	166

Because both copper and aluminum are also good thermal conductors, the second most important area of potential substitution is in heat-exchanger applications. Such applications include automobile radiators, refrigerators, and air conditioners of all sorts.

In addition to electrical-conductor and heat-exchanger applications, various miscellaneous areas of potential substitution exist, such as in structural parts, ordanance, and alloying and coating applications. In table V:2:2, which summarizes the areas where copper-aluminum substitution can take place, these miscellaneous areas have been combined into one category called "general applications". [4]

---

[4] The information summarized in table V:2:2 comes principally from the National Materials Advisory Board's Mutual Substitability of Copper and Aluminum (1972).

TABLE V:2:2

AREAS OF POTENTIAL COPPER-ALUMINUM SUBSTITUTION

Application	Areas of Substitution
Electrical Conductor	Transformers, appliance motors, busbars, AC induction motors, industrial relays, breakers and controls, building wire, communication cable, power wire and cable, automotive electrical
Heat Exchanger	Air conditioners, refrigerators, freezers, power stations, chemical and petrochemical plants, desalination plants, marine exchangers, aircraft oil coolers and fuel heaters
General	Coinage, brazing filler metals, electroplating and coating, alloying elements, ordnance, parts and equipment, bearings and bushings, powder metallurgy parts, springs, nonsparking devices, magnetic materials

V:2:2   Elasticities of Substitution

We have just examined the areas where substitution between
copper and aluminum can take place. The substitution that actually occurs, for given technology, depends on the relative costs
of purchasing copper and aluminum. We now estimate the amount
of substitution that can be induced by a change in the copper-
aluminum price ratio. Because the substitution process is
not instantaneous, a change in the price ratio of the two metals
will have a long-term effect on their market shares that is much
greater than the immediate effect. We therefore attempt to
measure the long-run elasticity of substitution (percent change
in consumption ratio due to a percent change in price ratio) between the two metals.

Historically, the price of aluminum has fallen relative
to that of copper, and the market for aluminum has increased
at the expense of copper. Figure V:2:1 shows plots of aluminum-
copper price and consumption ratios between 1954 and 1976
with the twenty-three-year trend in these ratios. As the price
ratio fell, the consumption ratio increased. In the future,
several factors, including the high price of energy and the depletion of low-cost copper ores, will change the relative costs of
producing copper and aluminum. It is to understand how these
cost factors will affect the future demand for the two metals
that we estimate substitution elasticities.

In the remainder of this section, the choice of production function and equilibrium condition used to estimate the elasticities of substitution, the class of distributed lags employed to capture long-run effects, and the empirical estimates of the substitution elasticities will be discussed.

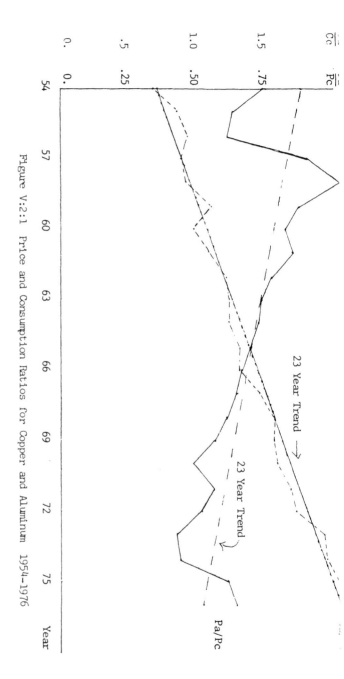

Figure V:2:1 Price and Consumption Ratios for Copper and Aluminum 1954-1976

V:2:2:1 The two-level CES production function

Demand for a metal is derived; that is, metal demand is induced by the demand for metal products. To model derived demand, we must make some assumption about the production function of the demanding sector. There are several possible production functions to choose from -- constant elasticity of substitution (CES) (Arrow, Chenery, Minhas, and Solow, 1961), two-level CES (Sato, 1967), and transcendental logarithmic (translog) (Christensen, Jorgenson, and Lau, 1972) -- to name a few.[5] The two-level CES will be used here because it provides sufficient flexibility without inordinate data requirements.

The two-level CES production function consists of several CES's within an overall CES

$$V:2:1 \qquad Q = [\sum_{s=1}^{S} (a_s \, Z_s^{-\rho})]^{-1/\rho} \qquad \rho > -1 \qquad a_s > 0$$

$$Z_s = [\sum_{i \in N_s} (b_i \, X_i^{-\rho_s})]^{-1/\rho_s} \qquad \rho_s > -1 \qquad b_i > 0.$$

---

5   A Cobb-Douglas production function was not used, because, with this production function, the elasticity of substitution is identically one. In section V:2:2:4, the hypothesis that the long-run elasticity of copper-aluminum substitution in each sector is equal to one is tested. In one half of the sectors the hypothesis can be rejected at the 95% confidence level.

In V:2:1, Q is the sector output and Z_s is an input group. A particular input X_i which contributes to Z_s can not contribute to any other Z ($i \in N_s \rightarrow i \notin N_j$, $j \neq s$).

The direct partial elasticity of substitution between any two factors within Z_s is σ_s, where σ_s is defined as

$$\sigma_s = \partial \ln(X_i/X_j)/\partial \ln(P_j/P_i).$$

Sato (1967) showed that

$$\sigma_s = 1/(1 + \rho_s).$$

σ_s measures substitution between a pair of factors in Z_s while holding output (Q) and all other inputs constant. Because the two-level CES production function is strongly separable,[6] the allocation of factors within each class is determined exclusively by relative factor prices within that class. Therefore, variations in Q do not affect factor ratios within Z_s. However, because other inputs from the same class are held constant, σ_s is an underestimate of the total elasticity of substitution σ_t, where σ_t is defined as

$$\sigma_t = d \ln(X_i/X_j)/d \ln(P_j/P_i).$$

---

[6]   A strongly separable production function is one where output, Q, is an additive function of the input groups, Z_s

$$Q = Q[\sum_{s=1}^{S} f_s(Z_s)]$$

211

σ_s can be estimated from the cost-minimizing equilibrium condition

$$X_i/X_j = (b_i/b_j)^{\sigma_s} (P_j/P_i)^{\sigma_s}$$

which is linear in logarithms.

As noted earlier, the five principal uses of copper and aluminum are in consumer durables, industrial machinery and equipment, electrical and electronic products, building and construction, and transportation. Because the substitution potential and appropriate lag structure can be expected to be different for each end use, [7] it is desirable to estimate a separate elasticity of substitution for each sector as well as an overall elasticity for total domestic consumption of copper and aluminum. If we assume that the supply of copper and aluminum to each demanding sector is infinitely elastic and that each sector produces its output according to a two-level CES production function, then

$$V:2:2 \qquad \ln(C_i/A_i) = c + \sigma_{l_i} \ln(Pa/Pc)$$

where C_i/A_i is the equilibrium value of the ratio of copper to aluminum sales to the i th sector per unit time, Pa/Pc is the equilibrium value of the copper-aluminum price ratio, and σ_{l_i} is the direct partial elasticity of substitution between copper and aluminum in the i th sector. Equation V:2:2 can be rewritten as

---

7   The hypothesis that the long-run elasticity of substitution
      is the same in each sector is tested in section V:2:2:4 and
      rejected at the 99% level of confidence.

$$(c/a)_i = c + \sigma_{\ell_i} (pa/pc)$$

where $(c/a)_i = \ln(C_i/A_i)$ and $pa/pc = \ln(Pa/Pc)$

If we assume that purchasers buy inputs on the basis of their expectations about the equilibrium price ratio, then, at time t,

V:2:3 $$(c/a)_{it} = c + \sigma_{\ell_i} (pa/pc)*_t$$

where $(pa/pc)*_t$ is the logarithm of the equilibrium price ratio expected at time t. If the rate of price change expected at time t is equal to a weighted average of the rates of price change observed at time t and ℓ previous time periods, it follows that

$$(pa/pc)*_t = \sum_{k=0}^{\ell} w_k (pa/pc)_{t-k} \qquad \text{where} \qquad \sum_{k=0}^{\ell} w_k = 1,$$

and V:2:3 is equivalent to

V:2:4 $$(c/a)_{it} = c + \sigma_{\ell_i} [\sum_{k=0}^{\ell} w_{ki} (pa/pc)_{t-k}]$$

In section V:2:2:4, equation V:2:4 will be used to estimate the long-run elasticity of copper-aluminum substitution, σ_{ℓ_i}, and the weights, w_{ki}, for each sector. First, however, the class of finite distributed lags used in the estimation of the w_{ki} will be discussed.

V:2:2:2 Shiller distributed lags

The general distributed lag problem is to estimate the parameters, β, in the equation

V:2:5
$$y_t = \sum_{i=0}^{\ell} x_{t-i} \beta_i + \varepsilon_i \qquad \ell \leqq \infty$$

or
$$y = X\beta + \varepsilon \qquad \varepsilon \sim N(0, \sigma_\varepsilon^2).$$

Equation V:2:5 can be rewritten as

V:2:6
$$y_t = \beta * \sum_{i=0}^{\ell} x_{t-i} w_i + \varepsilon_t$$

where
$$\beta * = \sum_{i=0}^{\ell} \beta_i \qquad \text{and} \qquad \sum_{i=0}^{\ell} w_i = 1.$$

In a dynamic system, $\beta *$ determines the magnitude of the long-run effect on y of a change in x, and the w_i define the time path of this effect. Both are important in determining the behavior and stability of the system.

A finite distributed lag is one in which the tail is (perhaps arbitrarily) cut off after a finite period ($\ell < \infty$). With a finite lag, the simplest method of estimating β is to apply ordinary least squares (OLS) directly to equation V:2:5. OLS yields unbiased estimates of β, but, because of multicollinearity, the standard errors of β may be large. The OLS solution is obtained by

$$\min (y - X\beta)'(y - X\beta).$$

214

To circumvent the problem of multicollinearity, Almon (1965)
proposed that the coefficients be constrained to lie along a polynomial of given degree d. Shiller (1973) noted that the Almon technique, the polynomial distributed lag (PDL), consists of imposing a
set of linear restrictions on β,

V:2:7 $Rd\ \beta = 0.$

where Rd is an $(\ell - d) \times (d + 1)$ matrix, which when multiplied by
β, gives the $d + 1$st differences of β. Instead of the exact PDL
restrictions on the coefficients, Shiller chose to make equations
V:2:7 stochastic by adding a disturbance term μ

$$Rd\ \beta = \mu \qquad\qquad \mu \sim N(0, \sigma_\mu^2).$$

Shiller presented his technique in terms of Bayesian smoothness
priors, the prior knowledge being that the lag coefficients should
trace out a smooth curve. Shiller's method is a compromise between
OLS (which may have problems with multicollinearity) and PDL (which
imposes arbitrary restrictions on the coefficients), and, in fact,
encompasses the two.

The Shiller solution is obtained by

$$\min_{\beta}\ (y - X\beta)'(y - X\beta) + k^2 \beta'Rd'Rd\ \beta$$

where $k^2 = \sigma_\varepsilon^2/\sigma_\mu^2.$

215

We can express the three methods in symmetric notation, using the fact that $Rd\beta = 0 \Longleftrightarrow \beta'Rd'Rd\beta = 0$. Let

$$F(\beta) = (y - X\beta)'(y - X\beta) \quad \text{and} \quad G(\beta) = \beta'Rd'Rd\beta.$$

Then we have

OLS
V:2:8
$$\min_{\beta} F(\beta)$$

PDL
V:2:9
$$\min_{\beta} F(\beta) \quad \text{subject to} \quad G(\beta) = 0$$

Shiller
V:2:10
$$\min_{\beta} F(\beta) + k^2 G(\beta).$$

In V:2:8, $k^2 = 0$ ($\sigma_\mu^2 = \infty$ or there is no constraint on the coefficients) whereas in V:2:9, $k^2 = \infty$ ($\sigma_\mu^2 = 0$ or the constraint is binding). In V:2:10, k^2 is known.

A problem with Shiller's method is that we must know k^2 _a priori_. [8] The problem is made more difficult because k^2 depends on the units chosen. A different (and perhaps more intuitive) interpretation of k^2 is given here. Equation V:2:10 has two parts -- the first half is the approximation to the data and the second is the smoothness constraint (approximation to a polynomial of

---

8   For a slightly different problem, Lindley and Smith (1972) suggested an iterative procedure for estimating k. Their procedure can be adapted to the Shiller lag situation, but it requires larger values of $\ell - d$ than those encountered in section V:2:2:4 of this chapter.

degree d). k^2 is a weight that determines which half is of greater concern. If k^2 is small, the solution will be near OLS; if it is large, the solution will be approximately the PDL solution. But, since $0 \leq k^2 \leq \infty$, it is hard to say what constitutes a "large" value of k^2. In practice, values of k that are moderately small (k=5) give solutions to V:2:10 that are numerically indistinguishable from the PDL estimates. Applying OLS to equation V:2:10 provides a very efficient method of computing a polynomial distributed lag (because no transformation of the data is required). Because k^2 need not be large, estimating a PDL by this method does not involve inverting a near-singular matrix.

In the next two sections, the class of finite distributed lags just presented is applied to obtain estimates of copper-aluminum long-run substitution elasticities. In estimating the price and output equations of the CAS model, a variable was usually dropped from an equation if the t-ratio of its estimated coefficient was less than one. Because the theoretical specification of the elasticity of substitution and derived demand equations is more precise that that of the price and output equations, variables are not dropped from the equations presented in this chapter if their estimated coefficients are insignificant.

V:2:2:3 The data

The data for the U.S. producer prices of copper and aluminum
were discussed in chapter III:4:4. Copper and aluminum sales to
each sector are recorded by the trade associations, Copper Development Association and The Aluminum Association (1960-1976). Dis-
aggregated consumption figures are yearly and have been kept only
since 1960. Therefore, in contrast to the equations in the rest of
the model, only the years 1960-1976 were used in estimating the
equations reported in this chapter. An equation was estimated for
the five demanding sectors as well as for total domestic consumption
of the two metals. Total comsumption of each metal is obtained by
summing consumption over sectors. For aluminum, two additional categories are included in the total -- containers and packaging and a
catch-all category called "other". No elasticity of substitution was
calculated for containers and packaging because little copper is
used in this category.

V:2:2:4 The elasticity of substitution equations

OLS estimates of σ_{ℓ_i} , the long-run elasticity of copper-aluminum substitution in the i th demand sector, can be obtained from the five equations

V:2:11
$$\ln(C_{it}/A_{it}) = c_i + \sum_{j=0}^{\ell} \sigma_{ij} \ln(Pa_{t-j}/Pc_{t-j}) + \varepsilon_{it} \qquad i=1,\ldots,5.$$

where C_{it} is sales of copper to the ith sector at time t

A_{it} is sales of aluminum to the ith sector at time t

Pc_t is the U.S. producer price of copper at time t

Pa_t is the U.S. producer price of aluminum at time t

and $\varepsilon_i \sim N(0, \sigma_{\varepsilon_i}^2)$.

The long-run elasticity of substitution, σ_{ℓ_i} , is the sum of the σ_{ij}

$$\sigma_{\ell_i} = \sum_{j=0}^{\ell} \sigma_{ij}.$$

A sixth equation was estimated for σ_ℓ, the long-run elasticity of copper-aluminum substitution in the U.S. economy as a whole, using total consumption figures. [9]

With the exception of consumer durables, where there is no detectable long-run response, a value of ℓ = 3 years gives good

---

[9]   It cannot be assumed that the supplies of copper and aluminum to the economy as a whole are infinitely elastic (as it was for the using sectors). The violation of this assumption results in simultaneous-equation bias in the estimated coefficients. However, because primary prices and output respond to changed underlying conditions with a lag, the bias should be small.

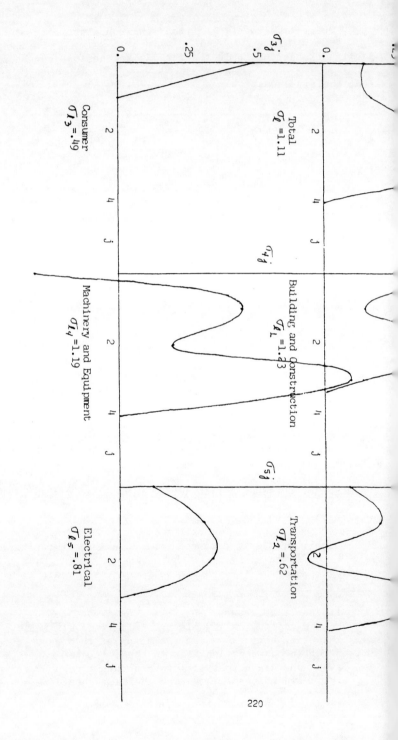

results.   Figure V:2:2 summarizes the OLS estimates.   The graphs

shown are the time paths of the response of the consumption ratio in

each sector to a change in the price ratio. σ_{ℓ_i} , the long-run elas-

ticity of substitution in each sector, is the area under the curve in

each graph.

Table V:2:3 shows the effect of varying ℓ , the length of the

lag, on σ_{ℓ_i} , the long-run elasticity of substitution for the trans-

port and building and construction sectors.   In these, as well as in

the other sectors, σ_{ℓ_i} is not very sensitive to the choice of ℓ .

TABLE V:2:3
STABILITY OF ELASTICITY ESTIMATES (OLS)

Building and Construction

ℓ	2	3	4	5
σ_{ℓ_i}	1.24	1.23	1.21	1.28

Transportation

ℓ	3	4	5	6
σ_{ℓ_i}	.615	.607	.600	.603

The justification for estimating five separate equations, one

for each sector, was that because copper and aluminum usage in each

sector is very different, the lag structure might vary from one

sector to another.   It is therefore of interest to test the hypothesis

221

that the elasticity of substitution is the same in all five sectors, making disaggregation unnecessary. To do this, a pooled time-series cross-section equation of the following form was estimated

$$\ln(C_{it}/A_{it}) = c_0 + \sum_{i=1}^{4} c_i D_i + \sum_{j=0}^{3} \sigma_j \ln(Pa_{t-j}/Pc_{t-j}) + \epsilon_{it},$$

where D_i are dummy variables that distinguish the five sectors. The null hypothesis is that

$$\sigma_{1j} = \sigma_{2j} = \sigma_{3j} = \sigma_{4j} = \sigma_{5j} = \sigma_j \qquad j = 0,\ldots,3.$$

The F-statistic to test the null hypothesis is computed to be 3.095, implying that the hypothesis of equal elasticities in all sectors can be rejected at the 99% level of confidence.

One rationale for choosing a two-level CES production function was that the simpler Cobb-Douglass (with elasticity of substitution $\equiv 1$) is too restrictive. It is therefore of interest to test the hypothesis that the estimated long-run elasticities of substitution are significantly different from one. Let the null hypothesis be that

$$\sum_{j=0}^{3} \sigma_{ij} = 1 \qquad i = 1,\ldots,5.$$

Table V:2:4 shows the t-statistics that test the above hypotheses. In one half of the sectors, the hypothesis of unitary elasticity of substitution can be rejected at the 95% level of confidence, therefore, the choice of the more elaborate two-level CES production function seems justified.

TESTS OF UNITARY ELASTICITY OF SUBSTITUTION

Sector	t	Significance
Total	1.78	5%
Construction	1.64	10%
Transport	-2.54	5%
Machinery	1.67	10%
Electrical	-.74	25%
Consumer	-2.78	1%

In three of the sectors -- building and construction, transportation, and machinery and equipment -- the shape of the distributed lag is somewhat erratic. Because lagged values of the price ratio are correlated with one another, we cannot obtain precise estimates of the individual coefficients using OLS. An intuitive feeling that the lag coefficients should trace out a smooth curve leads us to test the effect of varying the parameter k. Figure V:2:3 shows the results of varying k for the transport sector with $d = 2$ and $\ell = 3$. The OLS distribution is continuously transformed into the PDL solution. A value of $k = .1$ gives a good compromise between the two extremes; it retains some of the original shape while smoothing the curve. The same figure shows that the results are much the same if ℓ is chosen to be 4 instead of 3. $k = .1$ gives a good compromise in the other sectors as well.

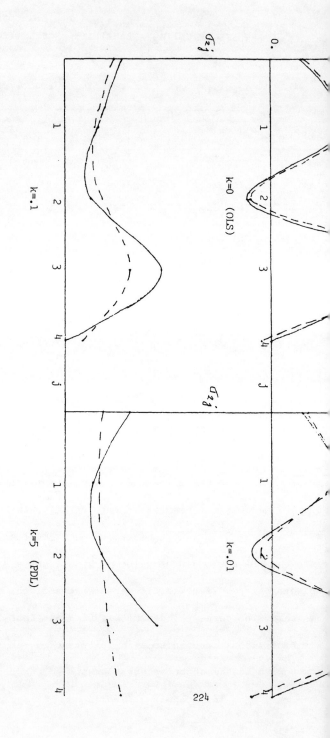

Different values of the parameter d, the degree of the polynomial or smoothness prior, were also tried. Because d must be less
than ℓ, values of d greater than 2 are not appropriate. With d = 1
and k near the PDL value, the coefficients are constrained to lie
along a straight line. Such severe restriction distorts the estimates of σ_{ℓ_i}. In general, a value of d = 2 was judged superior to
d = 1, and the results for d = 1 are not presented here. [9]

Figure V:2:4 and table V:2:5 summarize the Shiller lag estimates with k = .1, d = 2, and ℓ = 3. The statistical method used
to estimate the Shiller lags with autocorrelated errors is described
in appendix V:1. Figure V:2:5 gives the PDL estimates. Figures
V:2:2, 4, and 5 show that the estimates of σ_{ℓ_i} are hardly changed
when k is varied between the two extremes (OLS and PDL). However,
if it is necessary to choose among the estimates, several considerations are relevant. In a dynamic context, smoothing of
the lag coefficients can be very important. If the erratic shape
of the OLS distribution is due to multicollinearity and is not
a true representation of the time path, spurious dynamics can
be introduced into a simulation model when the OLS estimates are
used. For this reason, the Shiller lags with k = .1 are probably
superior to the OLS results. On the other hand, the smooth PDL

---

9   With a polynomial distributed lag, it is possible to test if
     the choice of d and ℓ is appropriate (Harper, 1977). However,
     with the more flexible Shiller lag, the choice of d is not
     very important. The results obtained using Shiller's method
     seem clealy superior to the PDL results for any ℓ. Therefore
     Harper's method was not used.

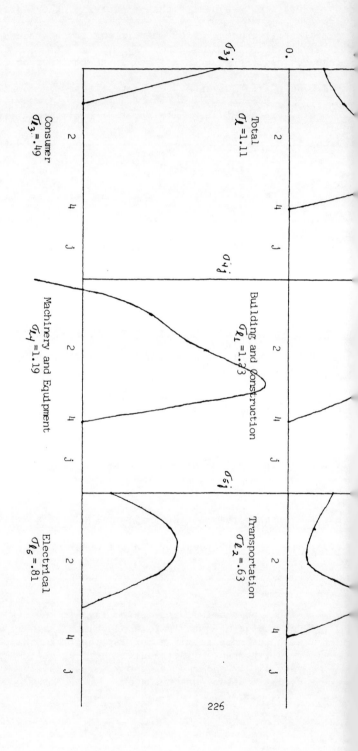

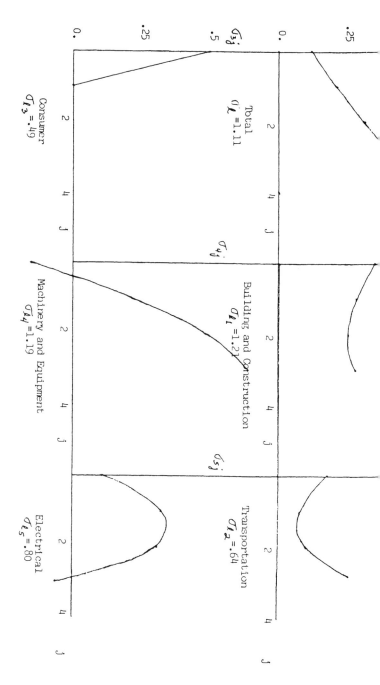

σ_{3j}

Total
$\sigma_{\ell} = 1.11$

σ_{4j}

Building and Construction
$\sigma_{\ell_1} = 1.21$

σ_{5j}

Transportation
$\sigma_{\ell_2} = .64$

Consumer
$\sigma_{\ell_3} = .49$

Machinery and Equipment
$\sigma_{\ell_4} = 1.19$

Electrical
$\sigma_{\ell_5} = .80$

estimates, without a zero restriction on the right-hand side, often
turn up in the last period, an unrealistic result. Therefore, the
Shiller lags are probably more representative of the true underlying distribution than are the more restrictive PDL estimates. Equations V:2:12 - 16 shown in table V:2:5 are the market-share equations
used in the CAS model.

TABLE V:2:5
ELASTICITY OF SUBSTITUTION EQUATIONS   SHILLER LAGS
ℓ = 3   d = 2   k = .1

	c_i	σ_{i0}	σ_{i1}	σ_{i2}	σ_{i3}	R^2	DW	ρ_i	No.
Total	.111	.127	.211	.331	.439	.97	2.1		
		(1.3)	(2.2)	(3.5)	(3.6)				
Const.	.075	.389	.271	.295	.274	.93	2.4	.40	V:2:12
		(2.4)	(1.9)	(1.9)	(1.6)			(1.4)	
Trans.	-.652	.171	.101	.075	.284	.91	1.5	.47	V:2:13
		(1.3)	(.92)	(.62)	(2.1)			(2.5)	
Consu.	.581	.488				.61	1.6	.62	V:2:14
		(2.7)						(3.2)	
Indus.	1.08	-.174	.251	.445	.670	.92	1.8		V:2:15
		(-.9)	(1.3)	(2.4)	(2.8)				
Electr.	.535	.111	.320	.315	.063	.93	1.6	.65	V:2:16
		(.76)	(2.6)	(2.3)	(.44)			(2.9)	

Years: 1960-1976

V:2:2:5 Comparison with other elasticity estimates

Previous attempts to measure copper-aluminum substitution potential statistically can be grouped into two classes -- those that fit logistic curves to historic market trends and those that estimate conventional demand equations with the price of the substitute metal as an explanatory variable. The first class is an outgrowth of dynamic input-output analysis. The emphasis is on determining changes in copper-aluminum market shares over time in order to modify input-output coefficients or to make demand projections. Because prices play only a minor role or no role at all, these results can not be directly compared to those obtained in this study. Ayres et al. (1971) and Rohatgi and Weiss (1974) present studies that fall into the first class.

The second class of studies offers useful comparisons. Because copper and aluminum are highly substitutable, demand equations in econometric commodity models of either metal usually include the price of the substitute material as an independent variable. From the demand equation it is possible to compute own-price and cross elasticities of demand. How these demand elasticities can be compared to the elasticity of substitution is shown here.

Let σ_ℓ be the direct partial elasticity of substitution, μ_ℓ be the own-price elasticity of demand, and η_ℓ be the cross-price elasticity of demand. Then

$$\sigma_\ell = \partial \ln(C/A) / \partial \ln(Pa/Pc)$$

229

$$\mu_\ell = \partial \ln(A) / \partial \ln(Pa) \quad [10]$$

and $\qquad \eta_\ell = \partial \ln(C) / \partial \ln(Pa). \quad [10]$

If output is produced according to a CES production function, a cost minimizing equilibrium condition is

$$C/A = c \ (Pa/Pc)^{\sigma\ell}$$

or $\qquad C = c \ A \ (Pa/Pc)^{\sigma\ell}$

Taking logarithms of both sides yields

V:2:17 $\qquad \ln C = \ln c + \ln A + \sigma_\ell \ln Pa - \sigma_\ell \ln Pc.$

Partially differentiating with respect to ln Pa and assuming that $\partial Pc / \partial Pa = 0$ (i.e., copper and aluminum prices are set independently) results in

---

10 The own-price and cross elasticities are defined here as partial derivatives, analogous to the direct partial elasticity of substitution. If the demand equation is of the form

$$\ln Ai = a0 + a1 \ln Pa + a2 \ln Pc + a3 \ln Qi + a4 \ln Ai_{-1}$$

where Qi is the sector output, then $-a1/(1-a4)$, the computed long-run own-price elasticity of demand, is obtained while holding Qi and all other inputs constant. The cete-ris paribus conditions of the demand equation insure that all other inputs have been held constant. The effect on d lnAi/d lnPa of the induced change in Qi (a3 d lnQi/d lnPa) is customarily not added to $-a1/(1-a4)$ in computing μ_ℓ.

230

$$\partial \ln C \, / \, \partial \ln Pa = \partial \ln A \, / \, \partial \ln Pa + \sigma_\ell$$

V:2:18 $\qquad \eta_\ell = -\mu_\ell + \sigma_\ell \qquad$ or $\qquad \sigma_\ell = \mu_\ell + \eta_\ell.$

The elasticity of substitution is equal to the sum of the own-price and cross elasticities of demand. [11]

Charles River Associates (CRA) (1971 and 1976) have estimated several econometric single-commodity models. In table V:2:6 the sum of the CRA long-run own-price and cross elasticities of demand are compared to the elasticities of substitution obtained here. The more recent CRA estimates are rather close to those of the present study, especially when we consider that one set of estimates was obtained from a demand equation and the other from a production function. The earlier CRA estimates are very different from those in either later study, but the discrepancy can probably be attributed to the lack of good data in 1971 rather than to any change in the true elasticities. The estimates of the present study are uniformly higher than those of CRA 1976. It is at least possible that we are observing an increase in industry substitution practice as technology improves.

---

[11] For equation V:2:18 to hold in a dynamic context, we must assume that purchasers of copper and aluminum make decisions on the basis of expected copper and aluminum prices. We then have

$$\ln C = \ln c + \ln A + \sigma_\ell \ln(Pa)* - \sigma_\ell \ln(Pc)*$$

$$\partial \ln C / \partial \ln(Pa)* = \partial \ln A / \partial \ln(Pa)* + \sigma_\ell$$

$$\eta_\ell = -\mu_\ell + \sigma_\ell$$

where price expectations, Pa* and Pc*, are formed as in section V:2:2:1.

TABLE V:2:6
LONG-RUN ELASTICITIES OF SUBSTITUTION COMPARED

	CRA [12] (1971)	CRA [13] (1976)	Slade (1979)
Building and Construction	2.06	1.16	1.23
Transportation	1.60	.62	.63
Machinery and Equipment	.89	.93	1.19
Electrical	2.30	.72	.81
Consumer	1.13	.33	.49

---

[12] Aluminum own-price, copper cross elasticity of demand.

[13] Copper own-price, aluminum cross elasticity of demand.

V:2:2:6 Interpretation of elasticity results

Both the long-run elasticities of substitution and the shapes
of the time paths of the substitution process vary considerably
from sector to sector. The variation in the elasticities has an
obvious interpretation -- more substitution is possible in some
sectors than in others and smaller price changes are required to
trigger it. For example, the computed elasticities in the building and construction and industrial-machinery and equipment sectors are greater than one. Copper and aluminum are highly substitutable in electrical wiring applications in both of these sectors.
In contrast, the computed elasticities in the transport and consumer-
durable sectors are less than one. Much substitution in these sectors is in heat-exchanger applications (in automobile radiators and
refrigerators, for example), where the substitution potential is less.
Therefore, both the high elasticities in the first two sectors and
the low ones in the second two seem reasonable. In only one sector,
electrical and electronic products, does the estimate obtained seem
too low. The copper-aluminum substitution potential in the electrical sector is probably greater than the estimated elasticity implies.
However, the hypothesis that $\sigma = 1$ in the electrical sector cannot
be rejected at any reasonable level of confidence. (See section
V:2:2:4).

233

The sector-to-sector variation in the distribution of the effect that a price change has over time is somewhat harder to interpret. However, with the Shiller estimates, the two sectors that have the most erratically shaped time paths -- building and construction and transportation -- are the sectors where demand for the final product is most cyclical. Cyclical demand for the output of these sectors may give rise to irregularity in adapting to changed relative factor prices.

234

V:3 The Demand for Copper and Aluminum

We have just seen how the market for copper and aluminum is divided between the two metals -- for a given state of technology, the division of the market is determined by past and present relative prices. In this section, the demand for copper and aluminum combined (the size of the market to be divided) is analysed. Equations defining the demand for copper and aluminum are derived from the production functions of the demanding sectors in section V:3:1, and econometric estimates of these equations are presented in section V:3:2.

V:3:1   Specification of a Derived-Demand Equation

If Qi is the output of the i th demanding sector, and Zs,
s = 1,...S, are input groups, then equation V:2:1 of the previous
section shows how output is determined (by the outer level of the
two-level CES production function).

V:2:1′ $Qi = [\sum_{s=1}^{S} (a_s \, Zs^{-\rho})]^{-1/\rho}$ $\rho > -1$ $a_s > 0.$

If Zs is sold in competitive markets, then the quantity of Zs
demanded by any sector, for a given price of Zs, will be determined
by the value of its marginal product (VMP_{Zs}), defined as

V:3:1 $VMP_{Zs} = Pi \; MP_{Zs} = Pi \; \partial Qi / \partial Zs,$ [14]

where Pi is the price of the i th sector's output. [15] The marginal
product of Zs can be derived from equation V:2:1′.

V:3:2 $MP_{Zs} = \partial Qi / \partial Zs = -1/\rho \, [\sum_{s=1}^{S} a_s \, Zs^{-\rho}]^{-\frac{1}{\rho}-1} (-\rho a_s \, Zs^{-\rho-1}).$

Simplifying we obtain

---

14   Just as with the elasticity of substitution equations, this
     specification of the demand equation is a partial derivative.
     The formulation ignores the change in the quantities of other
     inputs used as the price of Zs varies, and thus underestimates
     the elasticity of demand. It also ignores the effect of changes
     in the price of Zs on the sector output price, but, because copper
     and aluminum are not the principal inputs in any sector, the
     latter effect should be small.

15   If a market in which Zs is sold is monopolistic, $(1-1/\mu_i)Pi$ would
     be substituted for Pi in equation V:3:1, where μ_i is the price
     elasticity of demand for product i.

$$MP_{Zs} = a_s \ Qi^{(-\frac{1}{\rho}-1)}/-\frac{1}{\rho} Zs^{-\rho-1}$$

$$= a_s \ Qi^{\rho+1} \ Zs^{-\rho-1} = a_s (Qi/Zs)^{\rho+1}.$$

The value of the marginal product of Zs is then

$$VMP_{Zs} = Pi \ a_s \ (Qi/Zs)^{\rho+1}$$

If there are many demanding sectors and no one sector uses a significant proportion of the quantity of Zs produced, then we can assume that the supply of Zs to each sector is infinitely elastic at the price P_{Zs}. Figure V:3:1 illustrates the determination of the quantity of Zs used in each sector -- Zs is determined by the intersection of the sector supply (P_{Zs}) and demand (VMP_{Zs}) curves (i.e., purchasers of Zs increase the use of Zs to the point where its price is equal to the value of its marginal product).

$$P_{Zs} = a_s \ Pi \ (Qi/Zs)^{\rho+1}$$

Taking natural logarithms results in

$$\ln P_{Zs} = \ln a_s + \ln Pi + (\rho+1) \ln Qi - (\rho+1) \ln Zs.$$

Simplifying and solving for lnZs, we obtain

$$\ln Zs = \frac{\ln a_s}{\rho+1} + \ln Qi + \frac{1}{\rho+1} \ln Pi - \frac{1}{\rho+1} \ln P_{Zs}$$

or

$$\ln Zs = a0 + \ln Qi + a1 \ \ln Pi + a2 \ \ln P_{Zs} \qquad a1 > 0 \qquad a2 < 0$$

237

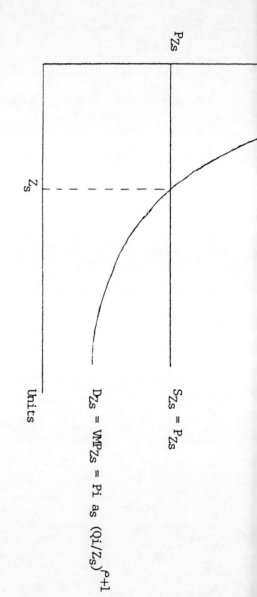

Figure V:3:1 The Determination of the Quantity of
the Input, Z_s, Used in a Sector

238

Equation V:3:5 specifies the quantity of Zs used in the i th

sector under conditions of equilibrium. However, equilibrium rarely

prevails, and we must specify the dynamic version of V:3:5. Sup-

pose that purchasers of Zs make their plans on the basis of their

expectations about the price of Zs, and the price of and demand for

their product. Then

V:3:6 $\qquad \ln Zs_t = a0 + \ln Qi_t* + a1 \ln Pi_t* + a2 \ln P_{Zst}* + u_t$

$$u \sim N(0, \sigma_\mu^2)$$

where the *'s denote expectations and u is a disturbance term that

indicates that it may be difficult to control the value of Zs pre-

cisely. If expectations are updated each period by a fraction, δ ,

of the discrepancy between the current observed rate of change of

the variables and the previous expected rates of change, [16] then

V:3:6 becomes

$$\ln Zs_t = a0(1-\lambda) + (1-\lambda) \ln Qi_t + a1(1-\lambda) \ln Pi_t + a2(1-\lambda)$$
$$\ln P_{Zst} + \lambda \ln Zs_{t-1} + u_t - \lambda u_{t-1}$$

---

[16]   This is an "adaptive expectations" model with rates of change
(implied by the natural logarithms) instead of values of the
variables. To see that equation V:3:7 results from V:3:6
combined with an adaptive expectations model, see Johnston
(1972, pp. 301-302). We have made the simplifying assumption
that the declining geometric weight, $\lambda = 1-\delta$, is the same
for all three variables.

or

V:3:7 $\qquad \ln Zs_t = b0 + b1 \ln Qi_t + b2 \ln Pi_t + b3 \ln P_{Zst} + \lambda \ln Zs_{t-1}$

$$+ u_t - \lambda u_{t-1}$$

$$0 < \lambda = 1 - \delta < 1 \qquad b1, b2 > 0 \qquad b3 < 0.$$

Equation V:3:7 specifies the quantity of an input group, Zs, used by each sector. In the next section, econometric estimates of equations based on V:3:7 will be presented.

V:3:2 Estimation of the Derived-Demand Equations

V:3:2:1 The data

A derived-demand equation was estimated for each of the five
copper- and aluminum-demanding sectors (building and construction,
transportation, electrical and electronic products, industrial machinery and equipment, and consumer durables) as well as for two sectors that use only aluminum (containers and packaging and "other"). [17]
Data on sales of copper and aluminum to each sector came from the
trade associations, Copper Development Association and The Aluminum
Association (1960 - 1976).

Equation V:3:7 contains Q_i, the level of output of the i th
sector. However, it was decided to use the index of industrial production as a proxy for Q_i for two reasons. First, the sectors, as
defined by the trade associations, are not standard industrial clas-
sifications (SIC's), whereas any measure of Q_i would have to correspond to some SIC. And second, better forecasts are available for
the index of industrial production than for its components. Industrial production was, therefore, used as a leading indicator for the
sector outputs.

---

17   There are "other" uses of copper as well as of aluminum (mostly
      military), but, unfortunately, they have been combined into
      the consumer-durable sector by Copper Development Association.

The data for sector output prices (Pi) are price indices used in computing the wholesale-and consumer-price indices. [18] Table V:3:1 lists the indices used. Each index was deflated by the wholesale-price index (1967 = 1); prices are thus in 1967 constant dollars. No satisfactory price was found for the industrial machinery and equipment sector. WPI 11, machinery and equipment, contains electrical machinery and equipment and construction machinery and equipment as subsets and is thus inappropriate. Therefore, the demand equation for this sector was estimated without an output price.

TABLE V:3:1
PRICE INDICES FOR SECTOR OUTPUTS

Sector	Index Name	Code
Construction	Construction Machinery and Equipment	WPI 112
Transport	Transportation Equipment	WPI 14
Consumer	Consumer Durable Commodities	CPI K2
Electrical	Electrical Machinery and Equipment	WPI 117
Containers	Metal Containers	WPI 103

The price of the input group (P_{Zs} in equation V:3:7) was computed as a weighted average of copper and aluminum prices with weights proportional to copper and aluminum usage in the sector in the previous

---

18   In contrast to the level of activity in each sector (where industrial production was used as a proxy), it is necessary to have a separate price for the output of each sector, because it is relative prices (the deviation of the sector output price from the overall price level) that determines demand for the output of the sector.

year. [19] Let

$$wi = Ci_{-1}/(Ci_{-1} + Ai_{-1})$$

where Ci and Ai are sales of copper and aluminum to the i th sector. Then

V:3:8 $Pwi = [Pa (1-wi) + Pc \, wi]/WPI$

where Pa and Pc are the U.S. producer prices of aluminum and copper respectively. The weights, wi, were chosen to be proportional to copper and aluminum sales on a weight basis (tons) because prices are computed on a weight basis, and, therefore, Pwi is proportional to the average expenditure per ton of metal purchased by the sector. Pwi was also deflated by the wholesale-price index.

V:3:2:2   The derived-demand equations

Table V:3:2 shows the final specification of the derived-demand equations for six sectors and for total consumption (the sum of consumption over all sectors). [20] Appendix V:2 describes the method

---

19   Sales from the previous year were used in constructing the weights because purchasers do not know Ai and Ci for the present year when they decide how much of each metal to buy.

20   If ρ_i is shown in parentheses in table V:3:2, it means that the correction for serial correlation was not performed. (See appendix III:1).

used in estimating the equations. Each equation in the table is
of the form

V:3:15 $\ln(C_i\hat{+}A_i)_t = b0 + b1 \ln IP_t + b2 \ln \hat{Pw}i_t + b3 \ln Pi_t$

$$+ b4 \ D75_t + b5 \ \ln(C_i+A_i)_{t-1} + u_t + \rho \ u_{t-1}$$

where (C_i+A_i) is consumption of copper plus aluminum
                                 in the i th sector

             IP   is the index of industrial production

             Pwi   is a weighted average of copper and alu-
                                 minum prices
                                 (deflated by the wholesale-price index)

             Pi   is the price of the i th sector's output
                                 (deflated by the wholesale-price index)

and   D75   is a dummy variable equal to one in 1975
                                 and zero elsewhere.

A dummy variable equal to one in 1975 and zero otherwise was
included in the equations because the effect of the 1975 recession
was unusually strong for the nonferrous-metals industries, especially for the copper industry.

244

Sector	B_0	IP	Pw_1	P_1	D75	$(C+A)_{1-1}$	R^2	F	DW	ρ_1	Years	No
Total	4.3	.81 (5.0)	-.42 (-1.9)		-.32 (-5.0)	.26 (1.8)	.97	78	1.8	(-.004)	61-76	
B and C	-3.7	-.20 (-.57)	-1.4 (-5.1)	2.3 (3.3)	-.59 (-6.9)	.85 (3.4)	.94	24	2.3	-.53	62-76	V:3:9
Trans	2.8	1.0 (5.7)	-1.6 (-4.4)	.83 (1.8)	-.33 (-4.1)	.19 (1.4)	.94	33	1.7	(.07)	61-76	V:3:10
C D	-3.2	.88 (4.1)	-1.1 (-3.1)	1.2 (2.9)	-.28 (-3.2)	.63 (3.6)	.90	14	2.0	-.24	62-76	V:3:11
E and E	-.28	.62 (2.1)	-.35 (-.85)	.38 (.81)	-.40 (-3.7)	.58 (2.8)	.94	30	1.8	(.04)	61-76	V:3:12
M and E	3.5	.42 (3.8)	-.62 (-2.8)		-.54 (-6.2)	.53 (3.5)	.84	12	2.2	-.31	62-76	V:3:13
C and P	-4.3	.73 (1.7)	-.06 (-.26)	-.68 (.73)		.69 (4.2)	.99	170	1.9	-.52	62-76	V:3:14

All of the estimated coefficients in table V:3:2 have the expected signs except for the coefficient of industrial production in the building and construction demand equation. However, construction is probably a counter-cyclical industry -- housing starts being high when interest rates are low.

It is possible to compute long-run elasticities from equation V:3:15. The long-run price elasticity of demand, μ_p, is

$$\mu_p = -b3/(1-b5)$$

and the long-run output elasticity of demand, μ_y, is

$$\mu_y = b1/(1-b5).$$

For total consumption of copper and aluminum μ_p is .57 and μ_y is 1.1. The demand for copper and aluminum combined is inelastic, even in the long-run, a reasonable result because the principal substitute for copper is aluminum and vice versa. As would also be expected, the long-run income elasticity of demand for the two metals combined is approximately equal to one.

A final equation was estimated for "other" uses of aluminum. Because much usage in this category is in military applications, no prices were included as explanatory variables. The demand for aluminum in this sector is a function of economic activity and of time. The final equation was

246

V:3:16 $\ln AO_t = -4.7 - 3.3 \ln t + 4.4 \ln IP_t$
                (-8.3) (9.6)

    $R^2 = .94$ $DW = 2.0$ $F = 105$ $\rho = .40$

                        Years: 1960 – 1976

where   AO   is consumption of aluminum in "other" applications

        t   is time measured in years $(1950 = 1)$

and   IP   is the index of industrial production.

This completes the analysis of the demand side of the market. In the next chapter, the way in which the difference between domestic production and consumption is met is discussed.

Appendix V:1   Estimation Method for the Elasticity of Substitution
Equations

To obtain the estimates of β in the equation

A:V:1:1 $\min_{\beta} (y-X\beta)' \, (y-X\beta) + k^2 \beta'Rd'Rd \, \beta$

OLS was applied to the equation

A:V:1:2 $\tilde{y} = \tilde{X}\beta + \eta$

where $\tilde{y} = \begin{bmatrix} y \\ 0 \end{bmatrix}$ and $\tilde{X} = \begin{bmatrix} X \\ k \, Rd \end{bmatrix}$

The t-statistics printed by a regression package after estimating equation A:V:1:2 are not correct because they are calculated
using the formula

$$\text{Var}[\beta] = \sigma_\eta^2 (\tilde{X}'\tilde{X})^{-1}$$

where σ_η^2 is the variance of η. The correct variance of β is

$$\text{Var}[\beta] = \sigma_\epsilon^2 (\tilde{X}'\tilde{X})^{-1}$$

where σ_ϵ^2 is the variance of ϵ in equation V:2:5. A correction
factor of $\hat{\sigma}_\epsilon / \hat{\sigma}_\eta$ was applied to the standard errors of the coefficients used to obtain the t-statistics reported in table V:2:5.

The transformation needed to go from the R^2 printed by a regression package to the correct R^2 for equation A:V:1:1 is not as simple as the correction for the t-statistics of the coefficients. Fortunately, the correct R^2 can be obtained by another method. It must be true that

A:V:1:3 $\qquad R^2_{OLS} \leqq R^2_S \leqq R^2_{PDL}$

where R^2_S is the correct R^2 for equation A:V:1:1. In all six equations estimated, the upper and lower bounds on R^2_S implied by A:V:1:3 were close enough to determine R^2_S with two-digit accuracy.

In four of the equations estimated, serial correlation was detected. Assume that the disturbance terms are of the form

$$\eta_t = \rho\eta_{t-1} + v_t \qquad\qquad v \sim N(0,\sigma_v^2).$$

We cannot use a regression package that corrects for serial correlation automatically to estimate equation A:V:1:2 with the new disturbance term, because the program will transform the last ℓ-d rows of $\tilde{X}$. However, a simple two-step procedure can be used to give consistent estimates of β.[1] First, $\tilde{y}$ is regressed on $\tilde{X}$ where

---

1   This procedure does not give efficient estimates of β, but, for the OLS and PDL distributions, the estimates obtained using the two-step procedure were compared to those using the Cochrane-Orcutt process and found to be very close.

$$\tilde{\tilde{X}} = \begin{bmatrix} y_{-1} & X & x_{\ell-1} \\ 0 & kRd & 0 \end{bmatrix}$$

The coefficient of y_{-1}, $\hat{\rho}$, is a consistent estimate of ρ. In the second step, $\tilde{y}_\rho$ is regressed on $\tilde{X}_\rho$ where

$$\tilde{y}_\rho = \begin{bmatrix} y - \hat{\rho}\, y_{-1} \\ 0 \end{bmatrix} \quad \text{and} \quad \tilde{X}_\rho = \begin{bmatrix} X - \hat{\rho}\, X_{-1} \\ kRd \end{bmatrix}$$

The coefficients in the second regression are consistent estimates of β except for the estimate of the constant term c. If $\tilde{c}$ is the estimate of the constant term in the second regression, a consistent estimate of c is

$$\hat{c} = \tilde{c} / (1 - \hat{\rho}).$$

Appendix V:2 Estimation Method for the Derived-Demand Equations

The method used in the CAS model to estimate equations with lagged endogenous variables and serially correlated errors was described in appendix III:1. The demand equations are of this form and result from an adaptive-expectations model. The only difference between the method of estimation of the derived-demand equations and the method described in appendix III:1 is in the treatment of the endogenous variables. In the CAS model, the instruments used in the copper equations were all of the predetermined variables in the copper model, while those used in the aluminum equations were all of the predetermined variables in the aluminum model. However, the demand equations include endogenous variables from both models (primary prices). If all of the predetermined variables from both models had been used as instruments in the demand equations, there would be thirty four instruments and only seventeen observations. Instead, a different approach was adopted.

Copper primary price, Ppc, was regressed on all of the predetermined variables in the copper model using the years 1954-1976, while aluminum primary price, Ppa, was regressed on all of the predetermined variables in the aluminum model using the same years. $\hat{P}pc$ and $\hat{P}pa$ were then used in calculating the weighted averages of copper and aluminum prices in each sector, $\hat{P}wi$. Then, the demand equations were estimated with $\hat{P}wi$, using only the years 1961-1976 (the first observation, 1960, having been lost in computing the weights).

251

CHAPTER VI: THE BALANCE BETWEEN DOMESTIC PRODUCTION
AND CONSUMPTION

Materials balance requires that the difference between domestic consumption and production of a metal be equal to net imports minus changes in inventories. Equation VI:1 states this fundamental identity

VI:1 $M - X - \Delta In \equiv C - Qp - Qs$

where   M   is imports of metal

            X   is exports of metal

            Δ In is changes in metal inventories

            C   is metal consumption

            Qp   is primary metal production.

In the last three chapters, we discussed the determinants of domestic production and consumption of copper and aluminum. In this chapter, we will see how the difference between domestic consumption and production of each is divided between net imports and changes in inventories.

VI:1 Copper and Aluminum Inventories

Inventories of metal consist of private (producer and consumer) inventories as well as of the government stockpile. Because the level of private inventories is determined by economic and technological factors and that of the government stockpile is determined by strategic and political considerations, the two types of inventories are discussed separately.

VI:1:1 Private Inventories

Private inventories are defined to include both producers' (refiners and smelters) and consumers' (mills, foundries and other semifabricators) stocks of metal, but not inventories of finished products. Stocks of metal consist of both refined and scrap metal (where the latter is measured on the basis of its metal content).

Copper Development Association publishes data on private copper inventories. Figure VI:1:1 shows private copper inventories (the solid line) and private inventories divided by copper consumption (the dashed line) from 1954 to 1976. This figure shows that copper inventories were very high in the last two years of the period. High inventories (and depressed copper prices) resulted from the worldwide excess supply of primary copper during that period.

253

The data for private aluminum inventories are not as complete as those for copper inventories. The Aluminum Association publishes figures for aluminum suppliers' inventories only as far back as 1967 (the year when the Bureau of the Census began collecting the data). These data include inventories of finished products as well as of ingot and scrap. Figure VI:1:2 shows private aluminum inventories and inventories divided by aluminum consumption from 1967 to 1976. Before 1967, the data for changes in private inventories used here were calculated as primary production minus primary shipments (changes in secondary stocks were ignored).

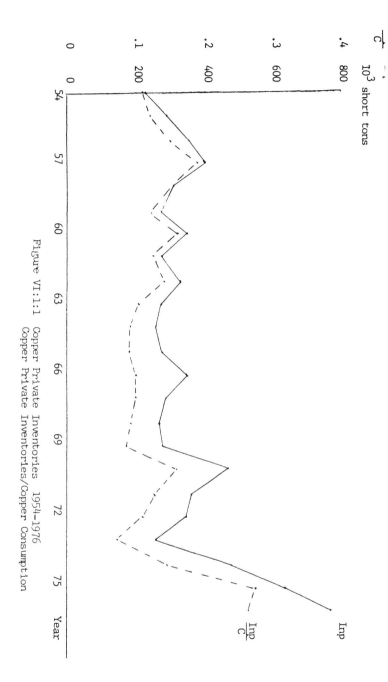

Figure VI:1:1   Copper Private   Inventories   1954-1976
                 Copper Private Inventories/Copper Consumption

255

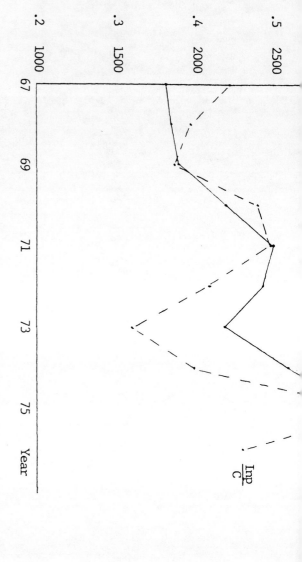

Figure VI:1:2   Aluminum Private Inventories   1967-1976
Aluminum Private Inventories/Aluminum Consumption

256

VI:1:2 The Government Stockpile

The commodity shortages experienced during World War II led
to the enactment of the Strategic and Critical Materials Stockpiling
Act (SCMSA) of 1946, which provided for the acquisition of certain
materials for use during a national emergency. Stocks of copper
and aluminum were acquired in the late 1940's and early 1950's under
both the SCMSA and the Defense Production Act (DPA) of 1951.
Materials purchased under the DPA were intended to induce entry
into the industry and expansion of existing capacity. Incentives offered included accelerated amortization, guaranteed loans,
subsidies, and a guaranteed market for new facilities. Between
1958 and 1965, stockpiles were maintained at levels of approximately
one million tons of copper and nearly two million tons of aluminum.
However, legislation in 1965 and later years authorized the disposal of both copper and aluminum from the strategic stockpile. Subsequent sales from the stockpile reduced government inventories of
both metals to virtually zero in 1976. On October 1, 1976 new stockpile goals were established. These goals include $1.3 \ 10^6$ tons of
copper but no aluminum for strategic purposes. [1] However, initial
purchases against the new goal for copper have not been scheduled.

Figure VI:1:3 shows the level of copper and aluminum in the
strategic stockpile between 1954 and 1976. Large sales of copper
took place immediately after they were authorized in 1965. In contrast, the biggest disposal of aluminum from the stockpile took place
in 1973-74.

---

1   The goals do include stocks of both bauxite and alumina.

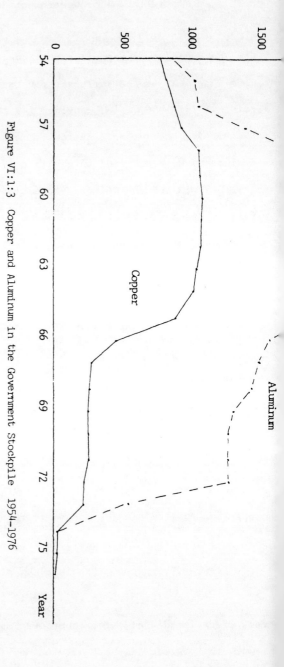

Figure VI:1:3 Copper and Aluminum in the Government Stockpile 1954-1976

258

VI:1:3   Specification of an Inventory Equation

From equation VI:1 we have

VI:1' Δ In $- (M - x) \equiv Qp + Qs - C$

$\equiv Q - C$ where $Q \equiv Qp + Qs$.

If changes in inventories were a constant fraction α of the difference between domestic production and consumption, then we
would have

VI:1:1 ΔIn $= \alpha(Q-C)$

VI:1:2 $-(M - X) = (1 - \alpha)(Q - C)$.

However, the division of $Q - C$ between the two (net imports and
changes in inventories) is not constant; several things affect
the choice between depleting stocks and purchasing imports. If
the domestic price of a metal is high, we can expect inventories
of that metal to accumulate because domestically produced metal
will be at a disadvantage relative to imports. In addition, if
the level of inventories is high relative to consumption, imports
are apt to be low because consumers are not likely to purchase
imported metal if they already possess large stocks of that metal.
Therefore, VI:1:1 should be modified as follows

259

VI:1:3 $\Delta \text{In} = a0 + a1 (Q - C) + a2 \text{Pp} + a3 (\text{In}/C)_{-1}$

           $a1, a2 > 0$ $a3 < 0.$

VI:1:3 is the equation that specifies the model for changes in inventories óf a metal. The level of inventories of that metal can be obtained by combining VI:1:3 with the identity

$$\text{In} \equiv \text{In}_{-1} + \Delta \text{In}$$

as follows

VI:1:4 $\text{In} = \text{In}_{-1} + a0 + a1 (Q - C) + a2 \text{Pp} + a3 (\text{In}/C)_{-1}.$

In equation VI:1:4, private and government inventories have been combined. However, it is preferable to consider that changes in government inventories are exogenous. This can be done by replacing In with Inp (private inventories) in equation VI:1:4, and by netting out changes in government inventories from production (i.e., by ignoring production for the government stockpile). Equation VI:1:4 then becomes

VI:1:5 $\text{Inp} = \text{Inp}_{-1} + a0 + a1 [(\dot{Q} - \Delta \text{Ing}) - C] + a2 \text{Pp}$

           $+ a3 (\text{Inp}/C)_{-1}.$

In the next section, equation VI:1:5 is used as a model for the econometric estimates of the inventory equations.

260

VI:1:4 Estimation of the Inventory Equations

The data for most of the variables in equation VI:1:5 were

discussed in earlier chapters. Data for inventories (both private

and government) are compiled by the trade associations, Copper

Development Association and The Aluminum Association (1954 - 1976).

The general discussions of chapter III:3 and appendix III:1 deal-

ing with the estimation of equations in the copper and aluminum

models apply to the inventory equations as well.

The final specification for the copper inventory equation,

based on VI:1:5, was

VI:1:6 $\widehat{Inp}_t = -292.9 + .256 \, (Q - \Delta \widehat{Ing} - C)_t + 11.1 \, \widehat{Pp}_t$
$\qquad\qquad\qquad\quad (2.3) \qquad\qquad\qquad\qquad (1.7)$

$\qquad\qquad + .712 \, \widehat{Inp}_{t-1}$
$\qquad\qquad\quad (1.5)$

$\quad R^2 = .67 \qquad DW = 2.0 \qquad F = 11 \qquad \rho = .73$

$\qquad\qquad\qquad\qquad\qquad\qquad\qquad\qquad$ Years: 1955 - 1976

where   Inp   is private copper inventories

            Q   is copper production (primary plus secondary)

            Δ Ing is changes in government inventories of copper

            C   is copper consumption

and   Pp   is the U.S. producer price of copper
                   (deflated by the wholesale price index).

All of the estimated coefficients in equation VI:1:6 have their

expected signs. The level of inventories divided by consumption was

261

dropped from the equation because it was not statistically significant. [2]

The presence of a lagged dependent variable in the equation
implies that the Durbin-Watson statistic is biased against detect-
ing serial correlation. However, if the Durbin-Watson statistic
indicates that serial correlation is present, then the correction
should be performed. The Durbin-Watson statistic for equation
VI:1:6, before the correction for serial correlation was performed,
was 1.0, indicating the presence of autocorrelation in the error
term and the necessity to correct for this condition (as has been
done).

In equation VI:1:5, the coefficient of Inp_{-1} is one. In
estimating VI:1:6, no restriction was placed on the coefficient of
this variable; however, the estimated coefficient of Inp_{-1} is not
significantly different from one (the t-ratio to test the hypothesis
that $a3 = 1$ was computed to be .47, implying that the coefficient is
not significantly different from one at any reasonable level of
confidence).

A special problem arose in estimating the aluminum inventory equation. Good data on private aluminum inventories goes
back only as far as 1967. In addition, the U.S. government stockpile has at times been used as an economic, not just a strategic,

---

[2]   As can be seen in figure VI:1:1, Inp_{-1} and $(Inp/C)_{-1}$ are
       highly correlated and should not both be included in the
       inventory equation. It is only when estimating changes in
       inventories (as in the aluminum inventory equation of the
       next section) that $(In/C)_{-1}$ becomes significant.

stockpile. For example, in 1973-74, the aluminum stockpile was

virtually depleted at a time that coincided with world-wide

excess demand for most commodities. The domestic price of alumi-

num was not allowed to rise during this period of shortages

because price controls were in effect in the U.S. Without stockpile

sales, there would have been rationing in the industry, but little

rationing took place. The building and depleting of the aluminum

stockpile has helped to level out price and production behavior;

therefore, the government stockpile was included in the inventory

variable.

The level of aluminum inventories before 1967 can be

computed only from the data on changes in aluminum inventories,

which are incomplete. Because any errors in the data on inventory

changes become cummulative when the level of invenventories is

calculated,[3] the estimate of the aluminum inventory inventory

equation was based on VI:1:3 instead of VI:1:5.

---

3)   If inventories are calculated as

$$In = In_{-1} + \Delta In,$$

then any error in ΔIn never dies out in the calculation
of In.

The final specification for the aluminum inventory equation was

VI:1:7 $\quad \Delta \hat{In}_t = - 885.4 + .596\ (Q \overset{\frown}{-} C)_t + 45.2\ \hat{Pp}_t$
$\qquad\qquad\qquad\qquad\quad (5.1) \qquad\qquad\quad (2.1)$

$\qquad\qquad\qquad - 143.9\ (In/C)_{t-1}$
$\qquad\qquad\qquad\ (-1.5)$

$\qquad\qquad R^2 = .81 \qquad F = 26 \qquad DW = 2.1$

$\qquad\qquad\qquad\qquad\qquad$ Years: 1955 - 1976

where $\qquad \Delta In\ $ is changes in aluminum inventories

$\qquad\qquad\quad$ Q $\qquad$ is aluminum production (primary plus secondary)

$\qquad\qquad\quad$ C $\qquad$ is aluminum consumption

and $\qquad\quad$ Pp $\qquad$ is the U.S. producer price of aluminum
$\qquad\qquad\qquad\qquad$ (deflated by the wholesale price index).

A dummy variable, equal to one prior to 1967 and zero elsewhere, was included in equation VI:1:7 (to correct for the different
definitions of private inventories used in the two periods).
However, the estimated coefficient of the dummy variable was not
significantly different from zero (t-ratio = .37), and the variable was dropped from the equation.

Given the level of aluminum inventories in some base year,
the level of inventories in any other year can be calculated from
equation VI:1:7 and the identity

VI:1:8 $\qquad In_t \equiv In_{t-1} + \Delta In_t$

The U.S. is virtually self sufficient in the production of
both copper and aluminum (but not of bauxite). Net imports do
not play a large role for either metal; they oscillate, sometimes
being positive and sometimes negative, but are rarely more than
ten percent of annual consumption. For this reason, in the CAS
model, net imports are treated as a residual. The supply of
imports of both metals to the U.S. is assumed to be infinitely
elastic at the world price. When domestic production, consumption, and inventory changes have been determined, the residual
(whether positive or negative) is filled by imports.

VI:2:1 Historic Behavior of Net Imports

Data on imports and exports of both copper and aluminum
are reported in the U.S. Bureau of Mines' Minerals Yearbook (1954-
1976). Figure VI:2:1 shows net imports of both copper and aluminum between 1954 and 1976. The data plotted are for refined
copper and crude and semicrude aluminum. Aluminum net imports
were generally positive but showed no marked trend. In contrast,
copper net imports were generally negative but began an upward
trend in 1961.

265

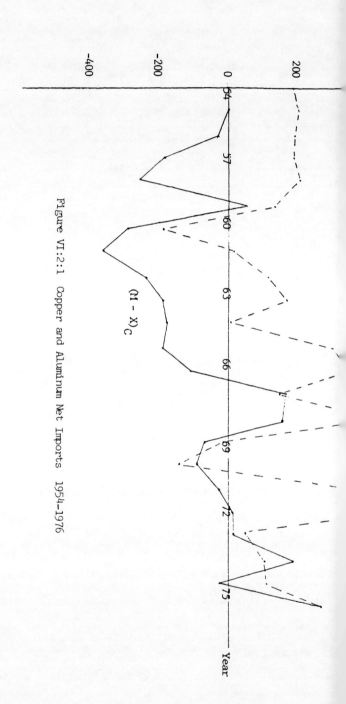

Figure VI:2:1   Copper and Aluminum Net Imports   1954-1976

266

VI:2:2   Specification of a Net-Import Equation

The final equations in the CAS model, the net import equations, are identities. Both the supply of imports of copper
and aluminum into the U.S. and the demand for U.S. exports of
copper and aluminum are assumed to be infinitely elastic at
world prices. When domestic production (primary and secondary),
consumption (in each sector), and inventory changes have been
determined, the gap (whether positive or negative) is filled
by net imports.

Equation VI:1 can thus be modified to specify the net quantity of imports of copper and aluminum into the U.S. as follows

VI:2:1 $M_t - X_t \equiv \sum_i Ci_t - Qp_t - Qos_t - Qns_t + \Delta Inp_t + \Delta Ing_t$

where   M   is imports of metal

            X   is exports of metal

            Ci   is consumption of metal in the ith using sector

            Qp   is primary production of metal

            Qos   is secondary production of metal from old scrap

            Qns   is secondary production of metal from new scrap

            Δ Inp is changes in private inventories of metal

and Δ Ing is changes in government inventories of metal.

This completes the analysis of copper and aluminum markets in the U.S. and the presentation of the related model equations. In the next chapter, model simulations over the historic and forecast periods are presented and analysed.

CHAPTER VII: SIMULATION, FORECASTING, AND POLICY ANALYSIS

Up to this point, we have analysed various aspects of domestic copper and aluminum markets, discussed the historic behavior
of the endogenous variables in the CAS model, developed models to
explain this behavior, and estimated equations based on these
models. We now look at the CAS model in its entirety to see
how it performs over the historic and forecast periods.   In
this chapter, we discuss the method used in simulation and
forecasting and compare the forecasts obtained using different
assumptions about the behavior of the exogenous policy and
geologic variables.

VII:1 Methodology -- An Overview

In the CAS model we attempt to capture the most important causal
or structural relationships of domestic copper and aluminum markets.
The model consists of a set of endogenous variables, whose behavior
is explained by the model (price, production, and consumption of
metal, for example) and a set of exogenous variables, whose behavior
is determined outside the model (industrial production and sector
output prices, for example). The model can be used as a sort of
experimental laboratory where the impact of external shocks on domestic metal markets can be investigated and the sensitivity of these
markets to changes in policy variables can be analysed.

The principal impacts considered here are the those that
changed cost factors (specifically energy prices and ore quality
and price) have on metal price, production, and consumption. Particular attention is given to the effects that these cost changes
have on substitution between copper and aluminum and on the fraction of consumption of each that comes from recycled metal.

Economic impacts are typically measured as deviations from a
set of "baseline" forecasts. However, a problem with designating
one set of forecasts as "baseline" is that these forecasts are often

interpreted as the "most likely" ones. In order to avoid this "most likely" interpretation, no set of energy-price forecasts was designated as "baseline". The simulations resulting from the three sets of energy-price forecasts -- low, intermediate, and high -- are presented together so that the deviations of any one from the other two can be seen. In simulating the impacts of changed world metal-market conditions (a successful bauxite cartel, for example), the intermediate energy-price forecasts were used. However, the high or low energy prices could have been chosen just as easily.

The method used for simulation and forecasting consists of two steps. First, values of the exogenous variables are forecast, and second, the model equations are solved for the endogenous variables in each future time period.

In performing simulations over the historic period, the exogenous variables take on their historic values. However, in order to simulate future conditions, the exogenous variables must be forecast. The three principal methods of forecasting these variables are time-series, econometric, and judgemental methods. Time-series (or purely statistical) forecasts require no knowledge of causal relationships. Forecasting by this method consists of examining the historic behavior of a variable to detect its systematic time response to exogenous disturbances and using this information to predict the future behavior of the variable. Econometric forecasts can be obtained from larger econometric models where the variable to be forecast is treated endogenously. For

271

example, forecasts of the index of industrial production can be obtained from well-known macro-economic models. Finally, judgemental forecasts are those obtained by means of subjective analysis. An example of a judgemental forecast would be the projection that the index of industrial production will grow at three percent per year for the next five years.

In the CAS model, forecasts of the exogenous variables (with the exception of energy price and ore quality) were made using time-series techniques. Econometric forecasts were not used for two reasons. First, it is virtually impossible to obtain econometric forecasts of some of the exogenous variables in the CAS model. And second, econometric forecasts merely shift the burden of forecasting from one level to another. For example, if we could relate the wholesale-price index to the money supply, we would still have to forecast the money supply. No matter how inclusive an econometric model is, there are always some exogenous variables that must be forecast. In contrast, pure time-series techniques rely only on the historic behavior of the variable of interest. Judgemental forecasts were used for the energy-price and ore-quality measures.[1] Energy prices were considered to be policy variables and, therefore, a variety of assumptions about their future behavior was tested.[2]

---

[1]   Both time-series and judgemental forecasts were used for the exogenous ore-quality measure in the model. See VII:2:3.

[2]   Unlike metal prices, energy prices are subject to a complex set of controls that can be changed by political decision. Therefore, energy prices should be considered policy variables.

Once the forecasts of the exogenous variables have been made, it is possible to perform model simulations. The model equations consist of a set of nonlinear differential equations whose solutions are time paths (the forecasts of the endogenous variables). Numerical techniques were used to solve the system of nonlinear equations simultaneously at each point in time. Newton's method was applied to obtain these solutions as follows.

At any time t, the problem is to find y_t such that

VII:1:1 $\qquad f_i(y_t) = 0 \qquad i = 1,\ldots,n$

where $\qquad y_t = (y_{i,t}) \qquad i = 1,\ldots,n$

is an n x 1 vector of endogenous variables and

$\qquad f = [f_i(y)] \qquad i = 1,\ldots,n$

is an n x 1 vector of continuous, differentiable functions -- the model equations. [3]

The method used to solve equations VII:1:1 simultaneously was a gradient method applied to the problem of minimizing the function

---

[3] The system must be complete. That is, there must be one equation for each endogenous variable. An incomplete system can be made complete by the addition of suitable identities. However, a unique endogenous variable does not have to appear on the lefthand side of each equation (i.e. the endogenous variables can be defined implicitly).

$$\min_{y_t} \ \Omega \ (y_t) \ = \ 1/2 \ \sum_{i=1}^{n} f_i(y_t)^2 \ = \ 1/2 \ f'f.$$

The gradient of Ω is

$$\partial\Omega/\partial y \ = \ J \ f$$

where J is the Jacobian

$$J \ = \ (\ \partial f_i/ \ \partial y_j).$$

The Newton-Raphson procedure was used to minimize Ω at each point in time. For a more complete description of this method, see Hall (1977), and for a discussion of the conditions under which the sequence of values of y converges to a unique solution for every t, see Saaty and Bram (1964).

Simulations for the historic period can be either static (if the lagged endogenous variables assume their historic values) or dynamic (if the lagged endogenous variables assume their solution values from previous time periods). In section VII:3:1, the dynamic simulation of the CAS model over the historic period is discussed.

Simulations for the forecast period must, of necessity, be dynamic. In section VII:3:2, various simulations of the forecast period are analysed, with each simulation corresponding to a different set of assumptions about the behavior of the exogenous policy variables. But before presenting these simulations, the exogenous-variable forecasts used in the simulations are discussed.

VII:2 Forecasts of the Exogenous Variables

In this section, the Box-Jenkins forecasting method that is used to predict most of the exogenous variables is described, and the forecasts obtained using this method are tabulated. After the purely statistical forecasts have been described, the judgemental forecasts of the policy and geologic variables are explained.

VII:2:1:1 The technique

To forecast most of the exogenous variables in the CAS model,
we will follow the approach developed by Box and Jenkins (1976).
Univariate Box-Jenkins forecasting models encompass a very broad
class of discrete time-series dynamic models and are constructed
using only the past data on the variable to be forecast. The
basic idea is to analyse the time response of the variable of
interest to random shocks, and to use this information to predict
the future behavior of the variable.

The class of models that will be used here can be fitted to
stationary time-series -- series whose parameters (mean, variance,
etc.) are independent of time. A series that is not stationary
can be made so by an appropriate transformation. For example,
if the mean shifts over time, the series can be made stationary
by taking its first difference. If the series has a trend, its
second difference will be stationary. If the variance is not
constant, an appropriate functional transformation, such as a
logarithmic transformation, can be applied.

The general class of time-series models can be defined as
follows. Let z_t, $t = 1,\ldots,$ be a series of observations taken at
equally-spaced intervals, let w_t be the d'th difference of the deviation of z_t from its mean level μ, and let ε_t denote a series of
random disturbances. $\varepsilon_t \sim N(0, \sigma_\varepsilon^2)$. The class of models is

VII:2:1 $\qquad w_t - \Phi_1 w_{t-1} - \ldots - \Phi_p w_{t-p} = \varepsilon_t - \Theta_1 \varepsilon_{t-1} - \ldots - \Theta_q \varepsilon_{t-q}$

where w_t is stationary. The parameters Φ_i are called the auto-regressive parameters and the parameters Θ_i are called the moving-average parameters. The model VII:2:1 is called a (p,d,q) model.

An intuitive feel for the meaning of the moving-average parameters can be obtained by noticing that the random shock ε_t hitting the system at time t will disturb the equilibrium level at times t, t+1, ..., t+q but will disappear after that. In contrast, even with a single autoregressive parameter, the effect of ε_t persists for long periods of time (though it gradually dissipates).

If we use the symbol B to denote the backshift operator defined as

$$B \, z_t = z_{t-1} \qquad\qquad B^n \, z_t = z_{t-n}$$

then VII:2:1 becomes

VII:2:2 $\qquad (1 - \Phi_1 B - \ldots - \Phi_p B^p) w_t = (1 - \Theta_1 B - \ldots - \Theta_q B^q) \varepsilon_t$

$$w_t = (1 - B)^d \, z_t \qquad\qquad d > 0$$

$$= z_t - \mu \qquad\qquad d = 0.$$

Box and Jenkins developed a three-step procedure to deal with the models defined by VII:2:2. The steps are

1) Identification -- determining the appropriate numbers p, d, and q.

2) Parameter estimation -- estimating Φ_i, $i = 1,\ldots,p$
   and Θ_j, $j = 1, \ldots,q$.

3) Diagnostic checking -- checking to see that the choice
   of p, d, and q was correct.

Step one makes use of the sample autocorrelation function
r_k of w_t, where r_k is defined as

VII:2:3 $$r_k = \sum_t (w_t - \bar{w})(w_{t-k} - \bar{w}) / \sum_t (w_t - \bar{w})^2 \qquad k = 1,2,\ldots$$

and $\bar{w}$ is the sample mean of w_t. r_k provides an estimate of the
correlations between w_t and its lagged values.

r_k tells a lot about the series w_t. For example, with a non-
stationary series, r_k of the original observations z_t will be
persistently large even for very large k. For a (0,0,q) model,
r_k will be approximately zero for k greater than q. For a (1,0,0)
model, with $0 < \Phi_1 < 1$, r_k will tail off geometrically. In general, one can identify a model tentatively by examining the behavior of the sample autocorrelation function. Figure VII:2:1 shows
plots of the most common autocorrelation functions encountered in
practice. The plots are drawn so that r_k appears on the horizontal axis and k is plotted on the vertical axis (k increases as you
go down the page).

278

Autocorrelation Functions

(p,q)

(0,1)

-1 0 +1   -1 0 +1

$\theta_1 > 0$ $\theta_1 < 0$

(0,2)

-1 0 +1   -1 0 +1   -1 0 +1   -1 0 +1

$\theta_1 > 0$ $\theta_1 > 0$ $\theta_1 < 0$ $\theta_1 < 0$

$\theta_2 > 0$ $\theta_2 < 0$ $\theta_2 > 0$ $\theta_2 < 0$

(1,0)

-1 0 +1   -1 0 +1

$\phi_1 > 0$ $\phi_1 < 0$

(2,0)

-1 0 +1   -1 0 +1   -1 0 +1   -1 0 +1

$\phi_1 > 0$ $\phi_1 > 0$ $\phi_1 < 0$ $\phi_1 < 0$

$\phi_2 > 0$ $\phi_2 < 0$ $\phi_2 > 0$ $\phi_2 < 0$

(1,1)

-1 0 +1   -1 0 +1   -1 0 +1   -1 0 +1   -1 0 +1   -1 0 +1

$\phi_1 > \theta_1 > 0$ $\theta_1 > \phi_1 > 0$ $\phi_1 > 0 > \theta_1$ $\theta_1 > 0 > \phi_1$ $0 > \phi_1 > \theta_1$ $0 > \theta_1 > \phi_1$

279

Once p, d, and q have been tentatively identified, it is necessary to estimate the parameters Φ and Θ. The program that was used to obtain forecasts for the CAS model variables (COMSHARE, 1976), employs a nonlinear least-squares method to compute maximum likelihood estimates of the parameters and their standard errors.

After a tentatively specified model has been fitted (i.e., after Φ and Θ have been estimated), it is necessary to perform diagnostic checking. One way of checking is to compute the auto-correlation function r_k of the residuals $\hat{a}_t$ computed from the fitted model. If the fitted model is correct, then r_k will be approximately zero for $k = 1, 2, \ldots$ On the other hand, if the model is not correct, then r_k provides valuable information for modifying its identification (repeating step one). For example, if the tentatively specified model were $(0, d, q)$ and the autocorrelation function of the residuals were $r_1 > 0$, $r_k \approx 0$, $k = 2, \ldots$, then the new identification would be $(0, d, q+1)$.

When the residual autocorrelation function is approximately zero, the model must be checked for stationarity and invertibility. To define these conditions, we must rewrite VII:2:2 as

VII:2:3 $\Phi(B)w_t = \Theta(B)\varepsilon_t$

where $\Phi(B) = (1 - \Phi_1 B - \Phi_2 B^2 - \ldots - \Phi_p B^p)$

and $\Theta(B) = (1 - \Theta_1 B - \Theta_2 B^2 - \ldots - \Theta_q B^q)$.

VII:2:3 is equivalent to

VII:2:4 $\qquad w_t = {}^\Theta(B)/{}^\Phi(B)\varepsilon_t$ [3]

$\qquad\qquad w_t = {}^\Psi(B)\varepsilon_t$

and to

VII:2:5 $\qquad {}^\Phi(B)/{}^\Theta(B)w_t = \varepsilon_t$ [4]

$\qquad\qquad {}^\Pi(B)w_t = \varepsilon_t$

For the process w_t to be stationary, the sequence $\Psi_1, \Psi_2,\ldots$ must be either finite or infinite and convergent. If the process is not stationary, the ultimate effect of a finite disturbance ε_t will be infinite (i.e. the system will eventually blow up). The condition that must be satisfied for the process to be stationary is that the roots of the polynomial

$$1 - {}^\Phi_1 x - {}^\Phi_2 x^2 - \ldots - {}^\Phi_p x^p$$

lie outside the unit circle.

For the process to be invertible, the sequence $\Pi_1, \Pi_2, \ldots$ must be either finite or infinite and convergent. If the process is not invertible, the effect of past values of w_t on future values grows without bound. The condition for invertibility of the process is that the roots of the polynomial

$$1 - {}^\Theta_1 x - {}^\Theta_2 x^2 - \ldots - {}^\Theta_q x^q$$

---

3   Stationarity is needed to perform this division.

4   Invertibility is needed to perform this division.

lie outside the unit circle.

Finally, when the model has been identified, estimated, and checked, it is possible to use it for forecasting. Forecasts can be obtained from equation VII:2:5 as follows. If

$$w_t = \Pi_1 w_{t-1} + \Pi_2 w_{t-2} + \ldots + \varepsilon_t$$

Then

$$E[w_{t+1}] = \hat{w}_{t+1} = \Pi_1 w_t + \Pi_2 w_{t-1} + \ldots + \Pi_n w_{t-n+1}$$

where t-n+1 corresponds to the first observation in the series w_t. Similarly

$$E[w_{t+2}] = \hat{w_{t+2}} = \Pi_1 \hat{w}_{t+1} + \Pi_2 w_t + \ldots + \Pi_{n+1} w_{t-n+1}$$

and so forth.

In the next section, the Box-Jenkins techniques described here will be used to forecast the exogenous variables in the CAS model.

VII:2:1:2 The forecasts

Thirteen exogenous variables are to be forecast by means of
Box-Jenkins techniques. Most of the variables are prices (the prices
of the inputs to metal production and the sector output prices). In
general, variables are forecast as they are used in the model. For
example, it is possible to forecast prices in current dollars, then
forecast the wholesale-price index (WPI), and divide. Instead,
prices are forecast in 1967 current dollars. The price indices that
are WPI indices are normalized so that 1967 = 1.0. Wages for both
copper and aluminum primary production are corrected for labor productivity before forecasting (i.e., they are measured in constant
dollars per ton not constant dollars per man). The index of industrial production is normalized so that 1967 = 100. The two profitability measures, after-tax profits divided by stockholders' equity
and Moody's AAA corporate bond yield, are measured in percent.

The years 1947 - 1976 are used in fitting the forecasting
models. Because time-series techniquies are not appropriate for
very short series, it is necessary to use data from years prior
to 1954 (the beginning of the data used in fitting the model equations) to obtain the forecasting equations.

Table VI:2:1 shows the (p,d,q) models for each variable
together with the estimated autoregressive (AR) and moving average
(MA) parameters. Table VII:2:2 shows the forecasts of the exogenous variables produced by these models. In table VII:2:2, the 1976
values of the variables are their historic values, but those for
1977-1986 are their predicted values.

283

BOX-JENKINS MODELS FOR THE EXOGENOUS VARIABLES

Variable	(p,d,q) Model	AR1	AR2	MA1	MA2	MA3	MA4
$(W/LP)_c$	(0,1,1)			.54			
$(W/LP)_a$	(2,1,0)	0.	-.40				
Psa	(2,0,0)	1.16	-.40				
Pha	(2,0,0)	.76	-.35				
Pb	(2,1,0)	0.	.34				
Π/E	(1,0,0)	.55					
CBY	(0,2,4)			.61	.24	.88	-.78
IP	(2,2,0)	-.60	-.68				
Pbc	(2,2,0)	-.17	-.83				
Pt	(0,1,2)			-.40	.27		
Pcd	(0,1,2)			-.45	.27		
Pem	(1,1,0)	.36					
Pmc	(2,2,0)	-.46	-.68				

$(W/LP)_c$		Copper wage/Labor productivity
$(W/LP)_a$		Aluminum wage/Labor productivity
Psa		Price of sulfuric acid
Pha		Price of hydrofluoric acid
Pb		Price of bauxite
Π/E		After-tax profits/Stockholder's equity
CBY		Moody's AAA corporate bond yield
IP		The index of industrial production
Pbc		Building and construction
Pt		Transportation
Pcd	Sector out prices	Consumer durables
Pem		Electrical machinery
Pmc		Metal containers

BOX-JENKINS FORECASTS OF THE EXOGENOUS VARIABLES

Variable	Year										
	76	77	78	79	80	81	82	83	84	85	86
$(W/LP)_c$	2.50	2.72	2.72	2.72	2.72	2.72	2.72	2.72	2.72	2.72	2.72
$(W/LP)_a$	3.75	3.63	3.48	3.52	3.58	3.57	3.54	3.55	3.56	3.56	3.55
Psa	1.07	1.02	.97	.93	.90	.89	.88	.88	.88	.89	.89
Pha	1.14	1.13	1.11	1.09	1.09	1.10	1.10	1.10	1.10	1.10	1.10
Pb	6.18	6.08	5.94	5.90	5.86	5.85	5.83	5.83	5.82	5.82	5.82
Π /E	14.2	13.1	12.5	12.1	11.9	11.8	11.8	11.7	11.7	11.7	11.7
CBY	8.43	8.52	8.84	9.22	9.47	9.73	9.98	10.2	10.5	10.8	11.0
IP	130	135	128	134	140	137	139	144	145	146	150
Pbc	1.09	1.02	1.04	1.12	1.12	1.08	1.12	1.17	1.16	1.15	1.19
Pt	.86	.86	.86	.86	.86	.86	.86	.86	.86	.86	.86
Pcd	.84	.83	.83	.83	.83	.83	.83	.83	.83	.83	.83
Pem	.80	.80	.80	.80	.80	.80	.80	.80	.80	.80	.80
Pmc	1.11	1.11	1.17	1.20	1.21	1.24	1.28	1.30	1.32	1.36	1.38

Table VII:2:2 shows that most of the prices are forecast to increase at about the same rate as the wholesale-price index. However, some prices, such as the price of metal containers, increase significantly faster. The index of industrial production exhibits typical cyclical behavior about a positive trend. The two profitability measures behave differently from one another. Whereas the rate of return to equity (Π/E) falls back from a high level of 14.2% in 1976 to about its average (12%), the corporate bond yield continues to increase as it has in the past (reflecting continuing inflation in the future).

VII2:2   Energy-Price Forecasts

Energy prices, unlike metal prices, are subject to a complex
system of controls. Therefore, political decisions play an important role in determining their behavior. It is thus of interest
to see how domestic copper and aluminum markets react to different
energy-price policies.

Between 1966 and 1973, deflated energy prices remained relatively constant. Then, in 1973-74, as a consequence of the Arab oil
embargo and OPEC price increases, energy prices increased sharply.
Between 1974 and 1976, they continued to increase but at a somewhat
slower rate than in the 1973-74 period.

What can we say about future energy prices? It could be
claimed that the events of 1973-74 were extremely unusual, and that,
after the prices of all energy sources catch up with oil prices (on
a Btu basis), energy prices will increase in the future at a rate
equal to the rate of inflation (i.e., there will have been a shift
in their level but no trend). An OPEC price increase of 10% per
year is consistent with this hypothesis if the rate of inflation in
the U.S. is 10%.

However, it could also be claimed that, because both discovery
and production rates for petroleum have peaked in the U.S. (formerly
the world's largest producer), and because most new sources of petroleum
are located either offshore or in inaccessible areas such as northern
Alaska, energy prices will rise in the future at rates greater than
the overall rate of inflation. [5]

287

But what does "greater than the overall rate of inflation"
mean? One could claim that deflated energy prices have been
increasing linearly since 1974 and that they will continue to do so,
or one could claim that energy prices have been increasing expo-
nentially since 1974 and that exponential growth rates will persist.
Both claims fit the data very well (an exponential-growth curve is
usually indistinguishable from a linear-growth curve if the period
of observation is short).

We therefore have three possibilities for the future path of
deflated energy prices.

1) No growth after 1978.

2) Linear growth at 1974-76 rates.

3) Exponential growth at 1974-76 rates.

I call these three possibilities the low, intermediate, and high
energy-price scenarios. What actually happens to energy prices
will depend on many things such as OPEC pricing policy, U.S. policy
on energy-price deregulation, economic growth in the industrial
world (which influences the demand for energy), the success of
petroleum-exploration projects in new areas such as the Baltimore
Canyon, and technological advances in the production of energy from
nonconventional sources. These are only a few of the factors that
will influence future energy prices, all of which are difficult to
predict. The three cases outlined above are meant to   encompass

---

5   This argument must hold in the long-run, but we are inter-
     erested in ten-year forecasts of energy prices.

the most likely possibilities, from lowest to highest growth rates, that can reasonably be expected in the future. What actually happens will probably lie somewhere in between.

Figures VII:2:2 and 3 show plots of the three energy-price forecasts. Figure VII:2:2 shows forecasts of a weighted average of energy prices with weights proportional to energy usage in the copper industry, while figure VII:2:3 shows forecasts of electricity prices. The linear and exponential growth curves shown in the figures were fitted to 1974-76 trends, but it can be seen that actual 1977 prices (the circles on the graphs) lie very close to the predicted prices for 1977 on all three curves in both figures.

The weighted average of energy prices that corresponds to copper-industry energy costs grew faster than electricity prices (which are relevant for the aluminum industry), and it is projected that the faster growth of copper-industry energy costs will continue in the future. Because most aluminum smelters are located near cheap sources of power, the industry is partially insulated from energy-price increases. It therefore seems that the slower growth of energy costs for the aluminum industry obtained by extrapolating past trends is a reasonable assumption for the future as well.

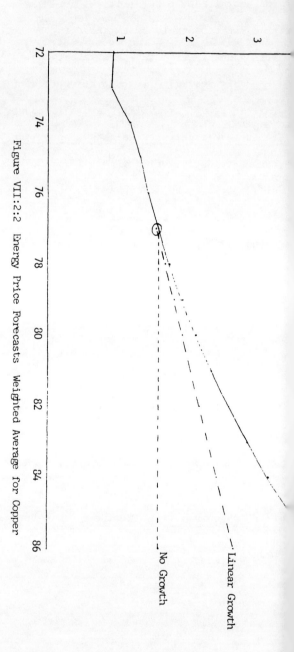

Figure VII:2:2 Energy Price Forecasts Weighted Average for Copper

No Growth

Linear Growth

290

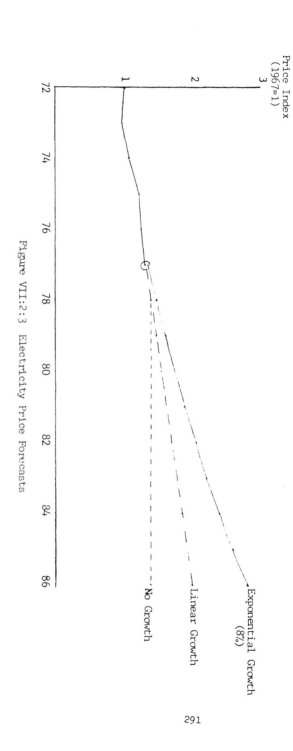

Figure VII:2:3   Electricity Price Forecasts

Price Index
(1967=1)

Exponential Growth
(8%)

Linear Growth

No Growth

VII:2:3 Ore-Quality Forecasts

Equation III:4:4, the equation for the U.S. producer price of copper, contains two measures of ore quality -- the average yield of copper ores mined and the level of primary production. Figures VII:2:4 and 5 show how copper-industry costs vary as yield and output vary. The first of these figures shows energy costs in primary production as a function of ore grade, [6] and the second shows how world copper costs vary as a function of primary production. These relationships were discussed in chapter III:2. Neither is used directly in the CAS model; however, they serve to illustrate the considerable variation in primary-copper production costs due to ore-deposit characteristics.

Figures VII:2:4 and 5 show how copper costs vary at a point in time. We are interested in the behavior of the two independent variables in the relationships -- yield and output -- as functions of time in order to estimate copper-industry costs at any point in time. The second of these variables, primary production, is an endogenous variable in the CAS model and need not be forecast. However, the yield of copper ores is exogenous.

Data exist on the average grade of each copper deposit in the U.S. that is being commercially produced as well as on planned capacity expansions in the industry. The data for each planned

---

6   Yield, which is approximately 70% of grade, is the variable
     to be forecast. However, the relationship plotted was calcu-
     lated in terms of grade.

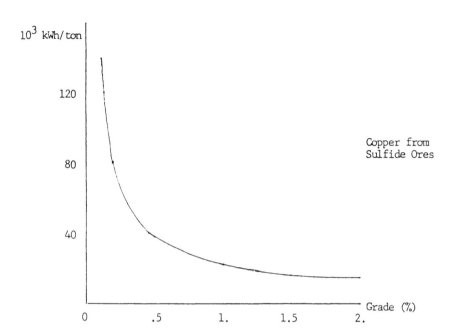

Figure VII:2:4 Energy Cost per ton of Copper as a Function of Ore Grade

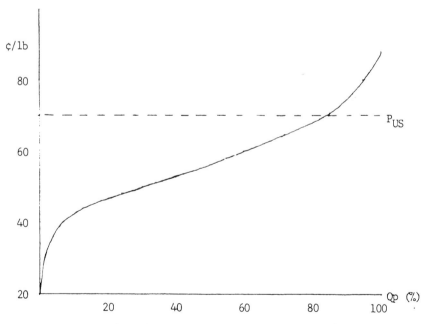

Figure VII:2:5 1976 World Refined Copper Cost as a Function of Output

293

expansion include the date when the investment project is scheduled to begin production and the average grade of each new deposit. [7]   In theory it would be possible to forecast average yield of copper ores in future years from this data. However, new mines do not always open when they are scheduled. For example, most copper industry investment projects were postponed in the 75-78 period due to poor economic conditions in the industry. In addition, when production is low, yield is apt to be high because high-cost mines close first in a recession. Therefore, forecasts of the average yield of copper ores mined in the future can not be calculated from this data in a mechanistic way.

To forecast yield it is helpful to look at its past behavior. Figure VII:2:6 shows the average yield of copper ores mined in the U.S. from 1954 to 1976. Since 1960, primary-copper production in the U.S. has fluctuated from year to year but has shown no marked trend. If prmary-copper production in the U.S. were to continue at about the same level, it would be valid to extrapolate the trend in yield seen in figure V:2:6. That is, U.S. copper production can remain constant in the future only by exploiting progressively lower quality ore deposits. If the demand for copper is high enough in the future to support the upward trend in copper prices that we have seen in the past, then the U.S. will continue to be a major copper producer. In this eventuality, statistical forecasting methods are probably as good as any for predicting future

---

[7]   The data are in a working computer file at the U.S. Geological Survey. However, the file contains proprietary information and is not publicly available.

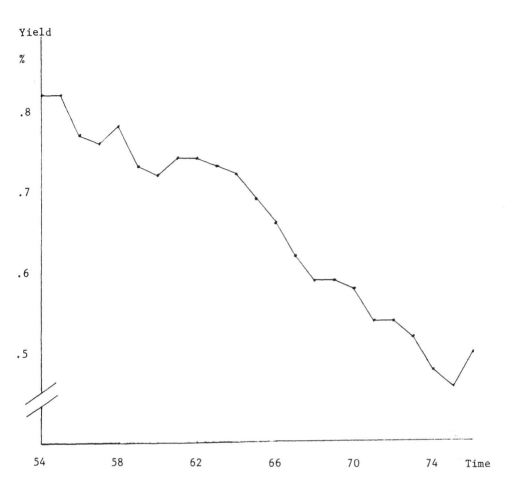

Figure VII:2:6   Yield of US Copper Ores as a Function of Time

295

copper-ore yields. Under most conditions envisioned (most simulations performed), primary-copper production in the U.S. does continue at historic levels and statistical forecasts can be used. However, in the final simulation performed, in which the world copper market remains depressed, U.S. production falls dramatically and yield must be forecast by judgemental methods. This simulation is discussed in section VII:3:3.

Table VII:2:3 shows the Box-Jenkins model fitted to the data for the average yield of copper ores mined in the U.S. and the forecasts produced from this model. [8] These forecasts are used in four out of the five simulations reported in the next section.

TABLE VII:2:3
BOX-JENKINS MODEL AND FORECASTS FOR THE AVERAGE
YIELD OF COPPER ORES MINED IN THE U.S.

(p,d,q)
Model   MA1

$(0,2,1)$ .92

Year	76	77	78	79	80	81	82	83	84	85	86
	.51	.50	.49	.47	.46	.45	.44	.43	.42	.40	.39

---

[8] These forecasts are not very different from those produced by more elaborate methods using the data from the computer file described earlier.

VII:3 Simulations

VII:3:1 The Historic Period 1962-1976

All the simulations discussed in this section were run on
Time Series Processor (TSP) Version 3.3 (1977). The first simulation is the dynamic simulation [9] of the historic period, 1962-
1976. [10] Figures VII:3:1-4 show plots of primary prices, consumption of copper and aluminum and the copper-aluminum consumption
ratio, and production of each metal from primary and secondary
sources. In the figures, the solid lines are the observed values
of the variables, and the dashed lines are their simulated values.
The overall behavior of the observed and simulated variables is very
similar, but many of the simulated time paths are somewhat smoother
than their historic counterparts. The simulated copper price for 1970
is not shown because that year was not used in estimating the copper
primary-price equation. Appendix D contains computer printouts of
the simulated values of all of the endogenous variables (not just
those shown here).

---

9   In a dynamic simulation, the lagged endogenous variables
assume their solution values from previous time periods.

10   The historic period for simulation purposes begins in 1962.
Data on consumption by sector goes back to 1960 but, due to
lags in the equations, 1962 is the first year that can be
simulated.

297

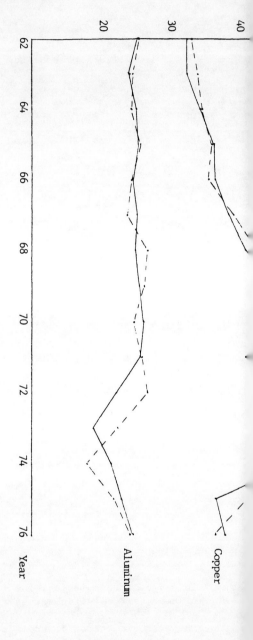

Figure VII:3:1 Copper and Aluminum Primary Prices 1962-1976
(Deflated by the Wholesale Price Index)

——— Observed
— — Simulated

298

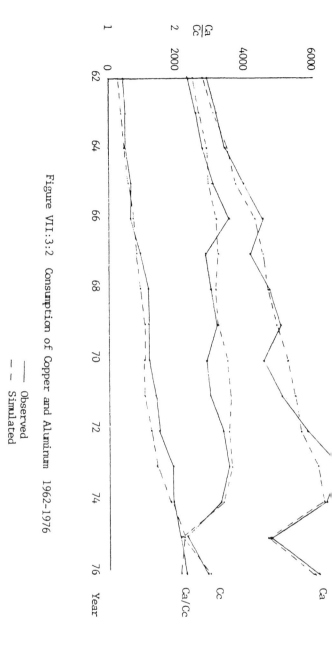

Figure VII:3:2 Consumption of Copper and Aluminum 1962-1976

—— Observed
— — Simulated

299

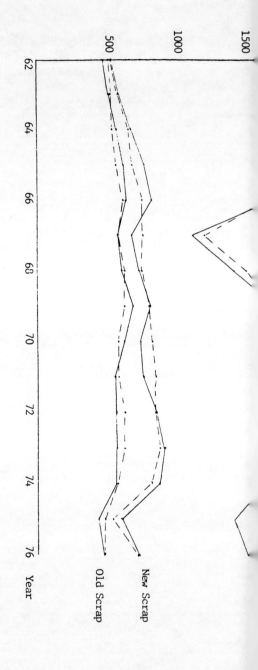

Figure VII:3:3 Copper Production 1962-1976

—— Observed
— — Simulated

300

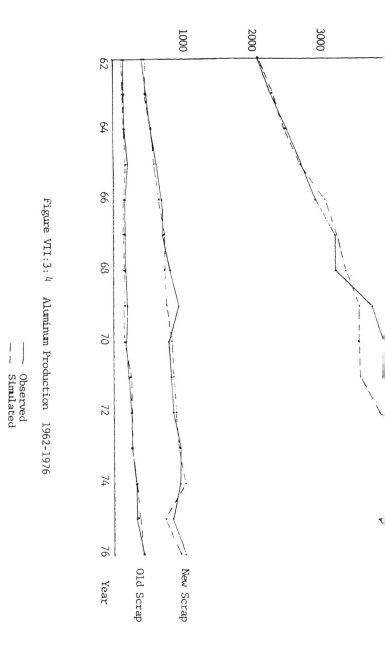

Figure VII:3:4   Aluminum Production   1962-1976

——— Observed
— — Simulated

301

VII:3:2   The Forecast Period   1977-1986

The five simulations presented in this section cover the ten-year forecast period, 1977 to 1986. The first three simulations correspond to different assumptions about the behavior of energy prices in the future, and the last two simulations test the sensitivity of domestic copper and aluminum markets to changes in world metal markets.

VII:3:2:1 Low, intermediate, and high energy price scenarios

In section VII:2:2, the three energy-price forecasts were discussed. Here we determine the impacts that different assumptions about future energy prices might have on domestic copper and aluminum markets. Figures VII:3:5 and 7-9 show plots of copper and aluminum primary prices, consumption, and production from primary and secondary sources between 1962 and 1986. For the period 1962 to 1976, the graphs show the observed values of each variable. For the forecast period, 1977 to 1986, the dotted lines correspond to the high energy-price forecasts (exponential growth), the solid lines correspond to intermediate energy prices (linear growth), and the dashed lines correspond to the low energy-price forecasts (no growth). The circled points in the year 1977 are observed values of the variables and can be compared with their forecast values.

302

Figure VII:3:5 shows that, whereas the price of aluminum is very sensitive to the assumed behavior of energy prices, the price of copper hardly changes under the very different assumptions about future energy prices. Aluminum price responds predictably to changes in energy cost. Because primary-aluminum production is very energy intensive, and because the U.S. producer price of aluminum is based to a large degree on long-run average cost, the sensitivity of aluminum price to energy cost is easy to understand. In all three simulations, the upward trend in aluminum prices noticed in the 1972 to 1976 period continues. However, the rate of increase of aluminum prices in each of the simulations is very different. In the year 1986, the forecast deflated aluminum price ranges from a high of 48 to a low of 30 cents per pound (or approximately $1.40 to $.88 in 1986 current dollars).

In contrast, the forecast deflated copper price in 1986 is approximately 50 cents per pound ($1.46 in 1986 current dollars) regardless of the price of energy. Because primary copper production is also very energy intensive and because the U.S. producer price of copper is also based to a large extent on long-run average cost, the result of unvarying copper prices is counterintuitive. The explanation for the lack of sensitivity of copper price to energy cost can be found in the depletable nature of copper ores. When energy price is low, demand is stimulated, primary production of copper is high, and lower quality ore deposits must be worked, implying higher mining costs. Conversely, when energy price is high, primary-copper production is low and the marginal ore

303

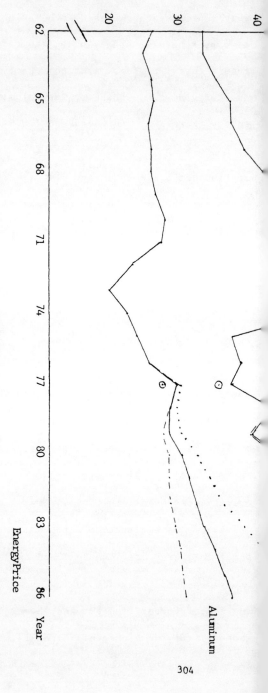

Figure VII:3:5 Copper and Aluminum Primary Prices
(Deflated by the Wholesale Price Index)

EnergyPrice

···· High
—— Intermediate
— — Low

304

deposit worked is of higher quality. Therefore, the two cost factors -- energy and mining cost -- act on copper price in opposite directions. The net effect is that they cancel each other. A diagram may make this reasoning clearer. Figure VII:3:6 shows that, when energy price goes up, the direct effect on copper price is positive. However, a higher copper price means lower demand for and production of copper and, therefore, higher quality ore deposits are worked and mining costs are lower. The indirect effect on copper price (through mining cost) is thus negative. The fact that the two effects are nearly equal (with resulting zero net effect) is coincidental, but the direction of the effects would be the same for any exhaustible resource.

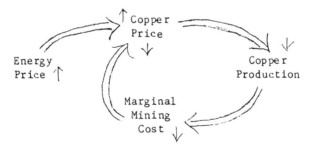

Figure VII:3:6   The Direct and Indirect Effects of an Increase in Energy Price on Copper Price

Figure VII:3:7 shows that the consumption of aluminum is much more sensitive to energy price than is the consumption of copper, a result to be expected because aluminum price (which determines consumption) is more sensitive. However, the ratio of aluminum consumption to copper consumption is close to two in all three simulations. The consumption ratio increased in the historic period from 1.09 in 1962 until it reached a high of 2.08 in 1976. Table VII:3:1 shows the value of the aluminum-copper consumption ratio in 1986 corresponding to the three energy-price assumptions. The forecast rate of increase in the consumption ratio is not great under any energy-price assumption, and with the high growth in energy prices, the consumption ratio is considerably lower in 1986 than its 1976 value of 2.08. We can therefore conclude that, if energy prices increase rapidly, the competitive cost advantage that aluminum has had over copper in the past will not hold in the future.

TABLE VII:3:1

THE RATIO OF ALUMINUM CONSUMPTION TO COPPER CONSUMPTION IN 1986

	Energy Price		
	Low	Intermediate	High
Ca/Cc	2.25	2.11	1.95

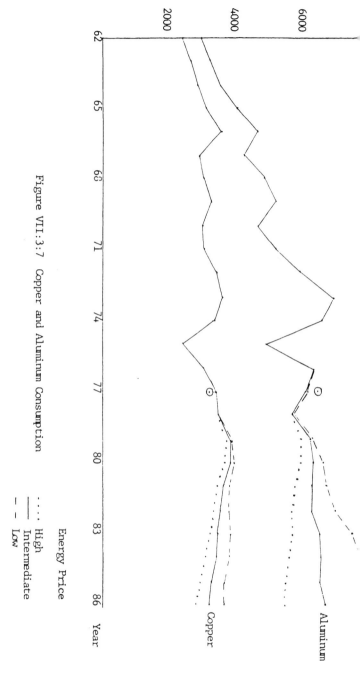

Figure VII:3:7 Copper and Aluminum Consumption

Energy Price

· · · · High
—— Intermediate
— — Low

Figures VII:3:8 and 9 show the forecast production of aluminum and copper, respectively, from primary and secondary sources. The primary production of both metals as well as production from new scrap, is negatively related to energy price as would be expected. When energy price increases, metal consumption falls and production of metal from new scrap (which is related to consumption) falls as a consequence. In addition, when energy price increases, the long-run average cost of primary metal production shifts upward and output from primary sources falls.

The analysis of the effect of an increase in energy price on secondary production from old scrap is more complex. An increase in energy price has three separate effects on the production of metal from old scrap. First, high energy price means high primary metal price which in turn means high secondary-metal price and high secondary production from old scrap. Second, high energy price means that marginal cost in secondary-metal production shifts upward, which in turn means lower secondary-metal production. And finally, high energy price means low metal consumption, implying a decrease in the stock of scrap available for collection and therefore lower secondary-metal production. Thus, one effect increases the incentive to recycle the metal contained in old scrap, while the other two decrease the incentive for recycling. Figure VII:3:10 illustrates the three effects that an increase in energy price has on secondary metal production from old scrap. Because the three pressures work in different directions, the direction of the net effect is an empirical issue.

308

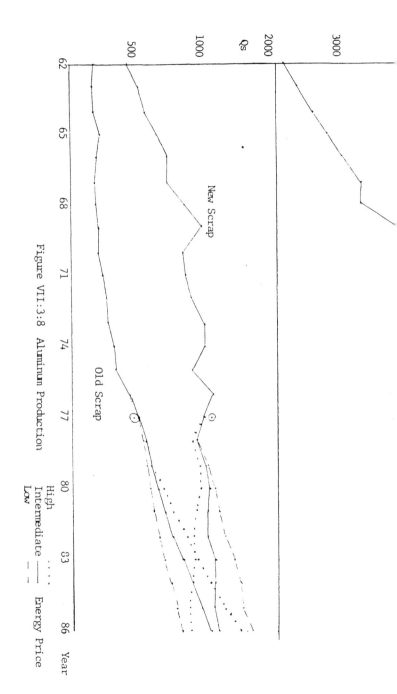

Figure VII:3:8 Aluminum Production

High
Intermediate ———
Low

Energy Price
— —

New Scrap

Old Scrap

Qs

3000
2000
1000
500

62 65 68 71 74 77 80 83 86 Year

309

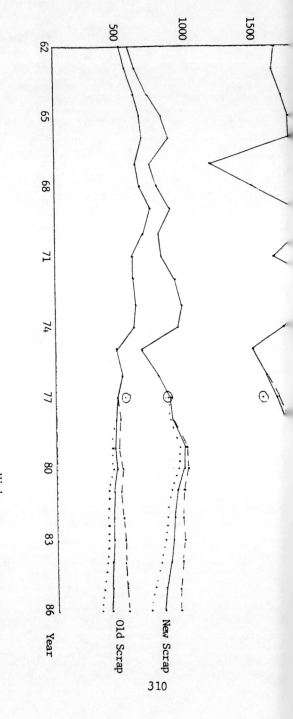

Figure VII:3:9 Copper Production

High
Intermediate ——— Energy Price
Low

310

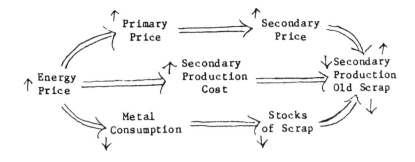

Figure VII:3:10　The Effects of an Increase in Energy Price
on Secondary-Metal Production from Old Scrap

Figures VII:3:8 and 9 show that an increase in the price of
energy increases the incentive to recycle the aluminum contained
in old scrap but decreases the incentive to recycle copper. This
result is logical because primary aluminum price increases sharply
with increases in energy price (providing the positive incentive),
but primary copper price hardly changes with changes in energy price
(implying that the negative incentives predominate).

Figure VII:3:11 shows the fraction of metal consumption that
is supplied by recycled material (defined as secondary production
from old and new scrap divided by metal consumption). For aluminum,
this fraction is positively related and very sensitive to energy
price. In contrast, for copper, the relationship to energy price
is negative but not strong. With the high growth in energy prices,
the fraction of aluminum consumption that is supplied by recycled
material increases from 24% in 1976 to nearly 40% in 1986, and
recycled metal provides a higher percent of aluminum consumption in the
last two years of the simulation than it does for copper consumption.
Most of the increase in aluminum recycling seen in the figures comes
from metal contained in old scrap.

311

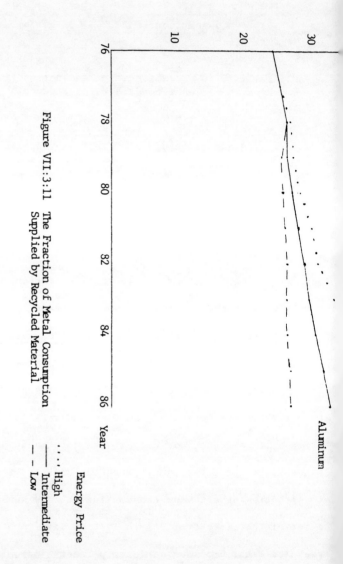

Figure VII:3:11   The Fraction of Metal Consumption
Supplied by Recycled Material

Energy Price

···· High
—— Intermediate
— — Low

VII:3:2:2 A "successful" bauxite cartel

In the simulations considered thus far, the price of bauxite
was forecast by statistical methods. The use of statistical forecasting techniques for bauxite price is valid only if the underlying structure of bauxite markets remains unchanged. If, for example,
the principal bauxite producers could collude to set prices to
maximize joint profits, the price chosen might be radically different
from the price forecast by statistical methods. Bauxite, a very
abundant mineral, is found in large quantity in many countries
of greatly differing economic development and political persuasion
(Australia, Brazil, Guinea, and Jamaica, for example). It is
therefore unlikely that actual and potential bauxite producers
could agree on a common tax policy in order to maximize bauxite-
industry profits in the long run. In addition, a high bauxite price
would stimulate bauxite supply in new areas and work against the success of the cartel. However, an assessment of the impact that substantially higher bauxite prices would have on the U.S. aluminum
industry is still of interest.

The price that would maximize bauxite-industry profits per ton
in the short run is that just below the ceiling established by the cost
of producing alumina from clay in the U.S. Charles River Associates
(1976) estimated this cost to be $40 per ton. A simulation was there-
fore made in which the price of bauxite rises gradually until it reaches
the limit of $40 per ton (in 1976 constant dollars) in the year 1986.
The calculation to obtain the appropriate bauxite price to use in the

313

model was made as follows. In 1973, before the royalty increases

adopted by the International Bauxite Association (IBA) members, the

price of crude, undried domestic bauxite (the price used in the model)

was $11 per ton. In the same year, the average price of imported,

dried bauxite was nearly $15 per ton. Therefore, a price of $40

per ton for imported dried bauxite corresponds to a price of $30

per ton for   crude domestic bauxite. [11] In the fourth simula-

tion, the successful bauxite-cartel simulation, the model price of

bauxite therefore rises until it reaches $30 per ton in 1976 constant

dollars ($16.50 in 1967 constant dollars) in the final year of the

simulation. Table VII:3:2 shows the forecasts of domestic bauxite

price used in the fourth simulation (the 1976 price in the table is

the historic price; all others are forecasts).

TABLE VII:3:2
FORECASTS OF THE DEFLATED PRICE OF CRUDE DOMESTIC BAUXITE

Year

76	77	78	79	80	81	82	83	84	85	86
6.18	7.23	8.26	9.26	10.29	11.32	12.35	13.38	14.41	15.44	16.5

Figures VII:3:12-15 show some of the results from the success-

ful bauxite-cartel simulation. In these figures, the solid lines

correspond to the statistical forecasts of bauxite price and the

dashed lines result from the cartel-pricing policy. The intermediate

---

11   There is a considerable amount of water contained in the
      crude bauxite.

energy-price forecasts were used for both simulations. The figures show that, with the highest possible bauxite price, the deflated price of aluminum rises to about 45 cents per pound in 1986 ($1.32 in 1986 current dollars). A three hundred percent increase in bauxite price therefore leads to a twenty five percent increase in the price of aluminum, about a fifteen percent fall in aluminum consumption in the U.S., and a six percent fall in primary production. The increase in aluminum price is substantial, but it is still considerably below the increase that occurs with the higher energy-price forecasts and no cartel. However, because copper price is not affected by the increase in the price of bauxite, the ratio of aluminum consumption to copper consumption falls more with a successful bauxite cartel than it does with the higher energy prices and no cartel.

Computer printouts of the values of the endogenous variables for this simulation and others can be found in appendix D.

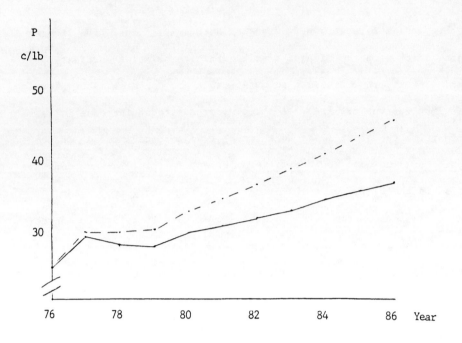

Figure VII:3:12   Aluminum Primary Ingot Price
                  (Deflated by the Wholesale Price Index)

———— No Cartel
— — Successful Cartel

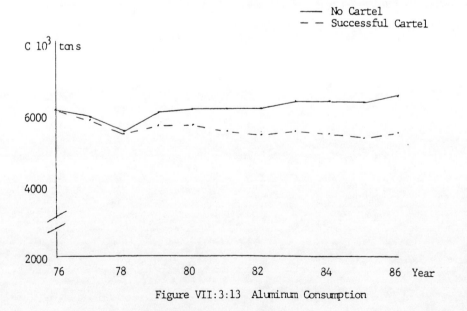

Figure VII:3:13   Aluminum Consumption

316

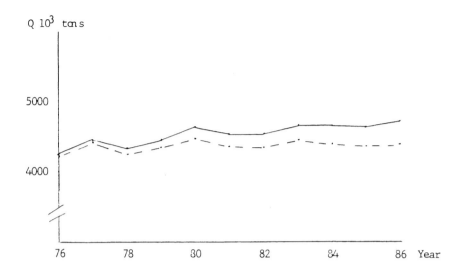

Figure VII:3:14 Aluminum Primary Production

—— No Cartel
— — Successful Cartel

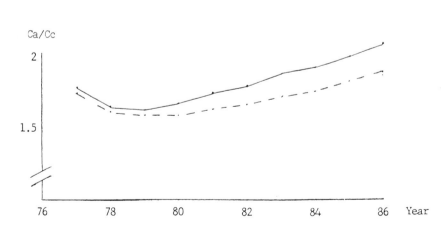

Figure VII:3:15 Aluminum Consumption/Copper Consumption

317

Closure of domestic copper mines due to a depressed world
         copper market

In the previous simulation, we considered the most unfavor-
able impact that changed world metal-market conditions could have
on the domestic aluminum market. Here, we look at the most extreme
impact that changed world copper-market conditions could have on
the U.S. copper industry. The the most damaging action that bauxite
producers could take, from the point of view of the U.S. aluminum
industry, is to raise the price of bauxite to profit-maximizing
levels; the most damaging factor for the U.S. copper industry
would be a very low world copper price.

In the past, the U.S. was able to maintain its position as
the largest producer of copper in the world through technological
improvements in exploiting lower and lower grade copper ores. Technological innovation gave the U.S. a competitive advantage, but
now these mining techniques are used abroad, and underdeveloped
countries that have higher quality ore deposits are able to mine copper
more cheaply than is possible in the U.S. The major mining companies have made large investments in new capacity overseas in recent
years, especially in Chile. A combination of slow economic growth
in the industrial world and large supply increases in Chile and
elsewhere could keep the world copper price at low levels and cause
many U.S. mines to close in the next decade. It is this possibility
that we want to consider now.

Large mining-cost differences exist that cause the copper

industry to be characterized by increasing costs as output expands.
Figure VII:2:5 from the previous section gives a rough idea of the
shape of the cost curve for world copper production; the cost curve
for the U.S. should be fairly similar in shape. With a constant-cost
industry like the aluminum industry, long-run supply is infinitely
elastic and shifts in demand are fully met by supply increases in the
long run. In contrast, in the copper industry, supply (cost) considerations are very important in determining production in the
long-range future. A low world copper price would not mean that,
without import controls, the U.S. copper industry would cease to
exist. It would mean, however, that many high-cost mines would be
forced to close.

The final simulation to be run is therefore based on the
assumption that world economic conditions in the copper industry
are such that one third of U.S. mines must close by 1986. In this
simulation, primary output was adjusted exogenously so that it
reaches a low level of 1200×10^3 tons in 1986. A lower level of
production would mean that the average yield of copper ores mined
actually increases (as high-cost ore deposits stop producing). For
this reason, the statistical forecasts of yield from earlier simulations could not be used, and it was necessary to make judgemental
forecasts of future yields from the data on deposit characteristics.
Table VII:3:3 shows the forecasts of domestic copper primary
production and of the average yield of copper ores mined in the U.S.
that were used in the fifth and final simulation (the 1976 values
in the table are the historic values; all others are forecasts).

FORECASTS OF COPPER PRIMARY PRODUCTION (10^3 TONS) AND THE AVERAGE YIELD
OF COPPER ORES MINED IN THE U.S.   FIFTH SIMULATION

Year	76	77	78	79	80	81	82	83	84	85	86
Qp	1537	1490	1450	1410	1380	1350	1320	1290	1260	1230	1200
Yield	.50	.51	.51	.52	.52	.53	.53	.54	.54	.55	.55

Figures VII:3:16-18 show some of the results from the final
simulation. Computer printouts of these variables, as well as of
the endogenous variables not shown, can be found in appendix D. In
the figures, the solid lines are from the second simulation, in which
the intermediate energy-price forecasts were used. The dashed lines
correspond to the final simulation, where U.S. copper mines are forced
to close by depressed conditions in the world industry. The intermediate energy-price forecasts were used in this simulation as well.

Deflated copper price falls to a low of 31.5 cents per pound
in 1986 (93 cents per pound in 1986 current dollars). Copper consumption, stimulated by the low price, rises to a record high of
6220×10^3 tons in 1986, but this increase is supplied by imported,
not domestic copper. With a low price, there is little incentive
to reclaim the copper contained in old scrap, but secondary recovery
from new scrap increases dramatically (again, most of the new scrap
that is reclaimed was originally imported). The combination of
higher energy prices and lower copper prices than those of today
causes the aluminum-copper consumption ratio to fall to a level of
1.2 by 1986.

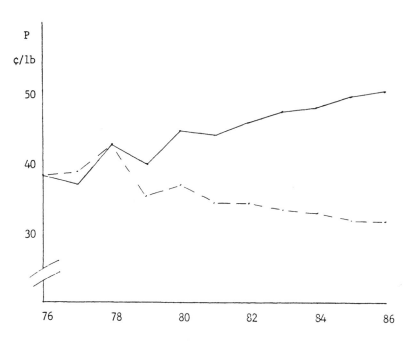

Figure VII:3:16 Copper Price
(Deflated by the Wholesale Price Index)

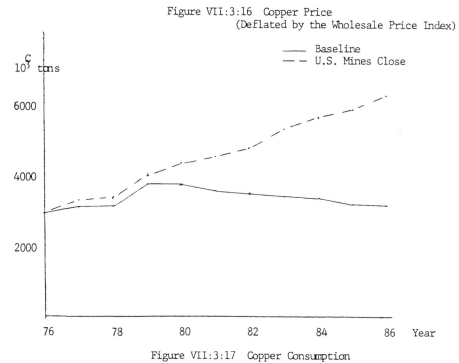

——— Baseline
— — U.S. Mines Close

Figure VII:3:17 Copper Consumption

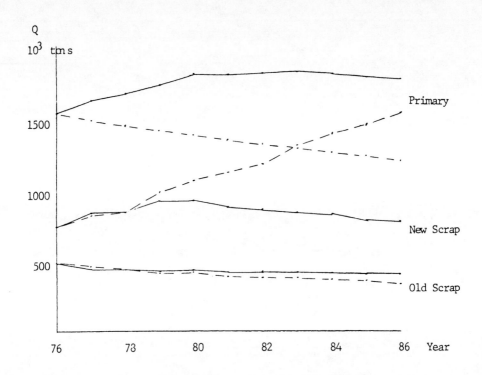

Figure VII:3:18 Copper Production

———— Baseline
– – U.S. Mines Close

The second and fifth simulations (intermediate energy price
with and without depressed world copper-market conditions) provide
two points on a copper price-output curve. This curve is defined
as the relationship between U.S. primary production of copper in
1986 and the U.S. producer price of copper in that year, given a
particular energy-price forecast (in these simulations, the intermediate forecast). Additional simulations could be run to trace
out more points on the curve. Figure VII:3:19 shows what such
a curve might look like. It is similar to figure VII:2:5, but,
whereas the earlier curve was based on cost conditions alone, the
curve in figure VII:3:19 is based on demand and substitution
relationships as well. [12]

---

[12]   The curve in figure VII:3:19, unlike that in figure VII:2:5,
will eventually bend backward when a high price leads to low
demand and production.

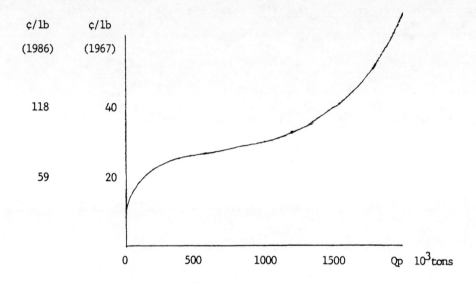

¢/lb   ¢/lb
(1986)   (1967)

118   40

59   20

          0   500   1000   1500   Qp 10^3 tons

Figure VII:3:19   Possible 1986 Copper Price-Output Relationship

324

The last two simulations reported are very pessimistic and represent improbable conditions. It is highly unlikely that the principal bauxite producers could maintain the simulated pricing policy. Not only are the political concerns of the members of the IBA very different, but such high bauxite prices would stimulate supply expansions that would ultimately hurt the cartel. On the other hand, although the world price of copper could fall in the future, the U.S. government is unlikely to allow imports to increase to the level reported in the final simulation without imposing controls on imported copper. The purpose of reporting the final simulations was to assess impacts, not to predict the future.

CHAPTER VIII   CONCLUSIONS AND POLICY IMPLICATIONS

In chapter II, where the CAS model was compared to and con-
trasted with other econometric models of copper and aluminum
markets, several innovations were noted. Among the most important
of these were: (1) the use of statistical cost functions for both
the primary and secondary producers, so that the effects of cost
changes on metal prices are estimated, not assumed; (2) the inclusion of ore quality measures as cost determinants, so that metal
production costs rise as high-quality ore deposits are exhausted;
and (3) the direct linkage of the domestic copper and aluminum markets through the derived demand and elasticity of substitution equations, so that the two markets can interact in a realistic fashion.
In this chapter, we summarize some of the most important conclusions
of this study and show how the innovations mentioned earlier make the
conclusions reached here different from those that would have resulted
if these issues had been ignored.

VIII:1 Metal Pricing

Primary-price determination in the CAS model is based to a
large extent on long-run average cost. The inclusion of ore-quality
measures as cost (and therefore price) determinants was found to be
extremely important for the copper industry, because high-quality
deposits are being depleted, but not for the aluminum industry,
because aluminum ores are very abundant and significant quality
deterioration is not apt to take place in the next decade. Variation
in copper-ore quality is important both in the short and in the long
run. In the short run, an increase in copper production means that the
marginal deposit mined is of lower quality; while in the long run,
an increase in cumulative production means that high-quality ore
deposits will be exhausted more rapidly and will have to be replaced
by deposits that are more costly to mine. [1]

Because the quality of copper ores is deteriorating significantly
whereas the quality of aluminum ores is not, a contrast is seen between
the reaction of copper price and that of aluminum price to an increase in
energy cost. If, for example, energy costs account for 30% of the cost
of producing primary aluminum and for 10% of the cost of producing primary
copper, and if energy prices double, after a simple calculation we might
predict that the resulting aluminum- and copper-price increases would be
30% and 10% respectively. However, although the simple calculation is

---

[1]   The distinction here is between cost as a function of annual
        production (tons/year) and cost as a function of cumulative
        production (tons).

roughly correct for estimating changes in aluminum price, it is very wrong for copper. In chapter VII, we saw that an increase in energy price discouraged the demand for and primary production of both copper and aluminum. However, the fall in aluminum production did not change the quality of aluminum ores mined, but the fall in copper production meant that the marginal copper deposit worked was of higher quality. Therefore, although the direct effect on copper price of an increase in energy cost is positive (because more expensive fuels must be purchased), the indirect effect is negative (because exhaustion proceeds more slowly). These two influences nearly cancel one another, implying that the net effect is very small. The insensitivity of copper price to a change in energy cost does not mean, however, that the domestic copper industry is unaffected by higher energy prices. It does mean that higher energy prices force high-cost mines to close and that the domestic copper industry declines.

Figure VIII:1:1 may clarify this distinction. The graph on the left-hand side (A) corresponds to the aluminum industry, a constant-cost industry, and that on the right-hand side (B) corresponds to the copper industry, an increasing-cost industry. In both industries, long-run average cost (LRAC) shifts upward by the same amount (from LRAC to LRAC'). In the aluminum industry, the change in price (ΔPa) is equal to the change in cost, but, in the copper industry, the change in price (ΔPc) is much less.

Figure VIII:1:1 shows only the short-run effect that a change in long-run average cost has on copper price. In the long run, when

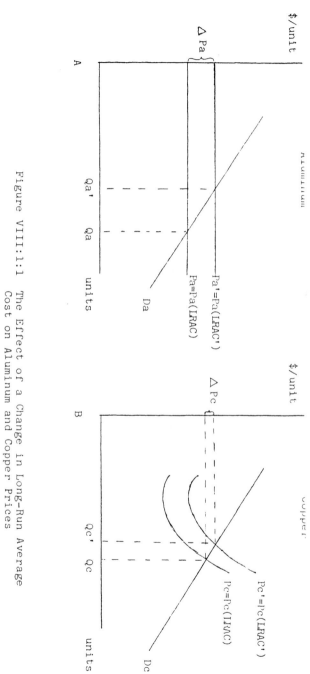

Figure VIII:1:1   The Effect of a Change in Long-Run Average
Cost on Aluminum and Copper Prices

production is lower, the LRAC curve will shift upward more slowly over time than it would have without the change in cost (because cumulative production is less), and the resulting price increase will be even smaller. We can therefore conclude that the inclusion of ore-quality measures as copper-cost determinants is very important in giving a realistic picture of copper-market pricing dynamics.

A final conclusion regarding metal pricing deals with the relative size of the impacts that increases in energy price and in bauxite price have on the U.S. aluminum industry. In the simulations presented in chapter VII, we saw that a forty percent increase in energy price (over the intermediate level) led to a considerably higher price for primary aluminum than did a tripling of bauxite price. Thus, the most pessimistic bauxite-producer-country pricing behavior from the point of view of the domestic aluminum industry, setting bauxite price to maximize profit-per-ton in the short-run, had less effect on the U.S. aluminum industry than did moderate energy-price increases at home. However, both issues -- bauxite-producer-country pricing policy and U.S. government-energy-pricing policy -- are very important in determining domestic aluminum price and therefore production, consumption and recycling rate.

VIII:2 Primary Production

In chapter II, we saw that the long-run elasticity of supply

of primary copper in the U.S., calculated from the CAS model primary-

production equation, was much lower than the Fisher-Cootner-Baily

(1972) estimate of the same elasticity. The low elasticity found

here was attributed primarily to two factors, both of which have

contributed to higher costs for capacity expansions in the domestic

copper industry than for existing facilities. First, in copper

mining, most of the very large, high-quality porphyry deposits have

been fully developed. Because newly discovered deposits tend to

be smaller, of lower grade, or more deeply buried, costs for new

mines are higher than costs for existing ones. And second, in

copper smelting, new air-pollution control regulations limiting

the emission of sulfur dioxide and particulates have led to increased

capital costs. Because new smelters have to meet New Source Perfor-

mance Standards, substantial price increases are required to bring

new smelting capacity on line. Not only are substantial price increases

required for capacity expansions, but moderately rising prices are

needed if the U.S. is to remain a major copper producer. The U.S.

can continue to produce copper at present levels only by exploiting

progressively lower and lower grade ores, and we saw that copper

mining and milling costs increase more than proportionately as ore

grades fall. However, the upward trend that we noted in deflated

copper price during the last twenty five years is projected to continue

in the future under all but the most pessimistic conditions, and the

331

domestic copper industry continues to produce at present, if not expanded, levels in most of the simulations performed.

The low elasticity of supply for primary copper found here gives rise to supply projections that are very different from those made using other econometric models of the U.S. copper industry. For example, table VIII:2:1 contrasts the forecasts of primary-copper production in 1986 obtained from the CAS model intermediate energy-price simulation with the baseline forecasts for the same year obtained by simulating the Arthur D. Little (ADL) model. The definitions of primary production used in the two studies are somewhat different. Therefore, it is necessary to focus on percent changes in primary production, not absolute levels. Primary-price and production forecasts from both studies are shown for 1977 and 1986. The price projections obtained from simulating the two models are very close to one another, although the CAS model forecasts are slightly higher in both years; the percent change in price over the period is also very similar. However, a 39% increase in deflated copper price results in a projected 36% increase in primary-copper production with the ADL model (elasticity of supply ≃ 1). In contrast, a 37% price increase results in only a 10% production increase with the CAS model (elasticity of supply ≃.25).[2]

---

2   Table VIII:2:1 also shows that the ADL forecast does not
     result from higher capacity utilization in later years
     than in 1977. Capacity utilization is about the same in
     1977 and in 1987 (1986 was not available), implying that
     capacity has expanded.

COMPARISON OF THE CAS MODEL INTERMEDIATE ENERGY-PRICE FORECASTS
WITH THE ARTHUR D. LITTLE MODEL BASELINE FORECASTS FOR U.S. COPPER

	ADL Model Baseline Forecasts	CAS Model Intermediate Energy Forecasts
Copper		
Primary Price 1974 ¢/lb		
1977	56.4	58.7
1986	78.3	80.3
%Δ	39 %	37 %
Copper		
Primary Production 10^3 tons		
1977	2061	1629
1986	2802	1785
%Δ	36 %	10 %
Capacity Utilization		
1977	87 %	
1987	88 %	

The difference in the two forecasts of primary-copper production results from the different assumptions made about the natural-resource base. In the ADL model, primary production can be easily expanded because ore quality is not considered, whereas in the CAS model, the costs incurred as high-quality copper ores are depleted are made explicit.

Discussions in chapter III led to the conclusion that the long-run supply of primary aluminum in the U.S. is infinitely elastic. Therefore, in the long run, increases in the demand for aluminum should be fully met by increases in domestic supply. However, the conclusion that the long-run supply of primary aluminum in the U.S. is infinitely elastic was based on economic considerations. It is possible that, for political reasons, new alumina refineries will be located abroad if pressures from bauxite-producing countries for downstream integration increase. Even though capital costs are high and skilled labor scarce in non-industrialized producer countries, these increased costs would be partially offset by the transportation-cost advantages of locating refineries near mines. However, forward integration beyond the refining stage (into smelting) would probably be difficult for most underdeveloped countries.

VIII:3 Consumption and Substitution

The direct linkage of domestic copper and aluminum markets
and the simultaneous determination of price and consumption in the
two models is a very important feature of this study. In the CAS
model, the structural relationships that link the two markets are
explicitly specified, and, in the simulations performed, the markets
interact through the derived demand and elasticity of substitution
equations. Of the econometric models classified in chapter II,
only one (Synergy, 1977) attempted to link the two markets directly.
However, the linkage was handled very differently in the Synergy
model (by including the price of each metal in the demand equation
for the other).

Considerable substitution potential was found in three out
of the five copper-aluminum-using sectors, with estimated elasticity of substitution greater than one in the construction and
industrial sectors, and not significantly different from one in
the electrical sector. In contrast, the estimated elasticities
for the consumer and transport sectors were found to be significantly less than one. Any cost increase that affects the two
industries unequally, such as an increase in energy price, will
cause changes in the market shares of the two metals; therefore,
any forecast of copper and aluminum usage that ignores this
substitution potential will be inaccurate.

With the high energy-price forecasts (exponential growth in

335

deflated energy prices at 1974-76 rates), the simulated aluminum-copper consumption ratio falls below its 1976 value of 2.13. Therefore, we can conclude that, if energy prices increase sharply, the aluminum industry will cease to have the cost advantage that has enabled it to take over a considerable share of the market for copper in the past.

VIII:4 Recycling

In the introductory chapter, it was noted that production of
copper and aluminum from scrap requires much less energy per ton of
metal than production from primary sources, so that an increase in
energy price might be expected to provide an incentive to recycle
both metals. However, a more thorough analysis (in chapters IV
and VII) showed that the issue is much more complex than initially
stated. An increase in energy price causes three separate pressures on secondary-metal production from old scrap. The first,
an increase in primary-metal price, provides a positive incentive
to recycle, but the other two, an increase in secondary-metal-
production cost and a fall in the stocks of scrap available for
collection, work in the opposite direction. Therefore, the direction of the net effect must be determined empirically.

For copper, the small increase in primary price induced by
higher energy costs, coupled with the large increase in marginal
energy reguirements for higher secondary-copper recovery efficiency,
means that the negative incentive will predominate as energy prices
rise. However, the disincentive to recycle is small. For aluminum,
the responsiveness of primary price to energy cost, coupled with
the less steep marginal energy-cost increases incurred with higher
secondary-aluminum recovery efficiency, means that there is considerable incentive to recycle the aluminum contained in old scrap
as energy prices rise. In fact, with the high energy-price forecasts, the fraction of aluminum usage that comes from recycled

337

metal in 1986 is greater than the fraction of copper usage (a considerable change from the present situation).

The disaggregation of copper and aluminum consumption into several using sectors was found to be very important in determining the fraction of consumption of each metal that will come from recycled material in the future. For example, the fastest growing aluminum-using sector -- the container and packaging market -- is one where products have very short average lifetimes and where the aluminum-price elasticity of demand is low. Therefore, that sector supplies an increasing proportion of the aluminum that is recycled in future years.

Just as with the primary industries, the use of statistical cost functions for the secondary producers (especially the consideration of the energy costs of secondary-metal production) was found to be very important in determining recycling potential. Because marginal cost in secondary production is a function of recovery efficiency, and because secondary-copper energy costs rise steeply when secondary-copper recovery efficiency improves, if these energy costs are ignored, the forecasts of future copper recycling rates obtained are too high to be met in practice.

Thus, many important issues face the domestic copper and aluminum industries in the next decade. Those considered here -- the consequences of higher energy prices, declining domestic ore quality, supply expansions abroad, and potential increases in producer-country royalties -- are by no means the only issues, but they are among the most pressing problems that must be confronted. Because metal prices, production, and consumption respond to changed conditions after a lag, the effects of decisions made today will continue to be felt for many years in the future. Therefore, the need to understand metal-market dynamics and to forecast market conditions is obvious, and forecasts obtained should be of interest to government policy makers as well as to industry long-range planners.

REFERENCES CITED

Almon, S., 1965, "The Distributed Lag Between Capital Appropriations and Capital Expenditures", Econometrica, Vol. 33, No. 1.

The Aluminum Association, 1954-1976, Aluminum Statistical Review, New York, N.Y.

American Metal Market, 1977, Metal Statistics 1977, Fairchild Publications, New York, N.Y.

Arrow, K.J., Chenerey, H.B., Minhas, B.S., and Solow, R.M., 1961, "Capital-Labor Substitution and Economic Efficiency", Review of Economics and Statistics, Vol. 43, No. 1.

Arthur D. Little, 1978, Economic Impact of Environmental Regulations in the U.S. Copper Industry, prepared for the Environmental Protection Agency, Washington, D.C.

Ayres, R.U., Noble, S., and Overly, D., 1971, Effects of Technological Change and Environmental Implications of an Input-Output Analysis for the U.S., 1967-2020, Part I: Technological Change as an Explicit Factor of Economic Growth, prepared for Resources for the Future by International Research and Technology Corp., Washington, D.C.

Bain, J.S., 1956, Barriers to New Competition, Harvard Univ. Press, Cambridge, Mass.

Banks, F.E., 1974, The World Copper Market: An Economic Analysis, Ballinger Publishing Co., Cambridge, Mass.

Barnett, H.J., and Morse, C., 1963, Scarcity and Growth, The Johns Hopkins Univ. Press, Baltimore, Md.

Battelle Columbus Laboratories, June, 1975, Energy Use Patterns in Metallurgical and Non-Metallic Mineral Processing, prepared for the U.S. Bureau of Mines, Washington, D.C.

Bennett, H.J., Moore, L., Welborn, L.E., and Toland, J.E., An Economic Appraisal of the Supply of Copper from Domestic Sources, U.S. Bureau of Mines IC 8598, Washington, D.C.

Box, G.P.E., and Cox, D.R., 1962, "An Analysis of Transformations, (with Discussion)," Journal of the Royal Statistical Society, Series B.

Box, G.E.P. and Jenkins, G.M., 1976, Time Series Analysis: Forecasting and Control, Revised Edition, Holden Day, San Francisco, Calif.

Bravard, J.C., Flora, H.B., and Portal, C., 1972, Energy Expenditures Associated with the Production and Recycling of Metals, Oak Ridge National Laboratory Report ORNL-NSF -EP-24, Oak Ridge, Tenn.

Brown, G.M., and Field, B.C., "Implications of Alternative Measures of Natural Resource Scarcity", 1978, Journal of Political Economy, Vol. 86.

Brown, M.S., and Butler, J., 1969, Production, Marketing, and Consumption of Copper and Aluminum, Praeger.

Brubaker, S., 1967, Trends in the World Aluminum Industry, The Johns Hopkins Univ. Press, Baltimore, Md.

Bureau of the Census, Oct. 1975, 1972 Census of Manufactures, Concentration Ratios in Manufacturing, Washington, D.C.

Chapman, P.F., Feb. 1974, "The Energy Costs of Producing Copper and Aluminum from Primary Sources", Metals and Materials, Vol. 8, No.,2.

_____, June, 1974, "Energy Conservation and Recycling of Copper and Aluminum", Metals and Materials, Vol. 8, No. 6.

Charles River Associates, 1970, An Economic Analysis of the Copper Industry, prepared for the General Services Administration, Washington, D.C.

_____, 1971, An Economic Analysis of the Aluminum Industry, prepared for the General Services Administration, Washington, D.C.

_____, 1976a, Policy Implications of Producer Country Supply Restrictions: The World Aluminum/Bauxite Market, prepared for the National Bureau of Standards, Washington, D.C.

_____, 1976b, Policy Implications of Producer Country Supply Restrictions: The World Copper Market, prepared for the National Bureau of Standards, Washington, D.C.

Christensen, L.R., Jorgenson, D.W., and Lau, L., 1970, "Conjugate Duality and the Transcendental Logarithmic Production Function", Unpublished paper presented at the 2nd World Congress of the Econometric Society, Cambridge, U.K.

COMSHARE, 1976, The Box System, Ann Arbor, Mich.

Copper Development Association, 1954-1976, Annual Data, New York, N.Y.

Copper Range, 1955-1976, Annual Reports, New York, N.Y.

Council on Wage and Price Stability, Seot. 1976, Aluminum Prices 1974-75, Staff Report, Washington, D.C.

Dammert, A., and Kendrick, D., 1977, A World Copper Model, International Bank for Reconstruction and Development, Washington, D.C.

Desai, M., Jan. 1966, "An Econometric Model of the World Tin Industry", Econometrica, Vol. 34, No. 1.

Dhrymes, P.J., and Taylor, J.B., June 1976, "On an Efficient Two-Step Estimator for Dynamic Simultaneous Equations Models With Autoregressive Errors", International Economic Review, Vol. 17, No. 2.

Durbin, J., 1970, "Testing for Serial Correlation in Least Squares Regression When Some of the Regressors are Lagged Dependent Variables", Econometrica, Vol. 38.

Eckstein, O., Oct. 1964, "A Theory of the Wage-Price Process in Modern Industry", Review of Economic Studies, Vol. 31.

Fair, R.C., May 1970, "The Estimation of Simultaneous Equation Models With Lagged Endogenous Variables and Serially Correlated Errors", Econometrica, Vol. 38, No. 3.

Farin, F., and Reibsamen, G.G., 1969, "Aluminum -- Profile of an Industry", Metals Week, McGraw-Hill, New York, N.Y.

Fisher, F.M., Cootner, P.H., and Baily, N.M., Autumn 1972, "An Econometric Model of the World Copper Industry,", The Bell Journal of Economics and Management Science, Vol. 3, No. 2.

Fusfeld, H.I., Nov. 1976, "Energy Use in the Metals Industry", in Proceedings of the Mineral Economics Symposium, A.I.M.E., Washington, D.C.

Godfrey, L.G., Sept.1976, "Testing for Serial Correlation in Dynamic Simultaneous Equation Models," Econometrica, Vol. 44, No. 5.

Gordon, R.L., June 1967, "A Reinterpretation of the Pure Theory of Exhaustion," Journal of Political Economy, Vol. 75.

Guilkey, D.K., July 1975, "A Test for the Presence of First-Order Vector Autoregressive Errors When Lagged Endogenous Variables are Present", Econometrica, Vol. 43, No. 4.

Hall, B.H., May 1977, Time Series Processor, Version 3.3, User's Manual, Cambridge, Mass.

Harper, C.P., Nov. 1977, "Testing for the Existence of a Lagged Relationship Within Almon's Method", Review of Economics and Statistics, Vol. 59, No. 2.

Hatanaka, M., 1976, "Several Efficient Two-Step Estimators for the Dynamic Simultaneous Equations Model With Autoregressive Disturbances", Review of Economics and Statistics, Vol. 57, No. 3.

Herfindahl, O.C., 1959, Copper Costs and Prices: 1870-1957, The Johns Hopkins Univ. Press, Baltimore, Md.

_____, 1967, "Depletion and Economic Theory", in Gaffney, M., editor, Extractive Resources and Taxation, University of Wisconsin Press, Madison, Wisc.

Hotelling, H., April 1931, "The Economics of Exhaustible Resources", The Journal of Political Economy, Vol. 39, No. 2.

Johnston, J., 1972, Econometric Methods, McGraw-Hill, New York, N.Y.

Knight, R., and Davies, B.T., March 1978, "Financial Model Studies in Mineral Exploration", Mining Magazine, Published by Mining Journal, London, U.K.

Koyck, L.M., 1954, Distributed Lags and Investment Analysis, North-Holland Publishing Co., Amsterdam.

Lanzillotti, R.F., Dec. 1958, "Pricing Objectives in Large Companies", American Economic Review, Vol. 48, No. 5.

_____, 1961, "The Aluminum Industry", in Structure of the American Industry, Adams, W., editor, The Macmillan Co., New York, N.Y.

Lindley, D.V., and Smith, A.F.M., 1972, "Bayes Estimates for the Linear Model (With Discussion), Journal of the Royal Statistical Society, B Series.

McDivitt, J.F., and Manners, G., 1974, Minerals and Men, The Johns Hopkins Univ. Press, Baltimore, Md.

McMahon, A.D., 1965, Copper, A Materials Survey, U.S. Bureau of Mines Information Circular 8225, Washington, D.C.

McNicol, D.L., Spring 1975, "The Two Price Systems in the Copper Industry", The Bell Journal of Economics, Vol. 6, No. 1.

Metal's Week, Aug. 1968, "Aluminum Profile of an Industry, Part 2: The Secondary Producers", McGraw-Hill, Vol. 39, No. 33.

Metal's Week, Special Report, June 1977, "The Cost of Producing U.S. Copper: Why Companies are not Expanding".

Mikesell, R.F., July 1978, American Mining Congress Journal.

National Commission on Supplies and Shortages, Dec. 1976, Government and the Nations Resources, Washington, D.C.

National Materials Advisory Board, April 1972, Mutual Substitutability of Aluminum for Copper, Washington, D.C.

Page, N.J., and Creasey, S.C., Jan.-Feb. 1975, "Ore Grade, Metal Production, and Energy", Journal of Research, U.S. Geological Survey, Vol. 3, No. 1.

Peck, M.J., 1961, Competition in the Aluminum Industry, 1945-1958, Harvard Univ. Press, Cambridge, Mass.

Penner, P., and Spek, J.K., 1976, Stockpile Optimization: Energy and Versatility Considerations for Strategic and Critical Materials, Center for Advanced Computation, Univ. of Ill., Urbana, Ill.

Pindyck, Robert S., Autumn 1977, "Cartel Pricing and the Structure of the World Bauxite Market", Bell Journal of Economics, Vol. 8, No. 2.

Prain, R., 1975, Copper, An Anatomy of an Industry, Mining Journal Books Ltd., London, U.K

Rohatgi, P., and Weiss, C., 1974, Technology Forecasting for Commodity Projections: A Case Study of the Effect of Substitution by Aluminum on the Future Demand for Copper, The World Bank Science and Technology Report Series, No. 8.

Saaty,T.L., and Bram,J., 1964, Nonlinear Mathematics, McGraw-Hill, New York, N.Y.

Sargan, J.D., July 1961, "The Maximun Likelihood Estimation of Economic Relationships With Autoregressive Residuals", Econometrica, Vol. 29.

Sato, K., 1967, "A Two-Level Constant Elasticity of Substitution Production Function", Review of Economics and Statistics, Vol. 34.

Schultze, W.D., May 1974, "The Optimal Use of Non-Renewable Resources: The Theory of Extraction", Journal of Environmental Economics and Management, Vol. 58, No. 2.

Shiller, R.J., 1973, "A Distributed Lag Estimator Derived from Smoothness Priors", Econometrica, Vol. 41, No. 4.

Singer, D.A., June 1977, "Long-Term Adequacy of Metal Resources," Resources Policy, Vol. 3, No. 2.

Skinner, B.J., May-June, 1976, "A Second Iron Age Ahead?", American Scientist, Vol. 64.

Smith, V.K., 1978, "Measuring Natural Resource Scarcity: Theory and Practice", Journal of Environmental Economics and Management, Vol. 5.

Solow, R.M., May 1974, "The Economics of Resources or the Resources of Economics", American Economic Review, Vol. 64, No. 2.

Spendlove, M.J., 1961, Methods of Producing Secondary Copper, U.S. Bureau of Mines IC 8002, Washington, D.C.

Synergy, 1977, Final Report for the Joint Copper/Aluminum Forecasting and Simulation Model, prepared for the U.S. Bureau of Mines, Washington, D.C.

Taylor, C.A., 1978, A Quarterly Domestic Copper Industry Model, University of Arizona, Tucson, Arizona.

Tukey, J.W., 1957, "On the Comparative Anatomy of Transformations," Annals of Mathematical Statistics.

U.S. Bureau of Mines, 1954-1976, Minerals Yearbook, Washington, D.C.

_____, 1978, Mineral Commodity Profiles, Washington, D.C.

Vogely, W.A., editor, Dec. 1975, Mineral Materials Modeling, A State of the Art Review, Resources For the Future, The Johns Hopkins Univ. Press, Baltimore Md.

APPENDICES

Appendix A: Variable Names

In this appendix, each variable that appears in a model equation in the text is listed alphabetically. The variable name is followed by a brief description of the variable; its name in the computer printouts; whether it is endogenous (N), exogenous (X), or from an identity (I); the number of the equation that defines the variable in the text; and the number of the page where the equation can be found. All identities are endogenous. However, a variable is classified as endogenous if it is defined by an estimated (stochastic) equation and as an identity if it is defined by an exact (nonsotchastic) equation.

Symbol	Definition	Code name	Type	Reference
c	Apparent consumption $C=Qp+Qos+Qns+(M-X)-\Delta\,In$	AAC,CAC	I I^1	
C1	Copper consumption, 1th sector	CCBC,CCT CCCD,CCEE CCME	N	V:3:9- V:3:13
Cca_1	Consumption of copper and aluminum, 1th sector	CABC,CAT CACD,CAEE CAME	N	V:3:9- V:3:13 245
Cc/a_1	Copper-aluminum consumption ratio 1th sector	CRBC,CRT CRCD,CREE CRME	N	V:2:12- V:2:16 228
CBY	Corporate bond yield	CBY	X	
Dcs	Dummy variable, copper strike	DCS	X	
Dpc	Dummy variable, price controls	DPC	X	
Dn	Dummy variable, year n	D66,D74 D75	X	
In	Inventories In=Inp+Ing	AIN CIN	N	VI:1:7 264
Ing	Government inventories	AING,CING	X	
Inp	Private inventories	AINP	I	
IP	Index of industrial production	CINP IPI	N X	VI:1:6 261
(M-X)	Net Imports	ANTIMP CNTIMP	I	VI:2:1 267

A-2

Symbol	Description	Variable(s)	Type	Reference	Page
		...SATI... (header cut off)			
Pe	Energy price index	EEEPID EID	X	III:4:7	110
P1	Price of the ith sectors output	CMEPID,TMEPID CDPID,EMEPID MEPID,MCPID	X	III:4:6	105
Pp	Primary price	APPD CPPD	N	IV:3:3	176
Ps	Secondary price	ASPD CSPD	N	IV:3:2	175
Pw1	Weighted average of copper and aluminum prices, ith sector	PWBC,PWT PWCD,PWT PWME PWEE	I	V:3:8	243
Tr/E	After-tax profits/equity, All manufacturing	RPSE	X	IV:4:3	182
Qns	Secondary production, new scrap	AQNS CQNS	N	IV:4:2	181
Qos	Secondary production, old scrap	AQOS CQOS	N	IV:4:12	191
Qp	Primary production	AQP CQP	N	IV:4:13	192
SS	Stocks of scrap	APOS,CPOS	I	III:5:10	134
t	Time	TIME	X	III:5:7	131
W/LP	Wages/labor productivity	AWCLP,CWCLP	X	IV:4:10-	186-
Y	Yield of copper ores	YIELD	X	IV:4:11	187

1 Copper and aluminum consumption in each sector (C1 and A1) are computed from the derived demand and elasticity of substitution equations.

Appendix B: Model Equations

All of the equations and the most important identities in the CAS model are listed in this appendix. The aluminum-industry equations are shown first, followed by the copper-industry equations. The final equations are those that link the two models (the derived demand and elasticity of substitution equations). Two of the equations listed -- the total (aggregated over sectors) derived demand and elasticity of substitution equations -- are not used in the simulations but are shown for reference purposes.

Aluminum Industry Equations

$$\hat{P}pa = -49.5 + .83\ Pp\hat{a}_{-1} - .007\ In\hat{a}_{-1} - .004\ (Ma\hat{-}Xa)_{-1} + .64\ \Pi/E + 4.4\ Wa/LPa$$
$$\quad\quad\ \ (6.5)\quad\quad\quad\ (-7.6)\quad\quad\ (-2.9)\quad\quad\quad\quad (3.7)\quad\quad\quad\ \ (7.0)$$

$$+ 11.6\ Pea + .65\ Pb + 12.2\ Pca - 3.1\ Dpc$$
$$\ \ (3.5)\quad\quad (2.7)\quad\quad (5.7)\quad\quad (-4.5)$$

$$R^2 = .96\quad\quad DW = 2.8\quad\quad F = 31\quad\quad \rho = -.70\quad\quad Years:\ 1955\text{-}76$$

$$ln\hat{Q}pa = 2.8 - .25\ lnP\hat{P}a + .97\ lnIP + .20\ lnQp\hat{a}_{-1}$$
$$\quad\quad\quad\quad (-1.4)\quad\quad\ (4.9)\quad\quad (1.5)$$

$$R^2 = .98\quad\quad DW = 1.9\quad\quad F = 407\quad\quad Years:\ 1954\text{-}76$$

$$\hat{Ps}a = 5.4 + .56\ Ppa + .052\ IP + 7.0\ D74$$
$$\quad\quad\quad (4.2)\quad\quad (3.7)\quad\quad (9.7)$$

$$R^2 = .88\quad\quad DW = 1.7\quad\quad F = 38\quad\quad \rho = .33\quad\quad Years:\ 1957\text{-}76$$

$$ln\hat{Qn}sa = -1.9 + 1.01\ lnCa\quad\quad\quad (Qnsa = .15\ Ca)$$
$$\quad\quad (-5.6)\ (24.2)$$

$$R^2 = .97\quad\quad DW = 1.5\quad\quad F = 585\quad\quad Years:\ 1954\text{-}76$$

$$ln\hat{Qo}sa = -6.3 + 1.3\ lnSsa + .24\ lnPsa + .47\ lnPea - .99\ lnCBY$$
$$\quad\quad\quad\quad (9.5)\quad\quad\quad (1.01)\quad\quad\ (1.7)\quad\quad\ (-4.1)$$

$$R^2 = .95\quad\quad DW = 2.1\quad\quad F = 87\quad\quad \rho = -.22\quad\quad Years:\ 1954\text{-}76$$

$$SSa = SSa_{-1} + .36\ Ca_{-31} + .11\ Ca_{-21} + .20\ Ca_{-18} + .09\ Ca_{-6} + .21\ Ca_{-1} - Qosa_{-1}$$

$$Ina = Ina_{-1} + \Delta Ina$$

$$\Delta I\hat{n}a = -885.4 + 45.2\ P\hat{p}a - .60\ (Ca-Qpa-\hat{Q}osa-Qnsa) - 144\ (Ina/Ca)_{-1}$$
$$\quad\quad\quad\quad (2.1)\quad\quad\ (-5.1)\quad\quad\quad\quad\quad\quad\quad\quad\quad (-1.5)$$

$$R^2 = .81\quad\quad DW = 2.2\quad\quad F = 26\quad\quad Years:\ 1955\text{-}76$$

$$(Ma-Xa) = Ca - Qpa - Qosa - Qnsa + \Delta Ina$$

Copper Industry Equations

$$\ln \hat{P}pc = -2.1 - .17 \ln t + .31 \ln \hat{Q}pc - .14 \ln Inp\hat{c}/Cc - 1.4 \ln Y + .46 \ln \Pi /E$$
$$\quad (-2.4) \quad\quad (5.7) \quad\quad\quad (-2.8) \quad\quad\quad (-22) \quad\quad (7.8)$$

$$+ 1.7 \ln Wc/LPc + .46 \ln Pcc + .11 \ln Pec$$
$$\quad (7.3) \quad\quad\quad (6.2) \quad\quad\quad (.95)$$

$$R^2 = .98 \quad DW = 2.5 \quad F = 52 \quad \rho_1 = -1.2 \quad \rho_2 = -.44 \quad 1954\text{-}69,\ 71\text{-}76$$

$$\hat{Q}pc = 1163 + 6.9\ \hat{P}pc - 1271\ Inp\hat{c}/Cc + 3.0\ IP - .62\ Dcs \times Qpc_{-1} + .064\ \hat{Q}pc_{-1}$$
$$\quad\quad\quad (2.1) \quad\quad (-3.5) \quad\quad\quad (2.5) \quad\quad (-10.7) \quad\quad\quad\quad (.72)$$

$$R^2 = .92 \quad\quad DW = 2.4 \quad\quad F = 36 \quad\quad \rho = .49 \quad\quad \text{Years: } 1954\text{-}76$$

$$\ln \hat{P}sc = -9.3 + 1.15\ \ln Ppc + 1.8\ \ln IP - .30\ \ln \hat{P}sc_{-1} + .24\ D66$$
$$\quad\quad\quad (4.0) \quad\quad\quad (2.6) \quad\quad (-2.1) \quad\quad\quad (2.5)$$

$$R^2 = .79 \quad\quad DW = 2.1 \quad\quad F = 16 \quad\quad \rho = .94 \quad\quad \text{Years: } 1954\text{-}76$$

$$Qn\hat{s}c = .25\ Cc$$
$$\quad\quad (25)$$

$$R^2 = .97 \quad\quad DW = 2.0 \quad\quad \rho = .83 \quad\quad \text{Years: } 1954\text{-}76$$

$$\ln \hat{Q}osc = 4.2 + .11\ \ln SSc + .29\ \ln Psc - .47\ \ln Pec$$
$$\quad\quad\quad (3.3) \quad\quad\quad (7.0) \quad\quad\quad (-4.9)$$

$$R^2 = .88 \quad\quad DW = 2.0 \quad\quad F = 47 \quad\quad \text{Years: } 1954\text{-}76$$

$$SSc = SSc_{-1} + .47\ Cc_{-31} + .16\ Cc_{-21} + .14\ Cc_{-18} + .22\ Cc_{-6} - Qosc_{-1}$$

$$In\hat{p}c = -293 + .71\ Inp\hat{c}_{-1} + 11\ \hat{P}pc - .26\ (Cc - Qpc - \hat{Q}osc - Qnsc + Ingc)$$
$$\quad\quad\quad (1.5) \quad\quad\quad (1.7) \quad\quad (-2.3)$$

$$R^2 = .67 \quad\quad DW = 2.0 \quad\quad F = 11 \quad\quad \rho = .73 \quad\quad \text{Years: } 1955\text{-}76$$

$$(Mc - Xc) = Cc - Qpc - Qosc - Qnsc + \Delta_{Inc}$$

Elasticity of Substitution Equations

$$\hat{Cc/a_i} = c_i + \sum_{j=0}^{3} \sigma_{ij}(Ppa/Ppc)_{t-j} \qquad \sigma ca_i = \sum_{j=0}^{3} \sigma_{ij}$$

	c_i	$\sigma i0$	$\sigma i1$	$\sigma i2$	$\sigma i3$	R^2	DW	ρi
Total	.111	.127 (1.3)	.211 (2.2)	.331 (3.5)	.439 (3.6)	.97	2.1	
Building	.075	.389 (2.4)	.271 (1.9)	.295 (1.9)	.274 (1.6)	.93	2.4	.40
Transport	-.625	.171 (1.3)	.101 (.92)	.075 (.62)	.284 (2.1)	.91	1.5	.47
Consumer	.581	.488 (2.7)				.61	1.6	.62
Machinery	1.08	-.174 (-.90)	.251 (1.3)	.445 (2.4)	.670 (2.8)	.92	1.8	
Electrical	.535	.111 (.76)	.320 (2.6)	.315 (2.3)	.063 (.44)	.93	1.6	.65

$$A_i = Cca_i/(1 + Cc/a_i)$$
$$C_i = Cc/a_i \; Cca_i/(1+Cc/a_i) \qquad i = b, t, c, e, m$$
$$Ca = Ab + At + Ac + Am + Ae + Acp + Ao \; [2]$$
$$Cc = Cb + Ct + Cc + Cm + Ce \; [2]$$

---

[2]   In the simulations, total consumption is computed by summing consumption over sectors. However, a different definition of consumption was used in estimating the price and output equations. (See section V:1).

Derived Demand Equations -- Copper and Aluminum

$$\ln \widehat{Cca}_i = c_{10} + c_{11} \ln IP + c_{12} \ln \widehat{Pw}_i + c_{13} \ln P_i + c_{14} D75 + c_{15} \ln \widehat{Cca}_{i-1}$$

Sector	c_i	IP	Pw_i	P_i	D75	Cca_{i-1}	R^2	F	DW	ρ_i	Years
Total	4.27	.82 (5.0)	-.42 (-1.9)		-.32 (-5.0)	.26 (1.8)	.97	78	1.8		61-76
Building	-3.71	-.20 (-.57)	-1.4 (-5.1)	2.3 (3.3)	-.59 (-6.9)	.85 (3.4)	.94	24	2.3	-.53	62-76
Transport	2.8	1.0 (5.7)	-1.6 (-4.4)	.83 (1.8)	-.33 (-4.1)	.19 (1.4)	.94	33	1.7		61-76
Consumer	-3.2	.88 (4.1)	-1.1 (-3.1)	1.2 (2.9)	-.28 (-3.2)	.63 (3.6)	.90	14	2.0	-.24	62-76
Electric	-.28	.62 (2.1)	-.35 (-.85)	.38 (.81)	-.40 (-3.7)	.58 (2.8)	.94	30	1.8		61-76
Machinery	3.5	.42 (3.8)	-.62 (-2.8)		-.54 (-6.2)	.53 (3.5)	.84	12	2.2	-.31	62-76
Container[3]	-4.3	.73 (1.7)	-.06 (-.26)	.68 (.73)		.69 (4.2)	.99	170	1.9	-.52	62-76

$$\ln \widehat{Ao} = -6.4 \; \underset{(-9.1)}{-3.7 \ln t} + \underset{(10.2)}{5.0 \ln IP}$$

$R^2 = .91$ DW = 1.5   F = 58   Years: 1960-76

---

3   Aluminum only.

Appendix C: Data Sources and Listing

This appendix contains three tables. The first table lists
all data sources. The second table contains the name of each
variable in the model, a brief description of the variable and
its data source. And the final table lists the data, with the
name of the variable on the top and the year of the observation
on the left-hand side of each column.

TABLE C.1
DATA SOURCES

AA   The Aluminum Association, Aluminum Statistical
            Review

BLS EE   Bureau of Labor Statistics, Employment and Earnings

BLS PT   Bureau of Labor Statistics, Office of Productivity
            and Technology

BOM   Bureau of Mines, Minerals Yearbook

C   Variable constructed from other data

CDA   Copper Development Association, Annual Data

CPI   Bureau of Labor Statistics, Consumer Price Index

EEI   Edison Electric Institute, Statistical Yearbook

FED   Board of Governors of the Federal Reserve System,
            Industrial Production

FTC   Federal Trade Commission

MOODYS   Moodys Investor Service, Moodys Bond Survey

MS   American Metal Market, Metal Statistics

WPI   Bureau of Labor Statistics, Wholesale Price Index

Variable Name	Description	Data Source
APP	Aluminum primary price	BOM
ASP	Aluminum secondary price	MS
AQP	Aluminum primary production	BOM
AQOS	Aluminum production, old scrap	AA
AQNS	Aluminum production, new scrap	AA
AIMP	Aluminum imports	BOM
AEXP	Aluminum exports	BOM
AAC	Aluminum apparent consumption	C
ACBC	Aluminum consumption in building and construction	AA
ACT	Aluminum consumption in transportation	AA
ACCD	Aluminum consumption in consumer durables	AA
ACME	Aluminum consumption in industrial machinery and equipment	AA
ACEE	Aluminum consumption in electrical machinery and equipment	AA
ACCP	Aluminum consumption in containers and packaging	AA
ACO	Aluminum consumption, other	AA
AINP	Aluminum inventories, private	AA
AING	Aluminum inventories, government	AA
CPP	Copper primary price	BOM
CSP	Copper # 2 scrap price	BOM
CYIELD	Average yield of copper ores mined	BOM
CQP	Copper primary production	BOM
CQOS	Copper production, old scrap	CDA
CQNS	Copper production, new scrap	CDA
CIMP	Copper imports	BOM
CEXP	Copper exports	BOM
CAC	Copper apparent consumption	C
CCBC	Copper consumption in building and construction	CDA
CCT	Copper consumption in transportation	CDA
CCCD	Copper consumption in consumer durables	CDA
CCME	Copper consumption in industrial machinery and equipment	CDA
CCEE	Copper consumption in electrical machinery and equipment	CDA
CINP	Copper inventories, private	CDA
CING	Copper inventories, government	CDA

WPI	Wholesale-price index	WPI
RPSE	Ratio of after-tax profits to stockholders equity, all manufacturing	FTC
CBY	AAA corporate bond yield	MOODYS
AHEPA	Average hourly earnings, primary aluminum	BLS EE 1964-76 [1]
LPIPA	Labor productivity index, primary aluminum	BLS PT
BP	Price of crude domestic undried bauxite	BOM
EEEPI	Electricity price index, commercial and industrial large light and power	EEI
HAPI	Hydrofluoric acid price index	WPI 0611 0329 1959-1973 [2] WPI 0613 0222 1974-76
AHECM	Average hourly earnings, copper mining	BLS EE
AHEPM	Average hourly earnings, primary metals	BLS EE
LPICM	Labor productivity index, copper mining	BLS PT
LPIPC	Labor productivity index, primary copper	BLS PT
NGPI	Natural gas price index	WPI 0531 0101 1958-76 [3]
RFPI	Residual fuel oil price index	WPI 0574
MDPI	Middle distillate price index	WPI 0573
SAPI	Sulfuric acid price index	WPI 0611 0335 1947-73 WPI 0613 0281 1974-1976
IPI	Index of industrial production	FED
CMEPI	Construction machinery and equipment price index	WPI 112
TMEPI	Transportation machinery and equipment price index	WPI 14
CDPI	Consumer durable commodities price index	CPI K2
EMEPI	Electrical machinery and equipment price index	WPI 117
MCPI	Metal container price index	WPI 103
DCS	Dummy, copper strike	
DPC	Dummy, price controls	

1   For years prior to 1964, AHEPA was regressed on AHEPM
and backcasted. The backcasting equation is

$$\hat{AHEPA} = -.306 + 1.124 \text{ AHEPM}$$
$$(148)$$

$$R^2 = .999 \qquad DW = 1.5 \qquad F = 21962$$

2   For years prior to 1959, HAPI was regressed on the price
of fluorspar (FP, from BOM) and backcasted. Because
fluorspar is the raw material, lagged values of FP were
used in the regression. The backcasting equation is

$$\hat{HAPI} = .197 + .006 \text{ FP} + .021 \text{ FP}_{-1} - .012 \text{ FP}_{-2}$$
$$(1.4) \qquad (3.2) \qquad (-1.9)$$

$$R^2 = .97 \qquad DW = 1.2 \qquad F = 130 \qquad \rho = .41$$

3   For years prior to 1958, the price index for natural gas
from Gas Facts, The American Gas Association, was used.

Year	1	2	3	4	5	6
1959	26.9000	23.4000	1953.00	104.000	343.000	196.000
1960	26.0000	24.7000	2014.00	95.0000	343.000	255.000
1961	25.5000	22.6000	1904.00	156.000	330.000	377.000
1962	23.9000	21.2000	2118.00	167.000	416.000	466.000
1963	22.6000	21.1000	2313.00	159.000	495.000	453.000
1964	23.7000	22.1000	2553.00	162.000	545.000	620.000
1965	23.7000	24.2000	2754.00	205.000	624.000	679.000
1966	24.5000	24.7000	2968.00	187.000	700.000	539.000
1967	25.0000	24.8000	3269.00	175.000	700.000	793.000
1968	25.6000	25.0000	3255.00	181.000	704.000	558.000
1969	27.2000	26.8000	3793.00	200.000	816.000	468.000
1970	28.7000	27.7000	3976.00	197.000	950.000	690.000
1971	29.0000	27.9000	3925.00	216.000	803.000	794.000
1972	26.3000	27.0000	4122.00	250.000	834.000	614.000
1973	25.3000	30.6000	4529.00	258.000	876.000	629.000
1974	34.1000	50.2000	4903.00	304.000	977.000	550.000
1975	39.8000	43.9000	3879.00	519.000	978.000	749.000
1976	44.7000	47.8000	4251.00	416.000	863.000	1030.00

Table C:3   Listing of Data

Year	1	2	3	4	5	6
1954	50.0000	1402.00	0.000000	0.000000	0.000000	0.000000
1955	34.0000	2019.00	0.000000	0.000000	0.000000	0.000000
1956	68.0000	2196.00	0.000000	0.000000	0.000000	0.000000
1957	63.0000	1872.00	0.000000	0.000000	0.000000	0.000000
1958	82.0000	1802.00	0.000000	0.000000	0.000000	0.000000
1959	164.000	2490.00	0.000000	0.000000	0.000000	0.000000
1960	384.000	2072.00	608.500	427.500	166.500	0.000000
1961	238.000	2406.00	662.500	256.500	187.000	0.000000
1962	259.000	2844.00	718.500	501.000	278.000	0.000000
1963	292.000	3182.00	630.000	630.000	316.000	208.000
1964	349.000	3419.00	800.000	714.500	331.000	231.500
1965	315.000	3957.00	879.500	751.000	383.000	252.000
1966	330.000	4520.00	961.000	898.000	430.000	288.500
1967	366.000	4127.00	992.000	975.500	455.000	327.000
1968	351.000	4713.00	964.500	889.500	415.500	308.500
1969	575.000	5036.00	1125.00	989.000	493.500	339.000
1970	612.000	4556.00	1187.50	993.000	531.000	350.000
1971	293.000	5052.00	1125.50	773.000	466.000	302.500
1972	329.000	5801.00	1393.00	898.500	486.000	321.500
1973	561.000	6795.00	1597.00	1112.00	563.500	375.000
1974	524.000	6406.00	1813.00	1406.50	669.500	474.500
1975	439.000	4752.00	1572.50	1220.50	580.000	522.500
1976	481.000	6185.00	1478.50	1227.00	517.500	452.000

Year	1	2	3	4	5
1956	0.000000	0.000000	0.000000	1598.00	1057.00
1957	0.000000	0.000000	0.000000	1667.00	1404.00
1958	0.000000	0.000000	0.000000	1642.00	1758.00
1959	0.000000	0.000000	0.000000	1608.00	1841.00
1960	264.000	160.500	174.000	1756.00	1885.00
1961	307.000	175.500	211.000	1704.00	1937.00
1962	337.500	189.500	280.000	1637.U0	1978.00
1963	355.500	248.000	273.500	1596.00	1925.00
1964	419.000	287.000	323.000	1594.00	1889.U0
1965	541.000	328.000	341.500	1561.00	1563.00
1966	650.000	370.000	454.000	1571.00	1502.00
1967	624.000	434.000	508.500	1825.00	1446.00
1968	656.500	513.000	549.000	1862.00	1306.00
1969	712.500	597.500	537.500	1892.00	1281.00
1970	679.500	733.500	395.500	2193.00	1281.00
1971	711.500	756.000	362.500	2513.00	545.000
1972	768.000	905.500	422.500	2431.00	1275.00
1973	927.000	1028.00	555.000	2183.00	545.000
1974	922.000	1132.50	444.000	2578.00	34.0000
1975	608.000	1000.50	268.000	3000.00	32.0000
1976	664.000	1285.00	345.500	2820.00	23.0000

Year	1	2	3	4	5	6
1954	29.5000	24.6000	.830000	1212.00	503.000	477.000
1955	37.3000	33.6000	.830000	1342.00	606.000	496.000
1956	42.5000	31.6000	.780000	1443.00	554.000	501.000
1957	30.1000	20.1000	.770000	1454.00	510.000	452.000
1958	26.3000	17.6000	.790000	1353.00	489.000	434.000
1959	30.7000	22.6000	.740000	1098.00	557.000	509.000
1960	32.1000	21.2000	.730000	1519.00	488.000	494.000
1961	30.0000	21.8000	.750000	1550.00	477.000	471.000
1962	30.8000	21.6000	.750000	1612.00	486.000	540.000
1963	30.8000	22.2000	.740000	1596.00	511.000	590.000
1964	32.6000	26.0000	.730000	1656.00	571.000	675.000
1965	35.4000	34.5000	.700000	1712.00	614.000	776.000
1966	36.6000	44.7000	.670000	1711.00	634.000	828.000
1967	38.6000	33.2000	.630000	1133.00	579.000	684.000
1968	42.2000	32.8000	.600000	1437.00	609.000	731.000
1969	47.9000	42.9000	.600000	1743.00	692.000	818.000
1970	58.2000	39.5000	.590000	1765.00	627.000	746.000
1971	52.0000	27.6000	.550000	1592.00	555.000	763.000
1972	51.2000	31.4000	.550000	1873.00	561.000	867.000
1973	59.5000	49.8000	.530000	1868.00	582.000	916.000
1974	77.3000	54.9000	.490000	1655.00	569.000	883.000
1975	64.2000	33.9000	.470000	1443.00	440.000	608.000
1976	69.6000	49.6000	.510000	1537.00	483.000	730.000

Year	1	2	3	4	5	6
1956	192.000	223.000	2350.00	0.000000	0.000000	0.000000
1957	162.000	346.000	2110.00	0.000000	0.000000	0.000000
1958	128.000	385.000	1985.00	0.000000	0.000000	0.000000
1959	214.000	159.000	2247.00	0.000000	0.000000	0.000000
1960	143.000	434.000	2131.00	488.500	287.000	410.000
1961	67.0000	429.000	2216.00	530.500	285.000	431.500
1962	99.0000	337.000	2349.00	596.500	317.500	468.000
1963	119.000	311.000	2577.00	317.500	336.500	493.000
1964	138.000	316.000	2636.00	636.500	375.500	575.500
1965	316.000	325.000	2713.00	713.500	392.000	639.000
1966	137.000	273.000	3016.00	736.500	409.500	780.500
1967	164.000	159.000	3438.00	799.500	325.500	726.000
1968	331.000	214.000	2808.00	650.000	356.000	772.500
1969	400.000	200.000	2969.00	650.500	381.500	807.000
1970	131.000	221.000	3178.00	710.500	312.500	644.500
1971	132.000	188.000	2858.00	611.500	350.500	633.500
1972	164.000	185.000	2975.00	686.500	417.000	718.000
1973	192.000	189.000	3348.00	763.000	460.000	764.000
1974	203.000	127.000	3502.00	839.000	392.000	663.500
1975	314.000	172.000	3257.00	662.500	286.000	563.500
1976	147.000	115.000	2316.00	567.000	417.000	630.000
	384.000		2896.00	696.500		
	1	2	3	4	5	6

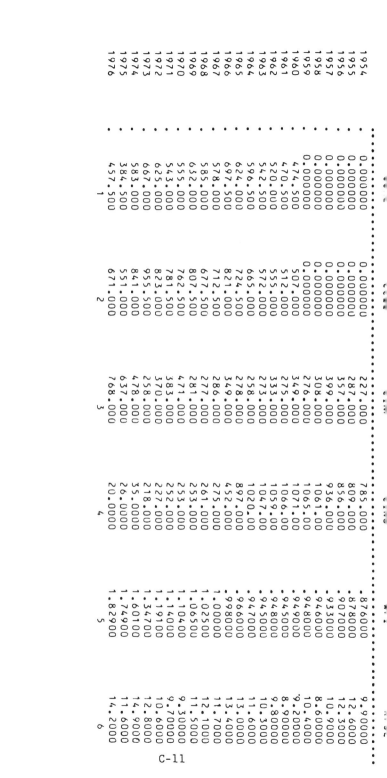

Year	1	2	3	4	5	6
1954	0.000000	0.000000	227.000	785.000	.876000	9.90000
1955	0.000000	0.000000	287.000	809.000	.878000	12.6000
1956	0.000000	0.000000	357.000	856.000	.907000	12.3000
1957	0.000000	0.000000	399.000	936.000	.933000	10.9000
1958	0.000000	0.000000	308.000	1061.000	.946000	8.60000
1959	0.000000	0.000000	276.000	1065.00	.948000	10.4000
1960	507.000	512.000	349.000	1071.00	.949000	9.20000
1961	474.500	555.000	275.000	1066.00	.945000	8.90000
1962	470.500	572.000	333.000	1059.00	.948000	9.80000
1963	520.000	665.000	273.000	1047.00	.945000	10.3000
1964	542.500	724.500	258.000	1020.00	.947000	11.6000
1965	596.500	821.000	278.000	897.000	.966000	13.0000
1966	697.500	697.500	349.000	452.000	.998000	13.4000
1967	578.000	712.500	286.000	275.000	1.000000	11.7000
1968	585.000	677.500	277.000	261.000	1.025000	11.0000
1969	632.000	807.500	281.000	253.000	1.065000	12.1000
1970	543.000	762.500	471.000	253.000	1.104000	11.5000
1971	555.000	781.500	383.000	252.000	1.140000	9.30000
1972	625.000	823.000	370.000	227.000	1.191000	9.70000
1973	667.000	955.500	258.000	218.000	1.347000	10.6000
1974	583.000	841.000	478.000	35.0000	1.601000	12.8000
1975	384.500	551.000	637.000	26.0000	1.749000	11.6000
1976	457.500	671.000	768.000	20.0000	1.829000	14.2000

	1	2	3	4	5	6
1956	3.36000	2.35000	.588000	6.94000	1.02220	.834000
1957	3.89000	2.50000	.597000	7.75000	1.04440	.979000
1958	3.79000	2.66000	.682000	7.66000	1.07780	1.07100
1959	4.38000	2.31000	.786000	8.98000	1.06670	1.16700
1960	4.41000	2.85000	.830000	9.51000	1.07780	1.01400
1961	4.35000	2.95000	.875000	9.78000	1.07780	.936000
1962	4.33000	3.04000	.904000	9.53000	1.06670	.889000
1963	4.26000	3.11000	.932000	9.57000	1.03330	.889000
1964	4.40000	3.22000	.944000	9.55000	1.01110	.889000
1965	4.49000	3.25000	.970000	9.52000	1.00000	1.00000
1966	5.13000	3.35000	1.00700	9.70000	1.00000	1.00000
1967	5.51000	3.43000	1.00000	9.70000	.988900	1.11600
1968	6.18000	3.71000	.945000	11.4600	1.00000	1.00000
1969	7.03000	3.96000	1.02500	11.5000	1.01110	1.11800
1970	8.04000	4.09000	1.06200	11.8800	1.05560	1.25700
1971	7.39000	4.45000	1.17300	11.8200	1.14440	1.40400
1972	7.21000	4.95000	1.16700	10.6000	1.21110	1.43600
1973	7.44000	5.37000	1.11800	11.5800	1.30000	1.43600
1974	8.57000	6.06000	1.23700	11.0100	1.72220	1.48200
1975	8.83000	6.63000	1.12800	11.5000	2.13330	1.93400
1976	8.43000	7.29000	1.06300	11.3000	2.30000	2.08800

	AHECM	AHEPM	LPICM	LPIPC	NGPI	RFPI
1954	2.01000	2.10000	.499000	.807000	.610000	.916000
1955	2.13000	2.24000	.564000	.886000	.620000	1.02800
1956	2.25000	2.36000	.575000	.891000	.660000	1.17000
1957	2.34000	2.50000	.651000	.907000	.730000	1.38800
1958	2.39000	2.64000	.698000	.914000	.752000	1.09600
1959	2.48000	2.77000	.715000	.752000	.832000	1.02900
1960	2.63000	2.81000	.733000	.867000	.905000	1.09700
1961	2.73000	2.90000	.752000	.944000	.949000	1.13300
1962	2.82000	2.98000	.823000	.990000	.968000	1.11500
1963	2.89000	3.04000	.820000	1.04800	.975000	1.07600
1964	3.04000	3.11000	.935000	1.06400	.977000	1.04800
1965	3.15000	3.18000	.962000	1.02000	.978000	1.05000
1966	3.22000	3.28000	1.01900	1.13100	.986000	1.07700
1967	3.26000	3.34000	1.00000	1.16000	1.00000	1.00000
1968	3.44000	3.55000	1.06200	1.12800	1.01600	.957000
1969	3.65000	3.79000	1.08300	1.13800	1.03200	.933000
1970	3.93000	3.93000	1.15200	1.11400	1.06100	1.25500
1971	4.16000	4.23000	1.21200	1.19200	1.12800	1.66000
1972	4.62000	4.67000	1.18100	1.29400	1.21000	1.53800
1973	4.78000	5.04000	1.17700	1.36700	1.31300	1.90400
1974	5.51000	5.60000	1.17600	1.26700	1.54600	1.85400
1975	6.33000	6.17000	1.28900	1.27800	2.15300	4.95500
1976	7.00000	6.80000	1.53200	1.46000	2.92000	4.52900
	1	2	3	4	5	6

	1	2	3	4	6
1956	.978000	.796000	61.1000	72.6000	91.5000
1957	1.03200	.796000	61.9000	78.2000	94.4000
1958	.946000	.796000	57.9000	81.2000	95.9000
1959	.961000	.796000	64.8000	84.1000	97.3000
1960	.905000	.796000	66.2000	85.9000	96.7000
1961	.949000	.796000	66.7000	87.3000	96.6000
1962	.936000	.796000	72.2000	87.5000	97.6000
1963	.939000	.796000	76.5000	89.0000	97.9000
1964	.865000	.796000	81.7000	91.0000	98.8000
1965	.919000	.837000	91.2000	93.6000	98.4000
1966	.937000	.900000	89.3000	96.5000	98.5000
1967	1.00000	1.00000	97.8000	100.000	100.000
1968	1.01900	1.13900	100.000	105.700	103.100
1969	1.02400	1.15000	106.300	110.400	107.000
1970	1.06500	1.15000	111.100	115.900	111.800
1971	1.10300	1.11900	107.800	121.800	116.500
1972	1.11300	1.11900	109.600	125.700	118.900
1973	1.39700	1.15200	119.700	130.700	121.900
1974	2.72000	1.42100	129.800	152.300	130.600
1975	3.09400	1.90200	129.300	185.200	145.500
1976	3.37000	1.95100	117.800	198.600	154.300

Not for publication

Year	1	2	3	4
1954	81.8000	81.?000	0.000000	0.000000
1955	82.9000	77.4000	0.000000	0.000000
1956	89.5000	82.4000	0.000000	0.000000
1957	96.4000	88.0000	0.000000	0.000000
1958	98.4000	90.6000	0.500000	0.000000
1959	99.9000	89.5000	0.000000	0.000000
1960	99.5000	89.6000	0.000000	0.000000
1961	98.2000	91.2000	0.000000	0.000000
1962	96.7000	92.7000	0.000000	0.000000
1963	96.7000	93.6000	0.000000	0.000000
1964	95.7000	94.3000	0.000000	0.000000
1965	95.1000	96.2000	0.000000	0.000000
1966	97.2000	98.3000	0.000000	0.000000
1967	100.0000	100.7000	0.000000	0.000000
1968	101.3000	103.7000	0.250000	0.000000
1969	102.9000	106.9000	0.500000	0.000000
1970	106.4000	112.6000	0.000000	0.000000
1971	109.2000	121.800	0.167000	0.000000
1972	110.4000	128.900	0.000000	0.000000
1973	112.4000	134.700	0.167000	0.000000
1974	125.000	164.700	0.000000	1.000000
1975	140.700	192.100	0.167000	1.000000
1976	146.600	202.300	0.000000	0.000000

Appendix D: Computer Printouts of the Model Simulations

Computer printouts of each of the six model simulations described in chapter VII are shown in this appendix. The left-hand
side of each table shows the year of the simulated values. The
variable names (as described in appendix A) are printed at the top
of each table. A "D" after a variable name implies that the variable was deflated by the wholesale price index, and an "S" after a
variable name indicates that the simulated, not the historic value
is shown. For example, if APP stands for aluminum primary price,
then APPDS means the simulated value of deflated aluminum primary
price.

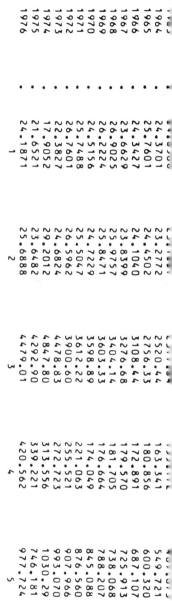

	1	2	3	4	5
1964	24.3701	23.2772	2520.44	163.341	549.721
1965	25.7601	24.4502	2756.33	180.856	600.320
1966	24.3427	24.1040	3108.44	172.891	687.107
1967	23.6629	23.8399	3276.68	179.570	725.913
1968	26.9025	25.9757	3404.14	181.705	738.068
1969	26.2224	25.8471	3603.33	176.664	788.207
1970	24.5156	24.7229	3598.89	174.049	845.088
1971	25.7488	25.5047	3612.22	221.063	876.560
1972	26.7601	26.5962	3900.60	255.521	907.966
1973	22.3827	24.6824	4478.83	272.723	993.070
1974	17.9052	29.2012	4847.80	313.556	1030.29
1975	21.6521	23.6482	4292.90	339.221	746.181
1976	24.1871	25.6888	4479.01	420.562	977.724

I: The Dynamic Simulation of the Historic Period 1962 - 1976

D-2

Year			
1962	15.7449	61.8946	2742.80
1963	-14.6315	73.1405	3050.26
1964	-66.2615	119.853	3419.61
1965	13.8342	206.799	3730.47
1966	-98.7586	195.756	4262.95
1967	-123.237	195.380	4500.78
1968	73.4831	324.816	4575.24
1969	4.81075	318.851	4882.24
1970	-243.379	368.838	5230.25
1971	-234.133	478.703	5422.67
1972	-82.3587	468.175	5614.62
1973	-179.641	210.097	6134.36
1974	-240.549	-70.7219	6361.47
1975	486.688	-266.681	4624.93
1976	18.9331	182.320	6040.68
	1	2	3

ACOS

Year	1	2	3	4	5	6
1966	1035.30	938.931	465.976	322.867	606.061	406.031
1967	1144.74	949.353	498.048	326.713	606.285	473.165
1968	1139.46	859.375	491.300	327.879	713.810	550.190
1969	1187.02	923.193	520.963	350.433	767.948	622.471
1970	1423.50	1018.16	559.303	387.300	812.001	663.032
1971	1596.65	971.778	567.806	382.401	828.525	739.165
1972	1539.48	956.301	573.426	374.023	851.180	875.445
1973	1446.88	1202.30	620.357	403.453	924.738	965.256
1974	1467.81	1328.43	603.393	413.495	984.384	1081.25
1975	1053.06	844.511	404.539	277.258	676.962	1106.43
1976	1434.13	1228.49	484.251	430.204	849.769	1242.41

ACOS

Year	7
1962	284.106
1963	289.567
1964	312.873
1965	385.958
1966	487.785
1967	442.478
1968	493.231
1969	510.215
1970	366.959
1971	336.353
1972	444.768
1973	571.373
1974	482.711
1975	262.176
1976	371.424

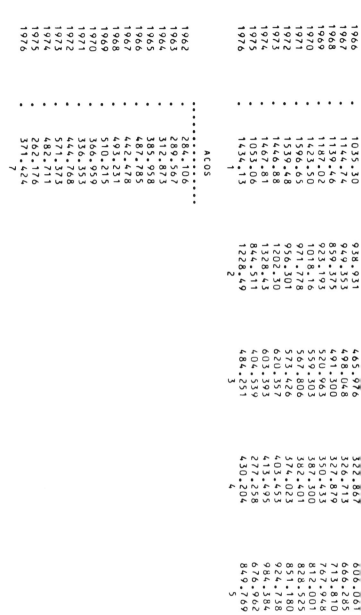

	1	CDELINPS 2	CNTIMPS 3	CACS 4	5
1970	58.6995	28.5055	1742.41	585.572	843.622
1971	40.9306	31.3065	1610.26	587.717	878.528
1972	45.1102	37.6119	1810.11	624.781	861.599
1973	42.2370	36.1397	1832.61	626.236	887.458
1974	46.7696	38.9957	1629.53	574.715	824.623
1975	41.3746	26.9581	1560.30	493.357	536.100
1976	36.5944	29.7926	1677.32	489.236	726.271
	1	2	3	4	5

	CDELINPS	CNTIMPS	CACS
1962	-24.5592	-240.306	2443.91
1963	-6.29809	-146.997	2607.64
1964	-7.45898	-53.5404	2824.10
1965	42.7397	-85.0872	2907.16
1966	85.3954	-246.657	3147.71
1967	-93.1668	368.465	3206.04
1968	45.8909	237.744	3123.63
1969	61.6396	116.298	3197.33
1970	-49.7350	231.518	3452.86
1971	-66.1698	439.433	3583.11
1972	82.7396	267.848	3506.59
1973	11.6523	259.983	3603.64
1974	88.9239	222.149	3345.09
1975	144.966	-274.079	2179.71
1976	-67.6087	-25.7332	2940.70
	1	2	3

	CCBCS	CCTS	CCCDS	CCMES	CCEES
1962	568.397	325.614	470.208	531.798	547.898
1963	616.661	337.305	518.591	556.042	579.042
1964	685.569	359.012	579.601	589.503	610.418
1965	693.468	350.709	624.183	595.361	643.436
1966	722.627	394.595	687.758	639.474	703.251
1967	749.036	385.265	690.947	647.652	733.140
1968	726.074	346.840	697.284	618.664	734.771
1969	726.283	365.607	737.899	613.487	754.052
1970	855.549	390.596	799.312	630.423	776.982
1971	971.503	377.497	808.958	642.932	782.221
1972	917.068	367.378	794.033	636.595	791.520
1973	814.107	452.351	813.078	695.890	828.209
1974	692.528	464.460	674.800	711.361	801.945
1975	489.002	293.860	527.048	380.663	489.136
1976	699.143	433.938	707.109	492.240	608.271
	1	2	3	4	5

II: Low Energy Price Forecasts

1985   29.6649   29.5779   4890.00   750.419
1986   29.9934   29.9674   5007.50   798.262   1308.56
            1   2   3   4   5

	ADELINS	ANTIMPS	AACS
1977	339.296	365.074	5932.69
1978	388.069	235.802	5573.01
1979	155.835	284.854	6156.09
1980	199.627	325.343	6439.79
1981	128.702	372.993	6566.63
1982	68.9270	433.686	6806.59
1983	-36.8841	541.593	7302.82
1984	-78.2377	641.373	7530.53
1985	-88.9852	697.615	7672.49
1986	-163.945	778.527	8056.79
	1	2	3

1983–1986

Year	1	2	3	4	5	6
1983	1721.88	981.874	501.818	414.706	939.800	2468.89
1984	1785.55	951.734	491.498	410.651	952.712	2690.19
1985	1732.89	928.231	480.948	407.717	957.858	2932.76
1986	1779.89	933.790	481.917	405.871	971.709	3243.54

Year	ACOS	CPPDS	CSPDS	CQPS	CQOSS	CQNSS
1977	398.012	36.7701	24.6867	1629.35	444.151	835.203
1978	271.620	42.3207	26.7648	1671.46	457.258	847.664
1979	291.776	39.3984	25.2451	1745.06	451.864	943.408
1980	324.790	43.8878	30.8972	1820.03	481.483	954.058
1981	264.365	43.5025	27.4024	1821.31	467.012	920.126
1982	253.995	45.1602	29.9393	1839.45	481.433	911.967
1983	273.854	46.8842	31.9483	1866.92	492.961	921.040
1984	248.197	47.8348	31.6865	1870.06	494.174	916.247
1985	232.086	49.1491	32.7448	1862.75	501.118	889.299
1986	240.077	50.1687	34.3449	1867.58	510.479	890.466
	7	1	2	3	4	5

```
1983   9.31686   422.431   3694.03
1984  14.8858    411.016   3676.61
1985  40.6837    357.272   3569.76
1986  39.1199    346.327   3575.73
          1          2          3
```

Year	CCBCS	CCTS	CCCDS	CCMES	CCEES
1977	790.281	390.734	745.151	623.862	776.072
1978	790.625	379.668	676.235	720.652	814.783
1979	974.924	422.976	729.789	775.657	868.506
1980	1010.79	414.288	718.754	784.846	889.953
1981	951.276	391.118	714.039	740.381	888.593
1982	959.599	386.951	698.772	727.633	882.339
1983	1029.98	378.545	697.023	704.597	883.886
1984	1059.29	366.810	686.812	688.913	874.789
1985	1012.92	354.235	670.342	667.533	864.731
1986	1030.48	353.498	669.147	656.902	865.700
	1	2	3	4	5

III: Intermediate Energy Price Forecasts

	1	2	3	4	5
	29.318U	29.U747	4625.06	627.558	1001.19
1981	30.2670	29.4720	4541.98	678.686	992.244
1982	31.4404	30.2300	4546.54	738.675	995.637
1983	32.6800	31.1937	4667.99	804.555	1033.31
1984	34.1677	32.0348	4648.21	874.702	1033.66
1985	35.4476	32.8028	4634.32	941.066	1029.30
1986	36.6848	33.6991	4713.20	1018.67	1055.70
	1	2	3	4	5

	ADELINS	ANTIMPS	AACS
1977	336.034	367.286	5934.84
1978	402.465	227.406	5562.87
1979	248.150	282.850	6046.90
1980	391.302	321.435	6183.94
1981	435.288	351.691	6129.32
1982	505.393	374.565	6150.03
1983	547.056	421.130	6379.93
1984	635.265	460.730	6382.04
1985	723.372	474.118	6355.43
1986	775.337	504.259	6516.49
	1	2	3

	ACOS
1977	398.012
1978	271.620
1979	291.776
1980	324.790
1981	264.365
1982	253.995
1983	273.854
1984	248.197
1985	232.086
1986	240.077
	7

	CPPDS	CSPDS	CQPS	CQOSS	CQNSS
1977	36.7150	24.6642	1629.33	447.209	835.866
1978	42.5651	26.9563	1671.73	445.403	845.039
1979	39.7451	25.4448	1741.12	425.894	928.061
1980	44.2842	31.1426	1809.34	440.003	923.305
1981	43.8338	27.5753	1801.60	414.604	875.425
1982	45.4345	30.0901	1810.25	415.568	853.287
1983	47.0547	32.0324	1826.64	414.431	845.344
1984	47.8724	31.6896	1816.90	405.160	824.413
1985	49.1358	32.7336	1795.54	401.406	786.381
1986	50.0374	34.2454	1784.69	399.688	770.122
	1	2	3	4	5

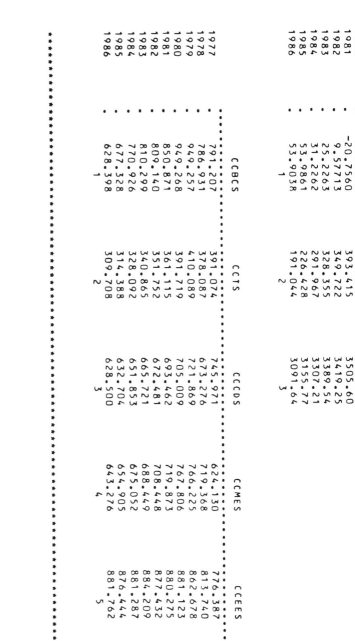

	CCBCS	CCTS	CCCDS	CCMES	CCEES
1977	791.207	391.074	745.971	624.130	776.387
1978	786.931	378.087	673.276	719.368	813.740
1979	949.257	410.089	721.869	766.225	862.678
1980	949.268	391.719	705.009	767.806	881.123
1981	850.871	361.115	693.462	719.873	880.275
1982	809.140	351.752	672.481	708.448	877.432
1983	810.299	340.865	665.721	688.449	884.209
1984	770.926	328.092	651.853	675.052	881.287
1985	677.328	314.388	632.704	654.905	876.444
1986	628.398	309.708	628.500	643.276	881.762
	1	2	3	4	5

1979	-124.192	490.034	3710.12		
1980	-37.1800	485.099	3694.92		
1981	-20.7560	393.415	3505.60		
1982	9.57713	349.722	3419.25		
1983	25.2263	328.355	3389.54		
1984	31.2262	291.967	3307.21		
1985	53.9861	226.428	3155.77		
1986	53.9038	191.044	3091.64		
	1	2	3		

1984	41.3856	36.0602	4390.93	1005.75
1985	44.5364	37.8717	4330.25	1106.27
1986	48.1663	40.1024	4346.72	1228.08
	1	2	3	4

	ADELINS	ANTIMPS	AACS
1977	378.701	377.946	5877.13
1978	498.400	245.091	5428.05
1979	422.189	287.378	5779.47
1980	646.910	317.354	5786.82
1981	775.724	337.196	5605.82
1982	943.081	355.485	5487.69
1983	1100.71	396.132	5547.44
1984	1299.04	443.253	5416.43
1985	1488.34	488.037	5291.29
1986	1676.76	558.370	5315.42
	1	2	3

875.539
855.069
859.017
5

IV: High Energy Price Forecasts

D-13

	ACOS					
1983	773.226	694.684	395.921	331.050	763.355	2315.35
1984	636.214	632.270	372.022	305.838	731.764	2490.13
1985	480.401	576.348	348.167	283.143	693.278	2677.86
1986	372.891	534.012	330.543	262.464	659.433	2916.00
	1	2	3	4	5	6

	ACOS
1977	398.012
1978	271.620
1979	291.776
1980	324.790
1981	264.365
1982	253.995
1983	273.854
1984	248.197
1985	232.086
1986	240.077
	7

	CPPDS	CSPDS	CQPS	CQOSS	CQNSS
1977	36.6805	24.6177	1626.37	445.091	830.515
1978	42.5154	26.9290	1664.45	438.112	832.539
1979	39.6463	25.3800	1729.16	412.609	904.379
1980	44.1197	31.0341	1791.97	419.965	891.424
1981	43.6414	27.4657	1777.8A	388.256	836.472
1982	45.1711	29.9265	1777.80	381.743	803.051
1983	46.6873	31.7986	1783.11	373.032	781.463
1984	47.4349	31.4278	1760.58	356.314	748.614
1985	48.7004	32.4832	1725.79	345.242	704.076
1986	49.6042	33.9850	1700.05	335.125	677.162
	1	2	3	4	5

	CCBCS	CCTS	CCCDS	CCMES	CCEES
1977	782.565	384.836	744.541	620.295	775.008
1978	762.628	365.888	669.741	711.058	811.806
1979	893.319	390.586	713.349	755.865	861.734
1980	862.375	369.327	692.919	759.065	882.999
1981	737.609	336.270	676.358	713.639	885.028
1982	659.505	321.372	651.233	700.248	884.818
1983	613.929	305.632	639.540	678.829	894.650
1984	536.144	287.926	619.867	663.208	895.163
1985	427.000	269.224	594.414	641.111	892.944
1986	353.096	256.957	581.586	625.829	900.242
	1	2	3	4	5

1983	36.6334	231.610	3132.58
1984	42.6017	179.404	3002.31
1985	61.8273	111.417	2824.69
1986	61.7876	67.1639	2717.71
	1	2	3

D-15

		1		2		3		4		5
1980	·	.		.		4404.32		696.011		916.427
1981	·	34.2655		31.7019		4377.56		688.995		888.934
1982	·	36.2537		32.9143		4356.84		750.282		873.216
1983	·	38.3858		34.3758		4447.70		816.942		889.377
1984	·	40.8003		35.7338		4405.78		887.386		876.607
1985	·	43.1162		37.0797		4368.05		953.491		866.240
1986	·	45.5998		38.6710		4413.66		1030.83		881.596

		ADELINS		ANTIMPS		AACS
		1		2		3
1977	·	394.293		384.571		5854.32
1978	·	529.764		261.518		5377.38
1979	·	471.780		306.923		5686.82
1980	·	694.984		334.509		5678.55
1981	·	811.935		354.757		5498.31
1982	·	948.555		370.452		5402.24
1983	·	1061.65		408.656		5501.02
1984	·	1202.13		455.323		5422.97
1985	·	1320.53		492.327		5359.58
1986	·	1421.02		548.398		5453.46

D-16

	ACOS	CPPDS	CSPDS	CQPS	CQOSS	CQNSS
1977	398.012	36.6182	24.5697	1625.06	446.814	828.777
1978	271.620	42.3020	26.7900	1661.39	444.599	829.554
1979	291.776	39.2949	25.1619	1724.90	424.508	900.458
1980	324.790	43.6218	30.7135	1787.90	438.227	890.364
1981	264.365	43.0446	27.1211	1775.39	412.404	839.334
1982	253.995	44.4587	29.4992	1777.73	413.175	810.190
1983	273.854	45.8668	31.2954	1786.49	411.627	793.526
1984	248.197	46.5093	30.8753	1768.99	402.086	766.462
1985	232.086	47.6754	31.8724	1741.17	398.270	727.761
1986	240.077	48.4698	33.2874	1723.75	396.350	707.662
	7	1	2	3	4	5

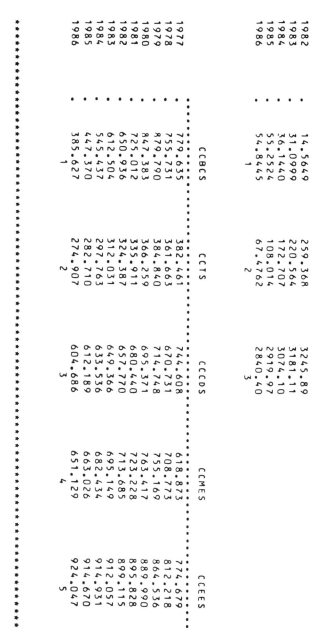

1979	-114.810	434.405	3599.08
1980	-30.1749	415.753	3562.42
1981	-16.0256	317.265	3360.42
1982	14.5649	259.368	3245.89
1983	31.0999	220.564	3181.11
1984	36.1440	172.707	3074.10
1985	55.2524	108.014	2919.97
1986	54.8445	67.4762	2840.40
	1	2	3

	CCBCS	CCTS	CCCDS	CCMES	CCEES
1977	779.635	382.461	744.608	618.873	774.679
1978	755.731	361.663	670.731	708.773	812.218
1979	879.790	384.840	714.748	755.169	864.536
1980	847.383	366.259	695.371	763.417	889.990
1981	725.012	335.911	680.440	723.228	895.828
1982	650.936	324.387	657.770	713.685	899.115
1983	612.504	312.031	649.366	695.149	912.057
1984	545.437	297.763	633.536	682.434	914.931
1985	447.370	282.710	612.189	663.026	914.670
1986	385.627	274.907	604.686	651.129	924.047
	1	2	3	4	5

	36.2050	33.1710	4568.47	886.422	1154.85
1984	37.7719	34.0991	4546.30	956.969	1166.72
1985	39.2627	35.1369	4616.92	1039.96	1214.01
1986	1	2	3	4	5

	ADELINS	ANTIMPS	AACS
1977	371.396	343.306	5863.88
1978	396.199	215.771	5563.73
1979	132.829	355.735	6276.02
1980	215.760	489.396	6572.75
1981	237.666	588.858	6600.42
1982	313.171	648.200	6641.16
1983	285.246	762.399	7028.29
1984	349.243	860.472	7120.97
1985	407.112	930.393	7193.27
1986	415.469	1025.91	7481.33
	1	2	3

VI: Low Domestic Copper Production

Year	1	2	3	4	5	6
1984	1772.05	841.524	521.924	380.163	793.815	2563.30
1985	1735.84	808.916	516.483	365.812	759.282	2774.85
1986	1799.94	791.149	520.867	349.850	732.440	3047.00

Year	ACOS	CPPDS	CSPDS	CQP	CQOSS	CQNSS
1977	398.012	38.5599	26.0698	1490.00	454.610	814.296
1978	271.620	42.4117	26.3887	1450.00	442.636	835.419
1979	291.776	35.0858	22.1973	1410.00	409.249	989.944
1980	324.790	36.7813	26.2394	1380.00	418.553	1067.88
1981	264.365	34.1499	21.8195	1350.00	387.060	1114.83
1982	253.995	34.0757	23.2339	1320.00	385.408	1188.43
1983	273.854	33.1045	23.1568	1290.00	377.040	1307.13
1984	248.197	32.6121	22.5263	1260.00	366.816	1392.62
1985	232.086	31.8922	22.1267	1230.00	358.182	1448.60
1986	240.077	31.4716	22.6740	1200.00	354.609	1547.93
	7	1	2	3	4	5

Year			
1982	29.8769	1903.41	4767.37
1983	47.9740	2320.91	5247.11
1984	34.5730	2607.98	5592.84
1985	22.6726	2805.46	5819.57
1986	40.0811	3157.93	6220.38
	1	2	3

Year	CCBCS	CCTS	CCCDS	CCMES	CCEES
1977	761.190	379.987	719.425	615.331	766.068
1978	769.641	379.683	668.858	710.665	803.862
1979	1042.59	444.518	792.140	795.529	884.264
1980	1201.12	435.971	836.289	849.533	953.587
1981	1278.89	420.609	882.342	873.133	1013.63
1982	1431.32	427.161	902.101	935.344	1071.45
1983	1720.71	439.567	954.452	985.273	1147.11
1984	1942.83	436.344	978.191	1030.21	1205.26
1985	2058.12	435.543	1000.43	1064.44	1261.03
1986	2305.21	443.603	1035.73	1107.95	1327.89
	1	2	3	4	5

D-21

For Product Safety Concerns and Information please contact our EU
representative GPSR@taylorandfrancis.com Taylor & Francis Verlag GmbH,
Kaufingerstraße 24, 80331 München, Germany

Printed and bound by CPI Group (UK) Ltd, Croydon, CR0 4YY
12/05/2025
01867561-0001